Comparable Corpora and Computer-assisted Translation

To Elia

Series Editor
Narendra Jussien

Comparable Corpora and Computer-assisted Translation

Estelle Maryline Delpech

iSTE

WILEY

First published 2014 in Great Britain and the United States by ISTE Ltd and John Wiley & Sons, Inc.

ISTE Ltd
27-37 St George's Road
London SW19 4EU
UK

www.iste.co.uk

John Wiley & Sons, Inc.
111 River Street
Hoboken, NJ 07030
USA

www.wiley.com

Library of Congress Control Number: 2014936484

British Library Cataloguing-in-Publication Data
A CIP record for this book is available from the British Library
ISBN 978-1-84821-689-1

FSC
www.fsc.org
MIX
Paper from responsible sources
FSC® C013604

Printed and bound in Great Britain by CPI Group (UK) Ltd., Croydon, Surrey CR0 4YY

Table of Contents

Acknowledgments

I would like to give Béatrice Daille and Emmanuel Morin my deepest thanks for having supervised and co-supervised this doctoral research. I felt so honored to work and learn by their sides. They both have shown an effective combination of academic rigorousness and pedagogy, which has helped me to progress over the past three years. Béatrice, thank you for suggesting this thesis to me – it was a very enriching experience. Manu, thanks again for being there whenever I needed you.

I extend my warm thanks to Nabil Hathout, Élisabeth Lavault-Olléon, Emmanuel Planas and Michel Simard for honoring me by attending my viva and being part of my committee in spite of their busy schedules. Their constructive comments were especially useful. I am glad to have profited from so many complementary points of view on my work. Special thanks to Michel Simard for coming to Nantes all the way from Canada.

I am particularly thankful to Emmanuel Planas, the former Scientific Director of Lingua et Machina, for trusting me and hiring me as a research engineer five years ago. Otherwise, I would probably not have had the chance to carry out a dissertation with LINA or to work on such a fascinating research subject within such a stimulating industrial environment.

Several people contributed to the work presented in this book. I would first like to thank Claire Lemaire from the University Stendhal in Grenoble, because she was an amazing colleague and co-doctoral candidate; and also for creating the resources for processing and assessing the German language. This would not have been possible without her and I am very thankful.

I would also like to thank Geoffrey Williams and Pierre Zweigenbaum for agreeing to be a part of my doctorate monitoring committee. Their shrewd comments and advice guided me in the right direction during this research project.

I would also like to thank Léa Laporte of the Toulouse Information Technology Research Institute (Institut de Research en Informatique de Toulouse (IRIT)) and Damien François from the Catholic University in Louvain for answering my questions on the statistical data-processing. Thanks also to Van Dang, from the University of Massachusetts, for answering my questions on the use of *learning-to-rank* algorithms.

I am immensely grateful to Clémence de Baudus, Kiril Isakov, Mathieu Delage from the Higher Education Institute of Translation and Interpreting (ISIT) and Nicolas Auger, for their extremely detailed annotation, without which it would not have been possible to evaluate the translation system.

My thanks go also to my colleagues at Lingua et Machina, François, Étienne and Jean-François, with whom I learned a lot and who I thank for their support. François's advice and experience were invaluable during the last year of my doctorate.

Unfortunately, I did not have the chance to spend a lot of time in the laboratory but it was always a pleasure to come to the team meetings. The welcome and atmosphere of the LINA is fantastic, and I greatly enjoyed talking with my colleagues – especially Amir Hazem and Prajol Shrestha, who were delightful fellow doctoral candidates.

Finally, I would like to thank my partner, Nicolas, for his unfailing support; my friends Émilie and Nathalie and my sister Laureen for their understanding about my lack of availability, as well as for their presence and logistical support on the day of the viva. Thanks to Loki, who is a wonderful alarm clock.

Introduction

I.1. Socio-economic stakes of multilingualism management

In the days of the globalization of exchanges, multilingualism is an undeniable socio-cultural asset, but it presents many challenges to our society.

First of all, the lack of knowledge of a language is often synonymous with limited access to information, and it is generally linguistic communities with little economic power, or whose language is not a prestigious one, who suffer as a result.

The case of the Internet is a good example: English – the most represented language on the web (54.8%)[1] – is the first language of only 26.8% of web users[2] whereas Chinese – the first language of 24.2% of the web users – is only sixth in terms of presence on the Internet (4%).

A significant portion of web-based information is therefore unavailable to many web users because of the language barrier.

In countries which are officially bilingual or multilingual or in international organizations such as the European Union, managing multilingualism falls within the remit of democracy: it is meant to ensure that each citizen has access to administrative services and legal texts in his own first language so she/he knows his/her rights and can benefit from the government's services in a language she/he speaks fluently. This has a considerable cost: the European Union spends 1 billion Euros every year in translation and interpretation costs [FID 11].

1 In May 2011, according to WEB TECHNOLOGY SURVEYS http://w3techs.com/technologies/overview/content_language/all.

2 http://www.internetworldstats.com/stats7.htm.

Multilingualism also has an impact on our economy: the ELAN report [HAG 06] claimed that in 2006 the lack of language skills had cost on average 325,000 Euros to a European SMB over three years.

To deal with this social and economic cost, research has been performed to speed up and improve the process of human translation. Today, there is a whole industry devoted to this issue. The language industry provides both human translation services and a wide range of software packages intended to bring translation costs down: translation memories, bilingual terminology-extraction and management software, localization software, etc.

This is the framework of research and development in computer-assisted translation (CAT) within which my doctoral research has taken place. This research was partially funded by Lingua et Machina[3] – a company specializing in multilingual content management in a corporate environment, and by the ANR project Metricc,[4] devoted to the leveraging of comparable corpora.

I.2. Motivation and goals

CAT has always used translation memories. This technique requires the translator to have a corpus of previous translations available, which the CAT software can use to generate bilingual lexicons, for example. This reality is problematic when the translator does not have such a corpus. This situation arises when the texts to be translated belong to an emerging field or to several languages for which few resources are available. To solve this issue, CAT research has looked into the leveraging of comparable corpora, i.e. a set of texts, in two or more languages, which deal with the same topic but are not translations of one another.

Comparable corpora have been the focus of academic research since the 1990s [FUN 95, RAP 99], and the existence of the *Workshop on Building and Using Comparable Corpora (BUCC)*, organized every year since 2008 on the fringe of major conferences, shows the dynamism of this research topic.

The current research mainly aims at extracting aligned pairs of terms or sentences, which are then used in cross-lingual information retrieval (CLIR) systems [REN 03, CHI 04, LI 11] or in machine translation (MT) systems [RAU 09, CAR 12]. While CAT is often mentioned as a potential applicative field, the input of comparable corpora has not, to our knowledge, been genuinely studied within this application framework. Yet it presents several issues such as scaling or the adaptation to the needs of the final users.

3 http://www.lingua-et-machina.com,

4 http://www.metricc.com.

This book had two primary objectives. The first objective is to assess the input of lexicons extracted from comparable corpora in the context of a specialized human translation task. Care has been taken to highlight the needs of translators and to understand how the comparable corpora can be best leveraged for CAT.

The second objective is to identify bilingual-lexicon-extraction methods, which best match the translators' needs. Determining the current limits of these techniques and suggesting improvements is the focus of this research. We will focus, in particular, on the identification of fertile translations (cases in which the target term has more words than the source term), the management of multiple morphological structures and the ranking of candidate translations (the algorithms usually return several candidate translations for a single-source term).

The experiments are carried out in two language pairs (English–French and English–German) and on specialized texts dealing with breast cancer. This research has significant emphasis on applicability, and our methodological choices are guided by the needs of the final users.

I.3. Outline

This book is organized in two parts:

Part 1 presents the applicative and scientific context of the research. In *Chapter 1*, a historical overview of the beginning of MT is presented and we show how the focus of research efforts gradually turn toward CAT and the leveraging of comparable corpora. This book presents the current techniques to extract bilingual lexicons and detail the way in which the writer created the prototype of a CAT tool meant to leverage comparable corpora. *Chapter 2* is devoted to the applicative assessment of this tool: we observe how the lexicons, thus extracted, enable translators to work more efficiently in their work. This assessment highlights the specific needs of human translation which are not dealt with in the classical techniques of term alignment. This is why this research took a different path, toward a different type of method, which aims to *generate* the translations of terms which can then be filtered using the corpus rather than to *align* terms that had been previously extracted from corpora. These techniques are described in *Chapter 3*. In this chapter, the focus is mainly on the so-called *compositional* approaches. Their limits are explored and *Part 1* concludes with an indication of possible fruitful avenues for future research.

Part 2 of the book is given over to the efforts to improve compositional translation. *Chapter 4* presents the methodological framework of the research: it describes the principle behind this approach, and attempts to highlight the contributions this work makes to compositional translation in terms of fertility, variety of the morphological structures processed and ranking of the candidate translations. The assessment methodology is also presented. *Chapter 5* describes the data which was used for experimenting with the translation method origin, nature, size and acquisition method. *Chapter 6* gives details of the implementation: the translation generation algorithm is mentioned here. The translation generation method is then assessed from a variety of angles (input of resources, input of translation strategies of productive translations, etc.). Finally, *Chapter 7* formalizes and experiments with several ranking methods for the generated translations.

This dissertation finishes with an assessment of the work carried out and suggestions of several research perspectives. The *Appendices* include an index of the measurements used throughout the book as well as extracts of the experimental data.

PART 1

Applicative and Scientific Context

1

Leveraging Comparable Corpora for Computer-assisted Translation

1.1. Introduction

This chapter starts with a historical approach to computer-assisted translation (section 1.2): we will retrace the beginnings of machine translation and explain how computer-assisted translation has developed so far, with the recent appearance of the issue of comparable-corpus leveraging. Section 1.3 explains the current techniques to extract bilingual lexicons from comparable corpora. We provide an overview of the typical performances, and discuss the limitations of these techniques. Section 1.4 describes the prototyping of the computer-assisted translation (CAT) tool meant for comparable corpora and based on the techniques described in section 1.3.

1.2. From the beginnings of machine translation to comparable corpora processing

1.2.1. *The dawn of machine translation*

From the beginning, scientific research in computer science has tried to use the machine to accelerate and replace human translation. According to [HUT 05], it was in the United States, between 1959 and 1966, that the first research in machine translation was carried out. Here, machine translation (MT) refers to the translation of a text by a machine without any human intervention. Until 1966, several research groups were created, and two types of approaches could be identified:

– On the one hand, there were the pragmatic approaches combining statistical information with trial-and-error development methods[1] and whose goal was to create an operational system as quickly as possible (University of Washington, Rand Corporation and University of Georgetown). This research applied the direct translation method[2] and this gave rise to the first generation of machine translation systems.

– On the other hand, theoretic approaches emerged involving fundamental linguistics and considering research in the long term (MIT, Cambridge Research Language Unit). These projects were more theoretical and created the first versions of interlingual systems.[3]

In 1966, a report from the Automatic Language Processing Advisory Committee [ALP 66], which assesses machine translation purely based on the needs of the American government – i.e. the translation of Russian scientific documents – announced that after several years of research, it was not possible to obtain a translation that was entirely carried out by a computer and of human quality. Only postedition would allow us to reach a good quality of translation.[4] Yet the point of postedition is not self-evident. A study mentioned in the appendix of this book points out that "most translators found postediting tedious and even frustrating", but many found "the output served as an aid... particularly with regard to technical terms" [HUT 96].

Although the study does not allow us to come to a conclusion on the point of postedition in relation to fully manual translation (out of 22 translators, eight find postedition easier, eight others find it harder and six were undecided), the report mostly highlights the negative aspects, quoting one of the translators:

> I found that I spend at least as much time in editing as if I had carried out the entire translation from the start. Even at that, I doubted if the edited translation reads as smoothly as one which I would have started from scratch. [HUT 96]

1 Several heuristic rules were implemented and tested on data until the result obtained was considered satisfactory.

2 A translation strategy, which does not involve any mediating processing layer: the very first translators used this approach by tokenizing a text into words, neutralizing inflections, looking for the translation of words in a bilingual dictionary, and after all this the translated words were reordered following several rules. Therefore, there was no syntactic or semantic analysis.

3 The interlingual method analyzes the source text so as to generate an abstract semantic representation of it, which is totally language-independent. The target text is then generated based on this representation. The generation module in the target language can only access the interlingual representation.

4 MT "presumably means going by algorithm from machine-readable source text to useful target text, without recourse to human translation or editing" – quoted in [HUT 96].

The report quotes remarks made by V. Yngve – the head of the machine translation research project at MIT – who claimed that MT "serves no useful purpose without postediting, and that with postediting the over-all process is slow and probably uneconomical" [HUT 96].

The report concludes on the fact that machine translation research is essential from the point of view of scientific progress, it however has a limited interest from an economic point of view. Thus funding was cut in the United States. However, research carried on in Europe (EUROTRA research project) and in Canada. This research was the source of the TAUM system, for example, (translation of weather reports from French to English) and of the translation software SYSTRAN.

1.2.2. *The development of computer-assisted translation*

While it signaled the end of public funding for machine translation research in the United States, the ALPAC report encouraged the pursuit of a more realistic goal for computer-assisted translation.[5] The report praised the glossaries generated by the German army's translation agency as well as the terminology base of the European Coal and Steal Community – a resource which foregrounded EURODICAUTOM and IATE – and came to the conclusion that these resources were a real help to translation. The final recommendations clearly encouraged the development of CAT, especially in the leveraging of glossaries initially created for machine translation.[6]

At that point, a whole range of tools intended to help the translator in his/her work rather than replace him/her started to be developed. The first terminology management programs appeared in the 1960s [HUT 05] and evolved into multilingual terminology databases such as TERMIUM or UNTERM. Bilingual concordancers are also of invaluable help: they allow the translator to access the word or term's context and compare the translation of the contexts in the target language. According to [SOM 05], the rise in computer-assisted translation happened in the seventies with the creation of *translation memory* software, which allows the translator to recycle past translations: when a translator has to translate a new sentence, the software scans the memory for similar previously translated sentences, and when it finds any, suggests the previous translation as translation model. The

5 "Machine-aided translation may be an important avenue toward better, quicker and cheaper translation" quoted in [HUT 96].

6 "research should be supported on: *[...]* 2. means for speeding up the human translation process; *[...]* 6. evaluation of the relative speed and costs of various sorts of machine-aided translation; 7. adaptation of existing mechanized editing and production processes in translation; *[...]* 9. production of adequate reference works for the translator, including the adaptation of glossaries that now exist primarily for automatic dictionary look-up in machine translation" quoted by [HUT 96].

time saved is all the greater when the texts translated are repetitive, which is often the case in certain specialized documents such as technical manuals.

These sets of translated documents make up what we call *parallel corpora*[7] [VER 00] and their leveraging intensified in the 1980s, allowing for a resurgence in machine translation. While the translation systems based on rules had dominated the field until then, the access to large databases of translation examples helped further the development of data-driven systems. The two paradigms arising from this turnaround are the example-base translation [NAG 84] and statistical machine translation [BRO 90], which remains the current dominant trend. The quality of machine translation is improving. Today, it generates usable results in specialized fields in which vocabulary and structures are rather repetitive. The last stronghold is general texts: machine translation offers, at best, an aid for understanding.

During the 1990s, CAT benefited from the intersecting input of machine translation and computational terminology [BOU 94, DAI 94a, ENG 95, JAC 96]. It was at that point that *term alignment* algorithms appeared, based on parallel corpora [DAI 94b, MEL 99, GAU 00]. The bilingual terminology lists generated are particularly useful in the case of specialized translation.

Automatic extraction and management of terminology, bilingual concordance services, pre-translation and translation memories, understanding aids: today, the translator's workstation is a complex and highly digital environment. The language technology industry has proliferated and developed itself, generating many pieces of CAT software: TRADOS[8], WORDFAST[9], DÉJÀ VU[10], and SIMILIS[11] to name just a few. The greater public is also provided for: on the one hand, Google has widened the access to immediate translation for anyone due to its GOOGLE TRANSLATE tool[12] and on the other hand, open access bilingual concordance services have appeared recently on the Internet (BAB.LA[13], LINGUEE[14]), and quickly become popular – for example LINGUEE reached 600,000 requests a day for is English–German version in 2008, a year after it had been created [PER 10].

7 "texts accompanied by their translation in one or more languages" [VER 00].

8 www.trados.com.

9 www.wordfast.com.

10 www.atril.com.

11 www.lingua-et-machina.com.

12 www.translate.google.com.

13 www.en.bab.la.

14 www.linguee.com.

1.2.3. *Drawbacks of parallel corpora and advantages of comparable corpora*

While they are useful, these technologies have a major drawback: they require the existence of a translation history. What about languages, which have few resources or emerging speciality fields? A possible solution is then to use what we refer to as *comparable corpora.*

There exist several definitions of comparable corpora. At one end of the spectrum is the very narrow definition given by [MCE 07]; within the framework of translation studies research. According to these authors, a comparable corpus contains texts in two or more languages, which have been gathered according to the same genre, field and sampling period criteria. Moreover, the corpora must be balanced: "comparable corpus can be defined as a corpus containing components that are collected using the same sampling frame and similar balance and representativeness (McEnery, 2003:450), e.g. the same proportions of the texts of the same genres in the same domains in a range of different languages in the same sampling period. However, the subcorpora of a comparable corpus are not translations of each other. Instead, their comparability lies in their same sampling frame and similar balance [MCE 07]. At the other end of the spectrum, we encounter the definition given by [DÉJ 02], within the framework of natural language processing research, which only underlines the fact that there should be "a substantial subpart" of vocabulary in common between the texts[15].

As for us, we have chosen a middle point, considering that sets of texts are comparable, if they are in two or more languages dealing with a same topic and if possible, if they have been generated within the same communication situation, so that there is a possibility of finding useful translations in them. We will only look at *specialized* comparable corpora, i.e. the texts generated by an expert in the field and addressed to other experts or the general public [BOW 02].

As well as being more easily available, comparable corpora also have an advantage in quality, which is emphasized by translation studies researchers. Parallel corpora are well-known for not being faithful to linguistic uses in the target language. For [MCE 07], "translated language is at best an unrepresentative special variant of the target language" [MCE 07]. For [ZAN 98], translated texts cannot represent all the linguistic possibilities of the target language and tend to reflect the idiosyncrasies of the source languages as well as those of the translator. As for [BAK 96], she

15 "*Deux corpus de deux langues l1 et l2 sont dits comparables s'il existe une sous-partie non négligeable du vocabulaire du corpus de langue l1, respectivement l2, dont la traduction se trouve dans le corpus de langue l2, respectivement l1*". Translation: two corpora in two languages l1 and l2 are comparable if there is a substantial subpart of the vocabulary of the corpus of language l1, l2 respectively, whose translation is in the body language of l2 and l1, respectively [DÉJ 02].

explains how the texts generated by a translation, like any other text, are influenced by their production context and the communication goals that they serve. Thus, they have specific characteristics, which differentiate them from "spontaneous" texts.

The term *translationese* is used to refer to this variation of language, which is generated in a translation situation. The existence of translationese has been widely studied and proven. Its characteristics are visible by comparing a translation corpus with a corpus of spontaneous texts covering the same topic.

[BAK 96] synthesize the results of several studies mainly based on the comparison between original texts and translations in English (newspaper articles and novels).

She highlights four characteristics:

Clarifying: clarifying is the tendency to avoid the implicit, and even to add additional information to replace the message in context. Translated texts are always longer than the source text, no matter what the translation direction or the languages are: from a lexical point of view, we notice more explanatory vocabulary (*cause, reason*) and connectives such as *because, consequently*.

Simplification: the language used is simplified. Sentences that are too long are cut up into shorter sentences. Punctuation is changed: weak punctuation marks are replaced by stronger punctuations (from *comma* to *semi-colon* to *period*). The translations have less lexical variety and a stronger proportion of tool words.

Standardization / conservatism: this aspect concerns the conformity or even the exaggeration of the typical characteristics of the target language, especially with regards to grammatical structures, punctuation and collocations.

Levelling out: translated texts show much less variety than spontaneous texts in numerous ways. For example, if we look at the variations of the type: token ratio (which measures the lexical variety) or of the sentence length over several texts, the variation of these characteristics is much lower for translated texts.

In the case of comparable corpora, several studies have underlined their usefulness for translation.

Two studies [FRI 97, GAV 97], mentioned by [MCE 07], estimate that specialized comparable corpora are useful in technical translation when it comes to checking translation hypotheses. [FRI 97] noticed improvements in quality, whether it is translated toward the translator's first or second language. The fact that there is an improvement even in the case of a translation toward the first language is proof of how hard it is to approach specialized texts. Indeed, being able to use everyday language does not mean that we know the terminology or linguistic uses specific to a field, or even the notions and concepts, which they deal with.

The works of [ZAN 98] on translator training highlight three possible uses of comparable corpora:

Researching translation matches: [ZAN 98] describes an experiment on the identification of translational matches in sport newspapers, which are said to employ a large amount of figurative language. The example given is the translation of the expression *salire il gradino più alto del podio* (to climb on the highest step of the podium) into English: can it be translated literally or should a matching term be chosen? The corpus study of the contexts of occurrence of the Italian expression show that this expression means to win the gold medal. A study of the joint occurrence of the word *podium* in English texts shows that although the meaning is the same as the Italian *podio*, *podium* does not appear with *the highest step* to denote winning the gold medal. A literal translation would thus be a poor translation, and the chosen translation will be *to win the gold medal.*

Learning terminology: [ZAN 98] underlines the strong proportion of translation matches between terms that are graphically similar in medical corpora (terms with common Greek and Latin origins, for example, i.e. *hépatique* ↔ *hepatic*). He explains that the observation of the collocations of similar terms such as these can help acquire knowledge of field-specific terminology. The example given is that of the translation of *biopsia epatica,* which intuitively in English would be *hepatic biopsy*. However, the context of *biopsy* never mentions the expression *hepatic biospy* whereas *liver biopsy* appears 39 times. A more in-depth study of the contexts of *liver* versus *fegato* (layman terms) and *hepatic* versus *epatico/a* (scholarly terms) show that the English and the Italian do not use layman and scholarly terms in the same way: in English, *hepatic* only occurs in the company of generic terms such as *lesion* or *disease* whereas in Italian, the scholarly term is used without any kind of restriction.

Exporting texts post- and pre-translation: in this case, we use comparable corpora to examine the uses specific to a field or a genre. The experiment described concerns a comparative study in the appearance of the word *Mitterand* in English and Italian newspapers. This study reveals that there are stylistic traditions in each language: in Italian, we tend to refer to politicians by their full name (*François Mitterand*) whereas in English, we use their title more often (*Mr. Mitterand, President Mitterand*). These uses are also different when it comes to introducing reported speech: in English, a small number of verbs is used (*say* and *add* are used in 60% of the cases) whereas in Italian, the verbs used to report speech are much more varied.

1.2.4. *Difficulties of technical translation*

To explain the difficulties of technical translation, we will rely on Christine Durieux's work ([DUR 10]), which subscribes to Danica Seleskovitch's interpretative theory of translation (or theory of meaning).

At first, one may believe that specialized human translation only focuses on the acquisition of translation matches between terms (learning terminology). Yet, as [DUR 10] explains, technical translation cannot be limited to the process of generating terminology matches. This approach is what she calls "transcoding", which is simply the transposition into the target language of terms that are not necessarily understood. The writer believes that a good technical translation can only exist if the translator is completely at home with the notions referred to in these terms: "one does not translate a sequence of words, but a message whose meaning was first understood"[16] [DUR 10]. Thus, the translator's work involves a dimension of self-improvement in the technical field, carried out through prior documentation enabling him or her to learn the field's terminology in context. Durieux suggests carrying out this documentation research in educational and outreach material such as encyclopedias in which the notions are described with an easily-accessible vocabulary rather than in specialized resources such as scientific journals. Specialized resources are only used later, to improve certain notions.

The situation is the same for stylistic uses: [DUR 10] remarks that there are specific turns of phrase for each field. Certain syntactic constructions or collocations can be more frequent in a specialized discourse than in everyday language. It is often the case that the collocations specific to a field of specialization involve a different translation of one of the collocations. For example, *répandre* can be translated as *to spread* in everyday language; however, when talking about insecticide, we use the verb *to spread* in English but *traiter* in French. *Unscheduled* is translated in everyday French by *imprévu* but an *unscheduled maintenance* becomes *un entretien curatif*. The translation of prepositions can be delicate since a preposition can change the meaning of a term: *exception detected by the program* has a different meaning from *exception detected in the programme*. Moreover, the choice of preposition can be idiosyncratic for the term: we talk of *filling out a form* but this is achieved by *filling it in*. Once again [DUR 10] suggests that systematic research and documentation, which enables the translator to notice the linguistic uses specific to each field.

We will understand when reading [DUR 10] that a specialized translator spends part of his/her time researching documentation with the sole goal of manually creating terminological records, which will match not just the terms, but also their contexts (defining contexts for the meaning of the terms, "language" contexts highlighting the collocations and stylistic aspects).

[DUR 10]'s conclusions have been supported by other studies. Thus, [DAR 79] believes that a specialized language is specific not only by its naming convention, but also by what he refers to as his discourse:

> When using what we call specialized languages, there is on the one hand the technical things that we have to be able to refer to exactly; and on the other hand, the text, which carries and actualizes these notions and

16 "On ne traduit pas une suite de mots, mais un message dont on a auparavant appréhendé le sens."

> which has to conform to certain form requirements. Therefore, the writer of the text has to have a dual competence: to be familiar with the naming convention of the topic and to be able to fully make use – in a certain register – of the language resources, which will highlight the elements of the naming convention. [...] With this in mind, we can consider that each specialized language presents itself under this dual aspect, and that naming convention and discourse must go hand in hand. Due to the appropriate documentation, it is often also easier to access the naming convention than the specialized discourse resources.

Echoing the distinction made by [DAR 79], [SCU 08] offers a fine analysis of the difficulties in translating French legal texts into Romanian. One point that we can highlight is that she considers that terms belonging to the naming conventions (e.g. technical terms) do not necessarily cause any difficulty in translation. [SCU 08] divides the naming convention into three categories:

Words which are exclusively judicial terms: these are technical terms used by the initiated. Some do not cause any difficulty in translation, because they have an immediate match in the target language (or are even borrowed from the source language) and have a formal resemblance to the source term, such as *abrogatif* and *abrogativ*. The terms that can be problematic in translation are terms that have no formal resemblance to the source term (e.g. *prononcé* and *pronunare*) and/or refer to a notion that does not exist in the culture of the target language (for example the French *communauté* and the Romanian *regim matrimonial legal*).

Words with dual allegiances: these are terms, which the legal system uses in very specific way. Among them we can mention:

– terms that are mainly judicial terms: these are judicial terms that have been appropriated by everyday language with a second meaning, such as *arbitrator, witness* and *guaranty*;

– terms that have a second legal meaning: these are terms whose main meaning is found in everyday language and who have acquired a specific meaning in the legal field, such as *act, mobile* and *enjoyment*.

The difficulty in translating these words with dual allegiances comes from the fact that they are shared with everyday language: their translation is only possible through context.

As for discourse, it covers several elements. We can find in it stylistic elements, specific phrasing and syntactic choices already highlighted by [DUR 10] as well as what [DAR 79] and [SCU 08] refer to as a support vocabulary. [DAR 79] defines support vocabulary as "the words whose technicality is low or non-existing and are used to actualize specialized words as well as provide the text with its organic nature." He lists the example of the legal field and the words "relationship *breakdown*", "*to hear* a witness", or "to cover" (in a financial sense).

Similarly, [SCU 08] mentions that – aside from words with dual allegiances – there are a certain number of terms that may not have a legal meaning but that, nonetheless, appear in texts with a specific meaning, which is different from the one they have in "common" language. For example, in French, *affaire* in legal documents does not have the meaning that is contained by its literal translation in Romanian (*afacere*). In a legal setting, it will be translated by *cauz* (so for example, "to take a case to court" would be in French *porter une affaire devant la Cour* and in Romanian *a duce o caus înaintea Curii*, while "to do business" is translated by *faire des affaires* in French and *a face afaceri* in Romanian).

Let us point out that [SCU 08] and [DAR 79] both deplore the fact that the resources available to the translator do not take supporting vocabulary into account:

> [We] can consider that each specialized language presents itself under this dual aspect, and that naming convention and discourse cannot be dissociated; it is often easier, due to the appropriate documentation, to access naming convention than specialized discourse resources. [DAR 79]

> The books in question often only include the terms specific to the field itself and exclude terms of everyday language, which elude the neophyte's understanding since they have acquired a specific meaning. [SCU 08]

According to [DAR 79], the lack of support vocabulary in technical glossaries can be explained by the fact that these resources are more aimed to help with understanding than with writing. Moreover, since the technical terms are striking due to their technicality, their presence naturally becomes necessary in a technical glossary. On the contrary, support vocabulary appears to be more transparent, and thus will be overlooked. However, it is just as essential. This point of view is also supported by [SCU 08]:

> Paradoxically, when writing or translating a text it is often not the technical word, which is the biggest issue (these technical words have been and continue to be the focus of terminological lexicographies). We can notice by going through legal language indexes that many terms that were used when writing legal and administrative texts have not been retained. This is even truer if we take into consideration the situation of

> bilingual dictionaries in the field. While it is true that in general the indexes target to understand more than writing. On the contrary, the terms of supporting vocabulary might appear to be marginal since they are transparent, but reveal themselves to be more delicate to manipulate, since they are required to go from mere lists of terms to a text: according to Darbelnet, it *is during the time of writing, and, therefore, we would add, during the time of translating, that this vocabulary effectively comes into its own* [DAR 79].

Since we situate ourselves in the perspective of facilitating translation and not knowledge engineering, our work does not focus on the extraction of translatable equivalences between terms. We focus instead on trying to identify the translations of any lexical element that might create translation difficulties. We will thus set aside in our research topic any information relating to syntax, style or text structure. We consider that any lexical unit that is not found in a general language dictionary might cause translation difficulties. Due to this definition, we exclude some terms that are frequently used in everyday language and whose translation has thus to be known by translators (e.g. *chemotherapy* is a medical term but its translation should not cause any issue for a professional translator). However we include elements such as *patient-centred,* which would not belong to a specific terminology but could create translation difficulties.

Therefore, from now on, our use of the word "term" should not be understood as corresponding to its official definition[17] but as a "problematic unit for a technical translator".

1.2.5. *Industrial context*

While there is a genuine qualitative interest in comparable corpora, they remain hard to use for translators. Compared to parallel corpora for which there are many existing tools, manual research and verification of informative contexts and translation matches in comparable corpora are time-consuming. This generates a loss in productivity and motivation for the translator.

There are very few computational tools that can help the translator when using comparable corpora. We can only mention two academic prototypes [BEN 00, SHA 06] and – as far as we know – when this doctoral research started, there was no commercial CAT tool that can process the comparable corpora. The technological transfer of the extraction techniques of bilingual lexicons from comparable corpora was our first task when we started to work as a research engineer

17 A term is a designation consisting of one or more words representing a general concept in a special language. [ISO 09].

for the LINGUA ET MACHINA corporation[18]. This company was created by Emmanuel Planas based on his research results [PLA 98, PLA 00]; it edits the translation memory software SIMILIS [PLA 05] whose specificity resides in the fact that it uses linguistic analysis. The texts are labelled morpho-syntactically and the sentences are broken down into *chunks*. The matching of the segments of previously translated text and of text to be translated also happens at a linguistic level (matching the lemmas and grammatical categories) – and not at a graphical level, as is the case for other translation memory software.

LINGUA ET MACHINA also edits a web application for multilingual management in a corporate environment called LIBELLEX. This platform integrates several translation aid tools (bilingual concordance services, terminology extraction and management tools, translation memories, CAT and translation project management tools). The platform is different from SIMILIS, because it is designed to be not only for professional translators, but also for all the collaborators in the company (see Figure 1.1).

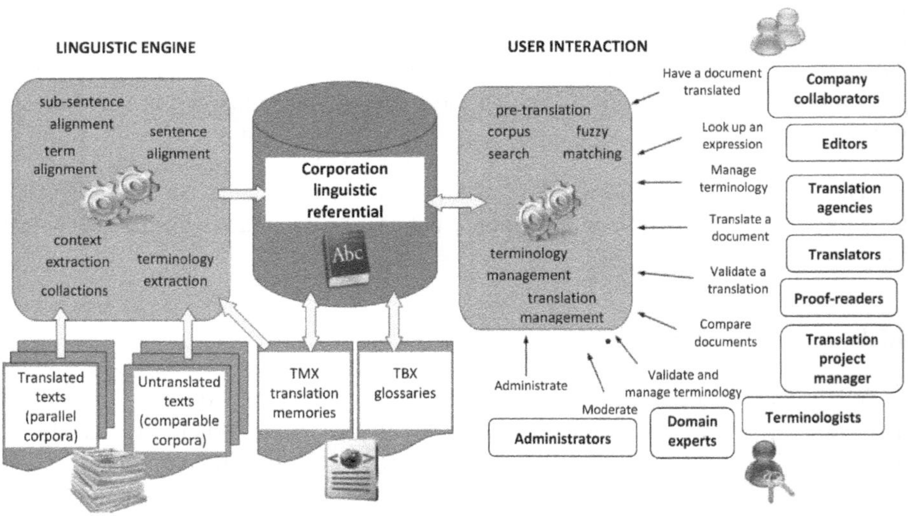

Figure 1.1. *Libellex: a multiservice platform for multilingual text management*

The possibility of using comparable corpora represents a major research and development axis at LINGUA ET MACHINA since fields of knowledge are constantly evolving and thus LINGUA ET MACHINA clients have to be able to quickly create translation resources even in fields in which there are little or no translation histories.

18 www.lingua-et-machina-com.

Part of the doctoral research work was thus to create a prototype which would enable the acquisition of bilingual lexicons from comparable corpora. We also developed an interface for looking up the extracted lexica. Generally speaking, the acquisition of bilingual lexicon from comparable corpora is carried out in two steps. First, the source and target terms are extracted from their respective corpora using terminology extraction techniques [BOU 94, DAI 94a, ENG 95]. Second, the terms extracted are aligned due to techniques based on the similarity of the terms' occurrence contexts. We describe these techniques in section 1.3.

1.3. Term alignment from comparable corpora: a state-of-the-art

Specific approaches have been developed to acquire bilingual lexicons from comparable corpora. There are methods based on frequency distribution [KOE 02] or the use of semantic relations [JI 09] but we will not describe them here in detail, for either their results are not very convincing or they rely on advanced information extraction tools, which led us to decide that they would be difficult to implement.

Other methods look to extract parallel segments from comparable corpora [FUN 04, RAU 09]. While this approach may be efficient in creating general language lexica, it is hard to apply it to specialized corpora since it requires large corpora[19]. However, in a specialized field, the texts not only have to belong to the same field, but also be limited to a very specific topic, which means that gathering a large number of texts is almost impossible.

The most common state-of-the-art method to align terms in comparable corpora is called the *distributional* method or *contextual similarity alignment* method. We describe its principle in section 1.3.1.

1.3.1. *Distributional approach principle*

Distributional semantics, whose origins can be found in the works of Z. Harris, consider that it is possible to semantically characterize a word thanks to its distribution, i.e. all the words with which it fosters syntactic relations. Extraction of bilingual lexicons based on distributional semantics hypothesizes that it is possible to calculate the distributional similarities between words in different languages and that similar distributions correspond to semantic equivalences, no matter what languages are involved. This hypothesis was successfully tested by [RAP 95] and the first alignment model was presented by [FUN 97].

19 For example, [FUN 04] use a Chinese corpus of 110,000 sentences and an English corpus of 290,000 sentences to obtain 2,500 pairs of aligned sentences, with a precision index of 65.76%.

[RAP 95] shows the relevance of distributional semantics for the alignment of terms by demonstrating that there is a correlation between co-occurrence patterns of words observed in corpora from different languages:[20] if words A and B co-occur in a significant manner in a language corpus $L1$, then their respective translations A' and B' in language $L2$ will also co-occur in a significant manner in a language corpus $L2$. For example, in a French–English medical corpus, we can expect *dépistage* and *radiographie* to co-occur in a significant manner in French, just like their respective translations – *screening* and *radiography* – do in English.

In his experiment, [RAP 95] represents the co-occurrences between the words by a matrix Aij in which the value at the intersection of row i and column j refers to the normalized count[21] of the co-occurrence of the word i with the word j. The experiment he carries out starts with two such matrices. The first matrix contains the co-occurrences observed in the source corpus (English) and the other matrix contains the co-occurrences observed in the target corpus (German). At first, the two matrices are aligned, i.e. the word i of the English matrix is the translation of the word i of the German matrix. Then [RAP 95] randomly switches the order of the words in the matrices to misalign them. He then observes that the similarity[22] of the source and target matrices decreases when the number of misaligned words increases.

[FUN 97] goes further with [RAP 95]'s experiment and uses a bilingual lexicon, which she projects onto the source and target corpora, which enables her to obtain attested translation pairs in both corpora. She then calculates a *context vector* for each source and target word whose translation is unknown. The context vector of a word w is an approximation of its distribution: it provides for each of the entries e of the bilingual dictionary a number of times in which m co-occurs with the entry e within a given contextual window (for example, three words to the right and three words to the left). Since the entries are attested in the source and target corpora, it is possible to compare the context vectors independently from their language. The closer two vectors are, the more plausible it is that their heads[23] have a similar meaning and are translations of each other.

---

20 One should point out that the author, like many of the works mentioned in the following, did not directly rely on syntactic analyzers. On the one hand, syntactic contexts are only available if the corpus used for alignment was syntactically analyzed, which involves using costly development tools, which are rarely available. On the other hand, as soon as the corpora reach a sufficient size, the syntactic context can be approximated due to a window of n words surrounding the word to be semantically characterized.

21 The measure used is the mutual information described in Appendix A1.1.3.

22 The similarity between two matrices matches the sum of the differences between the values found in identical positions in the matrix.

23 Here we use the terminology given by [PRO 10] and will henceforth refer to the word whose distribution is calculated as the *head* of the vector and each entry of the bilingual lexicon presents an *element* of the context vector in the vector.

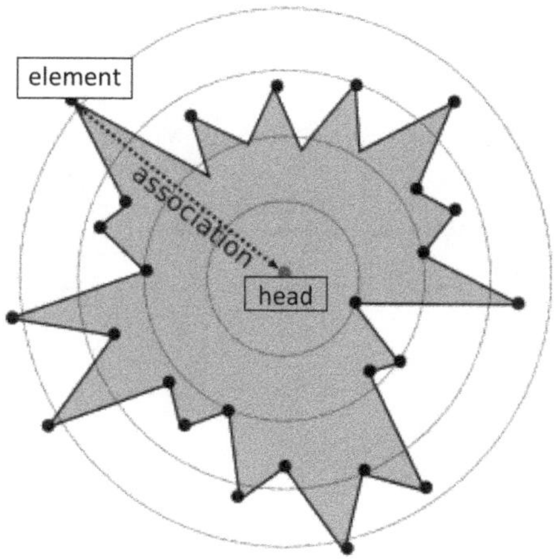

Figure 1.2. *Representation of a context vector – from [PRO 10]*

This alignment method can thus be summarized as follows:

1) Build the source and target term context vectors (see Figure 1.2):

- the vector of a term t matches $\vec{t} = \{(m_1, cooc_1), ...(m_n, cooc_n)\}$ in which each m_i is a co-occurring word with t at the heart of a given contextual window (for example five words to the left and five words to the right of t) and $cooc_i$ is the number of times this co-occurrence happens.

2) Normalize the number of co-occurrences due to a measure such as mutual information or the likelihood ratio (see Appendix A1.1).

3) Translate the source term vectors in the target language due to a bilingual dictionary (see Figure 1.3).

4) For each source term (see Figure 1.4):

- compare the translated context vector to the context vectors of the target words due to a similarity measure (see Appendix A1.2);

- rank the target term vectors by descending similarity;

- select the N vectors, which are most similar: the target terms associated to these N vectors are the candidate translations for the source term.

This alignment technique matches the state-of-the-art method, which was then used in a variation of ways, as we will see in section 1.3.3. However, before looking at these variations of the distributional method, let us first look at the evaluation methodologies of these alignment techniques.

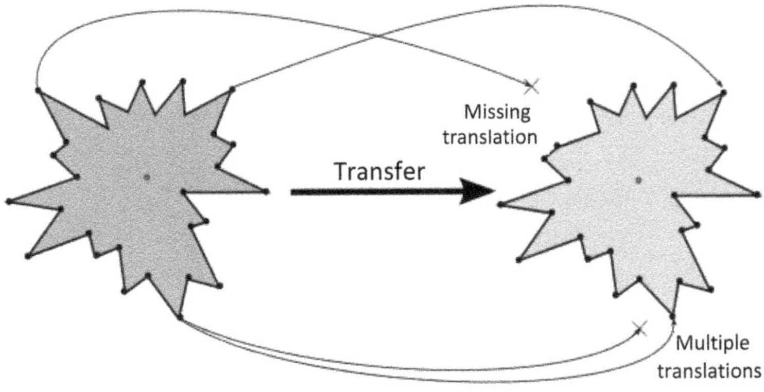

Figure 1.3. *Translation of a context vector – from [PRO 10]*

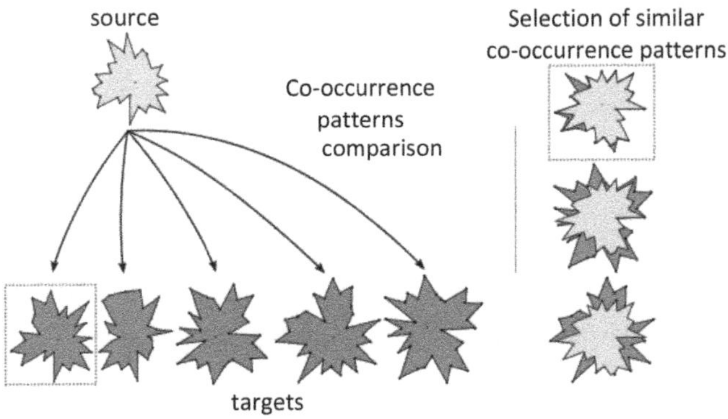

Figure 1.4. *Vector comparison and selection of the most similar vectors – from [PRO 10]*

1.3.2. *Term alignment evaluation*

The evaluation of alignment techniques is usually carried out by comparing the system outputs with a referential bilingual lexicon. The outputs of comparable corpora lexicon extraction system matches a list of pairs $(s, \{t_1, ...t_n\})$ in which s is a source term and $\{t_1, ...t_n\}$ is the ranked set of its candidate translations. Contrary to the parallel corpora lexicon extraction systems, it is very difficult to obtain a good-quality lexicon simply by selecting the first candidate translation. The measures usually used for parallel corpora such as *Alignement Error Rate* [OCH 00] are not the most relevant since we try, here more specifically, to assess the algorithm's ability to place the correct translation at the top of the list of candidate translations.

Literature presents three measures of evaluation: N-rank precision (also called *TopN*), MRR (*mean reciprocal rank*) and MAP (*mean average precision*).

1.3.2.1. *Precision at rank N or TopN*

This is by far the most common measure. It comes from the precision measure used in information retrieval. It represents the proportion of source terms, which have at least one correct translation in their N first candidate translations:

$$P_N = \frac{1}{|S|}\sum_{i=1}^{|S|} \alpha(T_{i^N}, R_i) \qquad [1.1]$$

$$\alpha(T_{i^N}, R_i) = \begin{cases} 1 \text{ if } T_{i^N} \cap R_i \neq \emptyset \\ 0 \text{ else} \end{cases}$$

in which:

– S is the set of source terms with at least one candidate translation;

– T_{i^N} is the set of the N first candidate translations for the source term i;

– R_i is the set of reference translations for the source term i.

It is also possible to calculate the recall on the N first candidate translations (R_N), which corresponds to the equation [1.1], except that the set S is the set of *all* the source terms, not just the source terms with at least one candidate translation. Increasing the precision makes the recall decrease, so $F1_N$, which corresponds to the harmonic mean of P_N and R_N, synthesizes the compromise between recall and precision [LAR 10b]. However, R_N and $F1_N$ are not often used. The bilingual lexicon extraction systems are mostly term *alignment* systems: they take a set of source terms and target terms at the input and calculate a translation result for each *source term, target term* pair. In effect, at least one translation is suggested for each source term.

1.3.2.2. *MRR*

The MRR measure matches the mean of the inverse of the correct translation ranks:

$$MRR = \frac{1}{|S|}\sum_{i=1}^{|S|} \frac{1}{rank_i} \qquad [1.2]$$

where S is the set of source terms with less than one candidate translation and $rank_i$ is the rank of the first correct candidate translation of the source term i [YU 09].

1.3.2.3. *MAP*

[LAR 10b] suggest using MAP, which is also an information retrieval measure. It corresponds to the average of the precision value obtained for the set of top k documents existing after each relevant document is retrieved, the average of the precision value obtained for the set of top documents existing after each relevant document is retrieved, and this value is then averaged over information needs:

$$MAP = \frac{1}{S}\sum_{i=1}^{|S|}\frac{1}{R_i}\sum_{j=1}^{R_i} Precision(T_{ij}) \qquad [1.3]$$

in which:

– S is the set of source terms;

– R_i is the number of referential translations for the term S_j;

– T_{ij} is the set of candidate translations given by the system for the term S_i with the reference translation j.

1.3.3. *Improvement and variants of the distributional approach*

Several variations and improvements on the distributional approach have been suggested. The latter focus on looking for distributional symmetry [CHI 04, SAD 03], the use of lexico-syntactic context (opposed to the contextual window) [OTE 05] and using anchor points, as is the case for parallel corpus sentence alignment [PRO 09]. Other variations have used second-order semantic affinities combined with semantic classes [DÉJ 02]. Finally, the work of [MOR 04] tried to align polylexical units.

1.3.3.1. *Favoring distributional symmetry*

[CHI 04] relies on the distributional symmetry hypothesis, which claims that "if two words are close in a translation direction as well as in the other (language A $\leftrightarrow$ language B) then there are greater chances that they might be a translation of one another than if they are close only in one direction" [CHI 04].

[CHI 04] thus uses what she calls *crossed similarity* in opposition to *classic similarity* [CHI 04]. After carrying out two alignment processes, one process in the direction of source to target and the other process in the direction of target to source, [CHI 04] calculates, for each pair of source and target terms (M_S, M_C), the harmonic mean of rM_C, M_C's rank among the candidate translations of M_S and rM_S, M_S's rank among the candidate translations of M_C:

$$MH(rM_C, rM_S) = \frac{2 \times rM_C \times rM_S}{rM_C + rM_S} \qquad [1.4]$$

Their experiments show that crossed similarity increases the number of translations found no matter what the type of the corpus (in the best case, the Top1 precision goes from 28% to 34%).

[SAD 03] also calculate a crossed similarity $SIM_{S \leftrightarrow C}$ between a source word M_S and a target word M_C based on:

$$SIM_{S \leftrightarrow C}(M_S, M_C) = SIM_{S \rightarrow C}(M_S, M_C) \times SIM_{C \rightarrow S}(M_C, M_S) \qquad [1.5]$$

in which $SIM_{S \rightarrow C}(M_S, M_C)$ is the similarity between M_S's vector translated into the target language and M_C's vector, and $SIM_{C \rightarrow S}(M_C, M_S)$ is the similarity between M_C's vector translated into the source language and M_S's vector.

The authors also apply a morphological filter to translations: a noun can only be translated by another noun, a verb can only be translated by another verb, etc. Alignments thus obtained are assessed through their input in a cross-lingual information retrieval system: the use of the lexicon acquired by crossed similarity significantly increases the R-precision[24] of the IR system by 27.1% (from 0.1417 to 0.1801) compared to the case in which the IR system only uses the lexicon acquired without crossed similarity.

1.3.3.2. *Using syntactic contexts*

[OTE 05] uses lexico-syntactic patterns acquired from a parallel corpus. For example, the pattern < *import of [NOUN]* > matches any noun appearing to the right of *import of*.

Bilingual syntactic patterns are acquired in three steps from an English–Spanish parallel corpus:

1) Acquisition of the English syntactic patterns on the source part of the corpus, for example: <import of [NOUN]>, <aid [VERB]>, <[NOUN] against fraud>

2) Acquisition of the Spanish syntactic patterns on the target part of the corpus, for example: <importación de [NOUN]>, <ayuda [VERB]>, <[NOUN] contra fraude>

3) Alignment of the English and Spanish patterns:

24 Average of precisions obtained for a recall level varying between 0 and 1.

<*import* of [NOUN]> → <importación de [NOUN]>

<*aid* [VERB]> → <ayuda [VERB]>

<*[NOUN]* against fraud> → <[NOUN] contra fraude>

The patterns are aligned using the Dice coefficient:

$$Dice(sourcepattern, targetpattern) = \frac{2|S \cap C|}{|S| + |C|} \qquad [1.6]$$

in which S corresponds to the number of sentences in which the source pattern appears, C corresponds to the number of sentences in which the target pattern appears and $|S \cap C|$ corresponds to the number of times in which the source pattern and target pattern appear in the same aligned sentences. Only the pattern pairs with the best coefficient are retained (the threshold is determined empirically).

These bilingual patterns are used instead of a bilingual lexicon: the context vector of a word w contains, for each bilingual syntactic pattern p, a score indicating how much w is encountered in p. For example, if w is a noun, its context vector will indicate how often it is associated with the <import of [NOUN]> and <[NOUN] against fraud>patterns. The weight of the association between the head of the vector w and a syntactic pattern p is calculated from the number of times in which w instances p,[25], from the number of patterns instanced by w and the number of words instancing p.

[OTE 05] obtains a precision of 89% on the Top1 and 96% on the Top5. These very good results can be explained by the nature of their data: the evaluation lexicon is made up of words whose number of occurrences is higher than 100 and the comparable corpus is composed of the unaligned parts belonging to a single-parallel corpus.

1.3.3.3. *Relying on trusted elements*

[PRO 09] uses anchor points, i.e. words used as trustworthy elements, for they are automatically identifiable, are not ambiguous and belong to the comparable corpus' topic. The authors suggest giving them more weight than other elements in the context vectors due to their properties making them highly discriminating elements. Working from Japanese to French and English, they use transliterations and classical compounds as anchor points. The association measure between head and elements of the vector is the likelihood ratio. This measure is recalculated to favor anchor points. To this end, the sum of the likelihood ratio of a single vector is redistributed between

25 For example, in *import of sugar* the noun *sugar* instances the pattern <import of [NOUN]>.

the co-occurrents in order to reinforce the anchor points and minimize those who are not:

$$TV(M,m) = \begin{cases} TVI(M,m) + \beta & m \in PA \\ TVI(M,m) - disparity_M & \text{if } m \notin PA \end{cases} \quad [1.7]$$

$$disparity_M = \frac{|PA|_M}{|\neg PA|_M} \times \beta \quad [1.8]$$

where $TVI(M,m)$ is the initial likelihood ratio between the vector head M and its co-occurent m, PA is the set of anchor points, PA_M the co-occurents of M which are anchor points, $\neg PA_M$ the co-occurents of M which are not anchor points, β is a coefficient varying between 1 and 20 (in the experiments, the best results were obtained with $\beta = 8$).

Compared to the state-of-the-art method, the use of anchor points enables them to increase precision by +18% (from 17% to 20%) on the Top1 for English–Japanese translations and by +10% (from 20% to 22%) on the Top1 for French–Japanese translations.

1.3.3.4. *Improving semantic information representation*

[HAZ 12] notice that the way in which information is represented in the state-of-the-art approach is not optimal since it contains redundant and potentially incomplete information at the same time.

The authors suggest improving the context vector representation by applying a transformation by independent component analysis (ICA). This transformation enables them to generate a new-representation space in which the information is as independent as possible. The approach takes four steps:

1) Reduction of the matrix size by applying a principle component analysis (PCA).

2) Transformation by ICA of the matrix, taking into account the information of global nature (bilingual dictionary entry context) in order to obtain a representation space called GICA then calculation of the distance between source terms and target terms in this new space.

3) Transformation by ICA of the matrix, taking into account the information of local nature (target term contexts) so as to obtain a representation space called LICA then calculation of the distances between source terms and target terms in this new space.

4) Calculation of the distances between source and target terms by linearly combining the LICA and GICA distances.

The results obtained show that the GLICA approach provides better results than the state-of-the-art approach from Top6 when using the best parameter combination.[26] The state-of-the-art approach obtains a precision level of 73.77% on the Top20 and the GLICA approach obtains 75.40% on the Top20. The approaches were tested on two corpora: a small specialized corpus and a large journalistic corpus.

1.3.3.5. *Using second-order semantic affinities*

The state-of-the-art method establishes the correspondence between the distribution of a source word and that of a target word by direct translation: each of the co-occurrences of the source word is "mapped" into the target corpus through the bilingual lexicon, then one tries to find a target word with a similar distribution to that of the "mapping". This method is highly dependent on the bilingual lexicon's coverage: only elements present in the lexicon and the two corpora will be present in the context vectors.

To overcome this issue of coverage, [DÉJ 02] suggests a method using distributional similarities between the terms to be aligned and the bilingual lexicon entries. They consider two terms whose semantic proximity with the bilingual lexicon entries are similar to be potential translations. The alignment method can be broken down into five steps:

1) Build the context vectors for the source terms and target terms to be aligned.

2) Build the context vectors for the source words and target words present in the bilingual dictionary.

3) Build, for each source term, and target term, its *similarity vector*: this vector indicates – for each of the entries e in the bilingual lexicon – the similarity between the context vector of the term and the context vector of the entry e. The size of the similarity vector can be parametrized, i.e. we can choose to only retain the n entries the most similar.

4) For each pair *(source term, target term)*, calculate the similarity between their respective similarity vectors.

5) For each source term, select the N target terms whose similarity vector is the closest to the source term's similarity vector.

This method thus enables the authors to translate any word in the corpus, even if no other element of the vector can be translated.

26 For the state-of-the-art approach, the best results are obtained with the likelihood ratio as the normalization measure of the co-occurrences count and the Jaccard as similarity measure. For the GLICA method, the best results are obtained with mutual information as the similarity measure. The similarity measure is the standardized Euclidian distance. These measures are given in Appendix 1.

[DÉJ 02] call their method "interlingual similarity translation"[27] and oppose it to the "direct translation"[28] advocated by [FUN 97]. Indeed, what is projected in the target language is the level of similarity between the lexical entries and the word to be translated, and not the context of the word to be translated.

The results obtained are not necessarily convincing. At best, the interlingual method enables the authors to obtain 51 correct translations on the Top20 whereas the state-of-the-art method obtains 57.

1.3.3.6. *Improving the bilingual resource with semantic classes*

[DÉJ 02] experiment with the use of the semantic classes of a thesaurus in combination with the interlingual method (see section 1.3.3.5). Instead of using a traditional bilingual resource, the authors use a thesaurus. The thesaurus is used to include new entries in the similarity vectors used in the interlingual method. For a term to be aligned t matching the similarity vector vs, the inclusion of new entries happens as follows:

1) E is an empty starting set.

2) Select the n entries of the thesaurus the closest to t, these entries are the set E_0.

3) For all the entry pairs (e_1, e_2) in E_0:

- add to E all the thesaurus entries, which can be found on the minimal path between e_1 and e_2;

- add e_1 and e_2 to E.

4) Add all the entries found in E to vs.

In the end, this technique enables them to obtain 63 correct translations on the Top20 against 57 for the state-of-the-art method.

1.3.3.7. *Translating polylexical units*

The works mentioned until now only focus on the translation of monolexical units (i.e. units made of a single word). [MOR 04] suggest adapting the interlingual similarity approach to polylexical units. This method is interesting for us, since we will need to translate such units within the context of CAT.

[MOR 04] suggest building the polylexical unit context vector as the union of the context vectors of each word which makes up the polylexical unit. The alignment method used also calls upon second-order semantic affinities:

1) Build the context vectors for source monolexical units.

27 "*traduction par similarité interlingue*".

28 "*traduction directe*".

2) Build the context vectors for source polylexical units as the union of the context vectors of each of the words that makes them up.

3) Build context vectors for target monolexical units.

4) Build context vectors for target polylexical units as the union of the context vectors of each of the words that makes them up.

5) For each source unit to be translated (see Figure 1.5):

- select the n entries in the bilingual lexicon, which are the closest to the source unit;

- select the target context vectors in the n bilingual entries;

- calculate the barycenter of these n target vectors: we obtain a mean context vector in the target language;

- compare this mean vector to the context vectors in the target units;

- select the most similar of the N vectors: the heads of these N vectors are the candidate translations for the source unit.

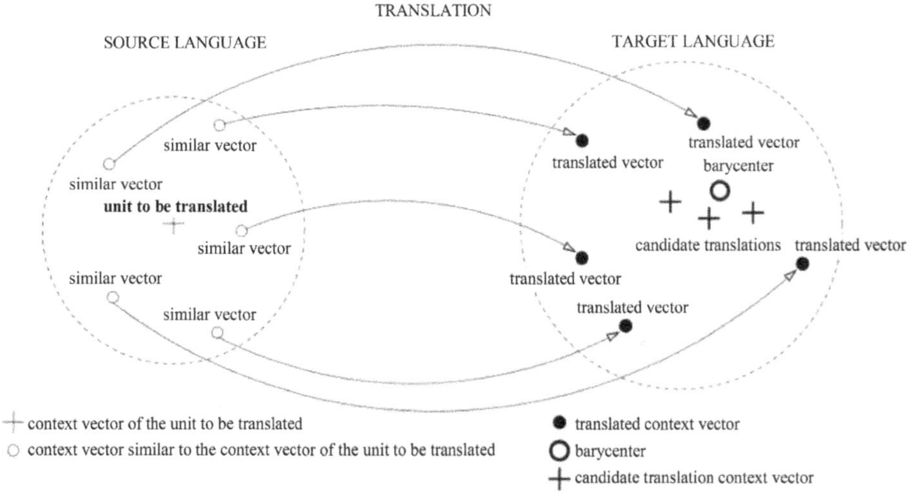

Figure 1.5. *Adapting the interlingual approach for the alignment of polylexical terms – from [MOR 04]*

This method provides good results for the polylexical terms whose translation is also a polylexical term (88% on the Top20). The results are more limited for polylexical terms whose translation is either a monolexical or a polylexical term (55% on the Top20). By comparison, the precision level obtained for monolexical terms whose translation is also a monolexical term is 51% on the Top20.

REFERENCE	LANGUAGES	ELEMENTS TO BE TRANSLATED			SUBJECT DOMAIN		BILINGUAL RESOURCES		METHOD	PRECISION		
		NB.	TYPE	NB OCC.		CORPUS	SIZE	TYPE		TOP1	TOP10	TOP20
[RAP 99]	DE → EN	100	UML		press	298M	16k	LG	direct	.65	.89	
[CHI 02]	FR → EN	95	UML	≥ 100	medical SC	1.2M	18k	medical	direct	.13	.61	.94
[DÉJ 02]	DE → EN	1800	UML		medical SC	200k	46k	LG	direct		.44	.57
							15k	medical thesaurus	interlingual		.43	.51
		180	UML	high	social sc. SC	8M	46k	LG	direct		.35	.42
							10k	social sc. thesaurus	interlingual		.79	.84
[MOR 04]	FR → EN	100	UML	≥ 5	environment	4.9 M	22 k	LG	interlingual		.41	.51
		100	UPL translated by UML or UPL	≥ 5	TECH						.45	.55
		100	UPL translated by	≥ 5							.87	.88
[MOR 07]	FR → JA	100	UML	≥ 2	medical SC + VG	1.5M	173k	LG, medical	direct		.51	.6
		100	UML et UPL	≥ 2	medical SC	659k					.3	.42
[PRO 10]	FR → EN	122	UML	≥ 5	medical SC	507k	173k	LG, medical	direct	.21	.47	.57
		648	UML	≥ 15						.13	.34	.41
[HAZ 12]	FR → EN	122	UML	≥ 5	medical SC	530k	244k	LG	ICA	.34	.64	.76
		500	UML		press	5M				.16	.32	.40

Table 1.1. *Results of the state of the art - alignment by contextual similarity*

We have seen in this section different alignment techniques – the state-of-the-art method, the interlingual method – as well as several variations on these methods – use of semantic classes, of anchor points, use of lexico-syntactic contexts, etc. Table 1.1 offers a synthesis of the results of this work. This table also specifies the type of terms to be translated (monolexical, coded as *UML* or polylexical, coded as *UPL*) as well as the size and nature of the corpora used: generalist texts (LG), scientific (SC), popular science (VG) or technical (TECH) specialized texts.

We can see that beyond the alignment techniques, the data used as well as the various parameters also influence the quality of the results. This impact is analyzed in section 1.3.4.

1.3.4. *Influence of data and parameters on alignment quality*

[LAR 10b] already provided a very good overview of the impact of data and parameters on the quality of the extracted lexicon. We have here added to their observations with an analysis of the results obtained through the approaches described in section 1.3.3. We start by describing the impact of the data (section 1.3.4.1) then the impact of the parameters (section 1.3.4.2).

1.3.4.1. *Data*

The factors which influence the quality of alignments the most are linked to the nature of the data:

Frequency of the elements to be translated – an element is all the better translated when it is frequent: its context is calculated from a greater number of occurrences and thus it is more representative and gives a better semantic characterization of the element to be translated. This is particularly well shown in the experiments by [PRO 10]: the less frequent words (maximum 25 occurrences) obtain approximately 7% on the Top20 whereas the most frequent occurrences (beyond 800 occurrences) obtain a score of 100% on the Top20.

Specialization of the elements to be translated – [CHI 04] mentions that the specialized elements are better translated than the general language elements, no matter their frequency. A similar result is obtained by [HAZ 12]: the alignment obtained are of better quality for the specialized corpus even though the press corpus is much bigger. This can be explained by the fact that the terms are generally semantically straightforward whereas polysemy or meaning variations are frequent in common words: this means that the context vector is more "fuzzy" and less discriminating.

Size of the corpus – when comparable corpora are large, the terms to be translated generally occur a great many times. This enabled us to build more representative context vectors. But the size in itself is insufficient. Corpora must also be sufficiently comparable.

Comparability of the corpora – [LI 10] defined a corpus comparability measure. This measure shows the expectation of finding the translation of a source word in the target corpus (and vice versa).[29] It is based on the projection of a bilingual dictionary in the corpus (see Appendix A1.3).

Relying on this measure, [LI 10] shows the impact of the comparability of corpora on the precision of alignments. [LI 10] starts from an original corpus called C from which they extract two highly comparable corpora called C^1 (comparability of 0.882) and C^2 (comparability of 0.916). The lexicons extracted from C^1 and C^2 are of better quality than those extracted from C: [LI 10] increase the precision of the results by between 5.3% and 9.5% on the Top20.

Specialization of the bilingual lexicon – in their experiments, [LAR 10b] compared the results obtained depending on the degree of specialization of the entries in the bilingual lexicon used to translate context vectors. For a bilingual lexicon of 5,000 entries, the results are slightly better when the lexicon is partially made of specialized lexies than when it is only composed of entries belonging to the general language (F1-measure on the Top1 goes from 38.9 to 39.4 and MAP goes from 0.471 to 0.473). It is the same for [PRO 10] who decides to reinforce the specialized elements (anchor points). In a personal experiment, we also observed that the presence of specialized elements in the bilingual lexicon improved the results (see section 1.4.1.5).

[CHI 04] obtains contradictory results. She mentions that adding words from the general language to the bilingual lexicon improves the results (from 59.4% to 100% on the Top20). This is particularly visible when the elements to be translated are terms and not words from the general language. However, the first lexicon is made of 4,963 entries, which only belong to the medical field, and the "improved" lexicon contains 6,210 entries belonging to the medical field and the general language. It is hard to say if the improvement of the results is only due to the addition of general vocabulary in the bilingual lexicon or the simple increase in the number of entries.

1.3.4.2. *Parameters*

The parameters involved in the distributional approach are:

– size and nature of the context in which the co-occurrences are gathered: sentence, paragraph, window of n words around the vector's head and syntactic context;

---

29 For the comparable corpus C, if we consider the translation process from the English part C_e to the French part C_f, a comparability measure M_{ef} can be defined on the basis of the expectation of finding, for each English word w_e in the vocabulary C_e^v of C_e , its translation in the vocabulary C_f^v of C_f. 645.

– normalizing the co-occurrences count: several measures are possible such as the likelihood ratio, the mutual information or the TF-IDF. These measures are detailed in Appendix A1.1;

– calculating the similarity between vectors, for example: cosine measure, Jaccard and Euclidian distance. These measures are described in Appendix A1.2.

These parameters are complicated to manipulate. [PRO 10] shows that the optimal combination of parameters depends on the corpus used and the languages involved and that it is impossible to determine it in advance.

Moreover, [LAR 10b] mentions that the choice of context can also depend on the final use of the bilingual lexicons. In their experiment, if the context matches the paragraph, they obtain a very good recall on the Top20, which can be useful for the semi-supervised creation of linguistic resources. However, if the context matches the sentence, we obtain a higher precision, which is ideal for the unsupervised creation of bilingual lexica.

[HAZ 12] shows that in a press corpus of large size, the best results are obtained with the likelihood ratio whereas on a small specialized corpus, the best results are obtained with mutual information. Only the size of the context can be anticipated: the elements with low frequency are better translated when the context vector is calculated in a short window [PRO 10].

A solution to this parameter problem would be to learn the best parameter configuration before extracting the lexicon. Several configurations could be tested by using translation pairs present in the bilingual lexicon as evaluation lexicon. The best configuration thus obtained could then be applied to align the terms.

1.3.5. *Limits of the distributional approach*

While parallel corpus alignment tools generate accurate translation pairs in more than 80% of the cases [DAI 94b, MAC 08, VIN 10], this is far from the case for comparable corpus alignment. We have seen in the previous section that the results obtained with comparable corpora vary between 30% and 89% on the $Top10$ and between 40% and 94% on the $Top20$ depending on the language pairs, the volume and quality of the data, the nature and frequency of the elements to be translated.

This contrast between the results obtained in comparable corpora and the results obtained in parallel corpora can be explained for two reasons:

Research space – in a parallel corpus, the research space is progressively diminished: one starts by looking for anchor points (cognates, figures) then aligns sentences, and then the translations of the terms are looked for within pairs of aligned sentences. In a comparable corpus, the translations of the terms are looked for in all the corpus.

Translation presence – in a parallel corpus, unless the translator has forgotten to translate a word, the source term always has a translation. In a comparable corpus, not only can a term not have any translation, it is also very hard to determine whether or not this translation might be present.

In addition, there are limitations inherent to the distributional method:

Semantic homogeneity of the vectors – if the element to be translated is polysemic or presents variations of meaning, its context vector will be less semantically homogeneous, since the element is used in varied contexts.

Term frequency – the element to be translated and its translation must be sufficiently frequent: the more the vectors are built from a great number of co-occurrences, the more representative they are of the distribution of the term.

Things are even more complicated when the alignment happens in a specialized corpus to acquire bilingual terminology lists:

Prior terminology extraction – there is a reliance on the term extractor: the target term can be found in the target corpus without having been extracted by the extractor.

Relevance of the bilingual dictionary – the bilingual dictionary used for the transfer can contain translations which are not appropriate in the subject domain of the texts and contribute to bias the projection of the source vector into the target language.

Size of the corpus – specialized corpora, since they correspond to a well-defined topic, are often small: their volume is closer to the hundreds of thousands of words [PRO 10] than the millions of words [RAP 99]. Therefore, the terms occur less often and their vectors are less representative.

Polylexical terms – we also try to align polylexical units. However, as it is mentioned in [MOR 07], complex terms have lower frequencies than simple terms, which make their context vectors less representative. If the complex term vector is a vector made of the vectors of the lexical words that create the term, then this lowers the semantic homogeneity of the vector.

In this section, we have presented a state-of-the-art of the comparable corpus alignment techniques. In section 1.4, we will describe the way in which we have created a CAT prototype that relies on the distributional method to extract bilingual lexicons from comparable corpora.

1.4. CAT software prototype for comparable corpora processing

In the industrial context of LINGUA ET MACHINA, comparable-corpus extraction is meant to provide impetus for the generation of linguistic resources in emerging fields or fields in which the corporation has very little translation memory. The provided corpora should be small specialized corpora (less than 2 million words). The precision scores thus obtained would be at best between 34% on the Top1 and 76% on the Top20. We can immediately anticipate the fact that translators will not be satisfied with a simple list of source terms and candidate translation alignments. To overcome these uncertain results, it is necessary to accompany these alignments with various pieces of information presented as a terminology record, which will allow the translation to decide which candidate translation is the right one.

The developed prototype is shown in Figure 1.9. It is able to extract terms from texts in the source and target languages and align them with a method based on the distributional approach (section 1.4.1). Then the prototype collects information from the texts in the corpus and on the web, which will be offered to the translator as a terminology record (section 1.4.3). A user interface for looking up the extracted lexicons was also developed (section 1.4.2).

1.4.1. *Implementation of a term alignment method*

1.4.1.1. *Implementation and data*

The point of this work is to create a first simple prototype, which could then be used to observe how the translators approach the lexicons extracted from comparable corpora and assess the contribution of these lexicons to specialized translation (Chapter 2). We have chosen to implement the state-of-the-art method due to its ease of implementation. The series of variations suggested required either specific resources (parallel corpora to learn lexico-syntactic patterns, thesauri), or the development of pre-processing tools (transliteration and neoclassical compound extraction), or these methods are time-consuming, which is always an issue in an industrial environment (crossed similarity, interlingual similarity, GLICA method). From all of the approaches mentioned, we will here only keep [MOR 04]'s approach for the alignment of polylexical terms. As it was demonstrated by [PRO 10], at the current level of research, it is impossible to decide at first what will be the best combination of parameters to use. In a corporate environment, we always apply the same parameter, regardless of the size or topic of the corpora. We have arbitrarily chosen to use the Jaccard index as the similarity measure and the likelihood ratio for normalizing the co-occurrences count. However, we have carried out a few experiments regarding the interactions between the size of the contextual window and the frequency of the terms to be translated. We have also assessed the input of specialized resources, which can be a simple and efficient means to improve the quality of lexica.

These tests were carried out on a small specialized English–French corpus (approximately 400,000 words per language) concerning breast cancer. This corpus is described in more detail in sections 2.3.2.1.1 and 5.2. To validate our experiments, we used two reference lexica:

Specialized lexicon: 177 English–French pairs of monolexical terms collected by [PRO 10] from the UMLS[30] and the *Grand dictionnaire terminologique*.[31]

Generalist lexicon: 1,842 English–French pairs extracted from our bilingual dictionary.

45 entries overlap between the two lexica. In accordance with the other research works, we ensured that each term to be translated appeared at least 5 times in the corpus. Translation was carried out from English to French.

The bilingual lexicons acquisition method implemented can be broken down into four steps:

– Extraction of the terms to be aligned (section 1.4.1.2).

– Gathering the context vectors (section 1.4.1.3).

– Translating the context vectors (section 1.4.1.5).

– Aligning the terms (section 1.4.1.6).

1.4.1.2. *Extraction of the terms to be aligned*

The terms to be aligned are extracted from source and target corpora. These terms are either polylexical terms extracted by the terminology extractor[32] integrated within SIMILIS (LINGUA ET MACHINA's translation memory software), or monolexical terms (e.g. simple words) belonging to the grammatical categories of noun, adjective, adverb and verb, occurring more than five times. The minimum threshold of five times was chosen for two reasons: (1) it reduces the number of terms to be aligned and thus the processing time; (2) it is the minimum occurence number chosen in the research works presented in section 1.3. We believe that below five occurrences, the context vector is not significative. The pre-processing of the corpus (tokenization, lemmatization and part-of-speech tagging) is carried out by the linguistic analyzer XELDA.[33]

30 Medical meta-thesaurus, www.nlm.nih.gov/research/umls.

31 www.granddictionnaire.com.

32 While this tool is called *terminology extractor* by LINGUA ET MACHINA, it does not actually extract terms *per se* (e.g. referring to a field-specific concept) but rather noun and verb phrases.

33 www.temis.com.

1.4.1.3. *Collecting context vectors*

1.4.1.3.1. Monolexical term context vectors

The size of the context was chosen after several attempts on our corpus. Contrary to [PRO 10], we have not observed any influence of the frequency of the terms to be translated on the size of the ideal contextual window (see Figure 1.6). In our prototype, the size of the context will thus be of three lexical words to the left and three lexical words to the right of the term to be translated, regardless of its frequency.

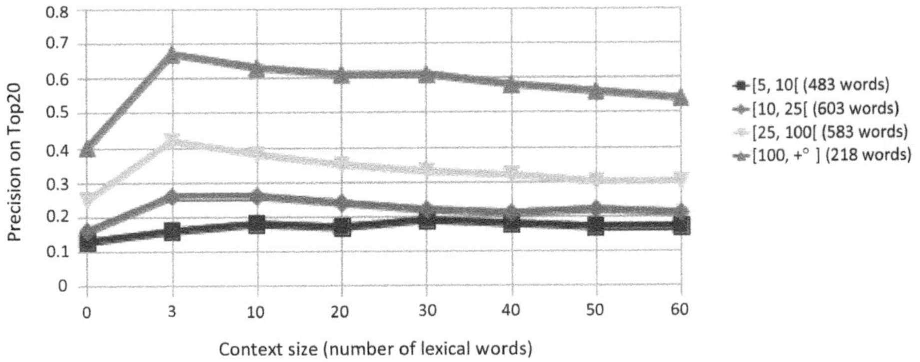

The units to be translated match the terminology entries and generalist entries. Each curve matches a frequency range, and the number of entries in this frequency range is mentioned in brackets.

Figure 1.6. *Influence of the frequency of terms to be translated on the size of the optimal contextual window*

The number of co-occurrences is standardized with the likelihood ratio [DUN 93]. Its calculation is detailed in Appendix A1.1.1.

1.4.1.4. *Polylexical term context vectors*

We calculate the context vector of a polylexical term, just like [MOR 04] did, from the context of each lexical term that is contained in it. [MOR 04] calculates the union of these vectors; as for us, we calculate an average vector:[34]

– The term *breast cancer* has two lexical words: *cancer* and *breast*

– Their context vectors are:

- cancer $= \{(cancer \leftrightarrow 50), (breast \leftrightarrow 30), (treatment \leftrightarrow 25)\}$

- breast $= \{(breast \leftrightarrow 60), (cancer \leftrightarrow 30), (ablation \leftrightarrow 20)\}$

34 This leads to a gain of about two points of precision on the Top20, but we do not know if this is specific to our corpus or independent of the data.

– The context vectors of *breast cancer* is thus:

- breast cancer $= \{(breast \leftrightarrow 45), (cancer \leftrightarrow 40), (treatment \leftrightarrow 12.5), (ablation \leftrightarrow 10)\}$

1.4.1.5. *Translation of the source context vectors*

Source context vectors are translated into target languages with several dictionaries. First, we use the bilingual dictionary integrated in our linguistic analyzer (XELDA). This dictionary has 37,655 entries (an English word is translated by 1.58 French words on an average). The size of the dictionary was increased with translation links extracted from Wikipedia and Wiktionary. This enables us to translate 18% more words in context vectors. Figure 1.7 shows the input of these two resources.

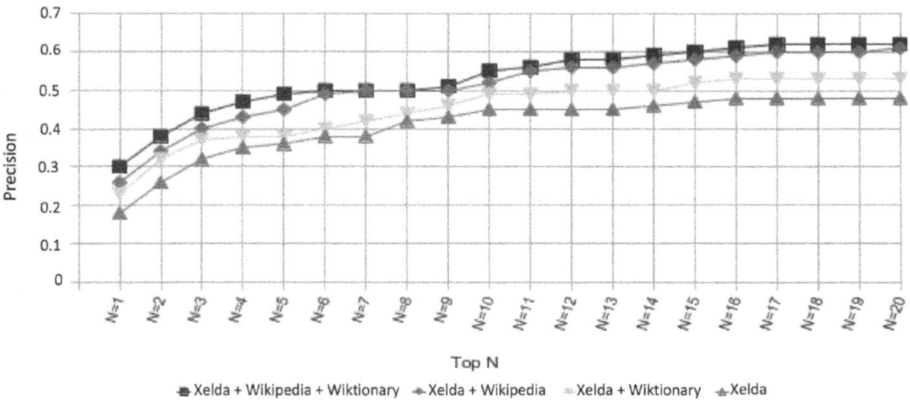

Figure 1.7. *Influence of the bilingual dictionary (Specialized lexicon)*

When a context word has several possible translations, its likelihood ratio is distributed over all its translations according to the frequency of each translation in the target corpus. For example:

– the vector of *patient* will contain the association $(related \leftrightarrow 60)$;

– *related* can be translated by:

- *parent*: 10 occurrences in the target corpus,

- *proche* (kin): five occurrences in the target corpus,

– The vector of *patient* thus translated into the target language will contain the associations:

- $(parent \leftrightarrow 40)$,

- ($proche \leftrightarrow 20$).

When several context words match one translation, the likelihood ratios add up. For example:

– the vector of *patient* contains the association ($rebuilding \leftrightarrow 10$) and the association ($reconstruction \leftrightarrow 20$);

- *rebuilding* is translated by *reconstruction*,

- *reconstruction* is also translated by *reconstruction*,

– the *patient* vector translated in the target language will thus contain the association:

- ($reconstruction \leftrightarrow \underline{30}$).

1.4.1.6. *Term alignment*

The similarity measure used to compare the source and target vectors is the Jaccard index [MOR 04], which is detailed in the Appendix A1.2.2. The alignment is carried out from English to French and we retain the Top 20 best candidate translations.

[MOR 04]'s experiments on the alignment between monolexical and polylexical terms had produced limited results, so we have separated these two types of unit. The monolexical terms can only be aligned with other monolexical terms and the polylexical terms can only be aligned with other polylexical terms.

For the monolexical terms, we added a grammatical category filter (as [SAD 03] had): nouns can only be aligned with nouns, adjectives with other adjectives, etc.

Figure 1.8 shows the differences in the results obtained on these two lexica. We can see that the terms from the specialized lexicons are better translated than those of the generalist lexica. Two reasons can explain this: (1) specialized entries are on average more frequent (166 occurrences against 54 for generalist entries), which means their context vector represents them better; (2) as specialized vocabulary, these terms are probably less subject to polysemy, which means their context vectors are more homogeneous.

1.4.2. *Terminological records extraction*

As we mentioned in section 1.2.3, a simple list of alignments is not sufficient for translators: they need to be able to access information, which will recontextualize the term and allow them to understand its meaning.

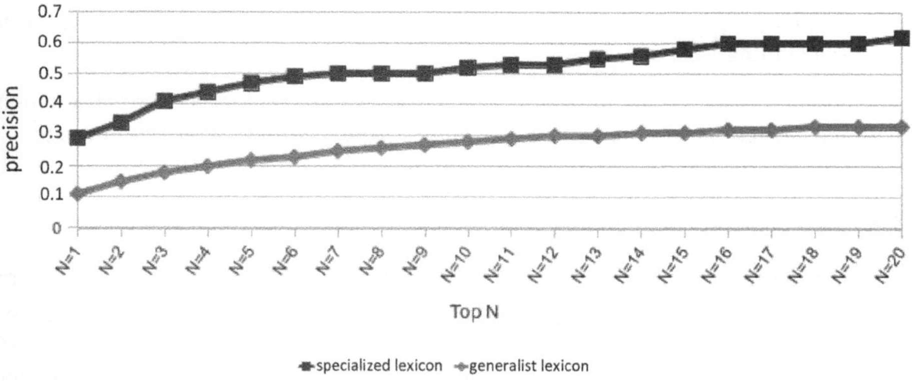

Figure 1.8. *Precision to the Nth rank according to the type of terms to be translated*

This is the reason why we developed a terminological record extraction module, which gathers the following information for each term:

The entry term – this is the lemma for monolexical terms and the most common inflected form for polylexical terms.

Part-of-speech – we display the part of the speech tagged by XELDA (monolexical terms) or a grammatical type tagged by SIMILIS (polylexical terms).

Frequency – the number of occurrences or frequency (number of occurrences divided by the number of words in the corpus) does not mean much to translators. We chose instead to use the three classes calculated from the distribution of the occurrences of lexical words:

– frequent use (number of occurrences of the term is above the 90th percentile);

– infrequent use (the number of occurrences ranges from the 51st percentile to the 90th percentile);

– rare use (the number of occurrences is below or equal to the 50th percentile).

Definition – when it exists, we provide a link to the Wikipedia or Wiktionary page.

Collocations – collocations are words whose appearance in the left or right context of the term is significantly frequent (we used the likelihood ratio to compute this). For example, *lymph node* is linked to *axillary lymph node*. To select collocations, we rank all the collocations found in the corpus by descending likelihood ratio and only keep those that belong in the top 25%.

Context – these are all the sentences in which the term appears. The term is set in bold in the sentence. A link to the document from which the sentence is taken is provided. Contexts are not ranked.

Variations – these are simply spelling variations (e.g. hyphens, alternation between *-or* / *-our* in English).

Close terms – these are the terms, which have at least one lexical word in common with the key term, for example *tumor* is linked to *benign tumor, tumor growth*, etc.

1.4.3. *Lexicon consultation interface*

Translators can look up the lexicons in a dedicated interface. Screen captures are provided in Appendix 3 and the prototype can be freely seen at the following address: http://80.82.238.151/Metricc/InterfaceValidation/.[35] This consultation interface offers tools to facilitate term searches. The translator has a query field, which allows him/her to explore the lexicon at ease, and "fuzzy" queries are possible. For example, the query "*lymph%*" will bring up all the terms starting with *lymph-*. If none of the terms match the request, a search is carried out directly in the corpus's texts.

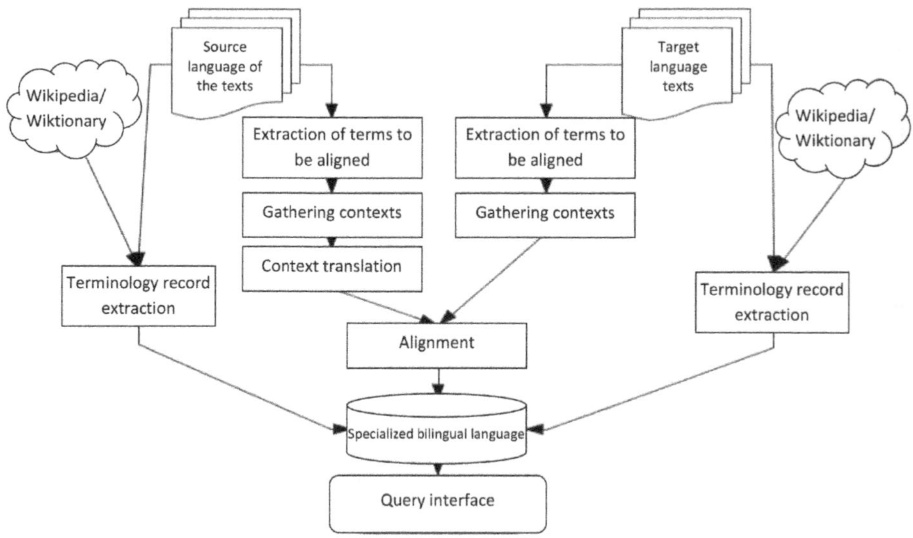

Figure 1.9. *Implementing a method to acquire bilingual lexicons and a search tool of the extracted lexica*

1.5. Summary

This chapter started with a short historical overview of the beginning of MT. We saw that the field of the *translation aid* – a field in which we have carried out our

35 The user name is "test". Leave the password field empty.

research – arises from the first disappointing machine translation tools. Computer-aided translation tools have a less ambitious but more realistic goal: the objective is to provide the translator with a tool to improve his productivity, not to replace him/her.

Until recently, translation aid software always required the existence of a translation memory to operate correctly. This created issues when there was no such translation memory (languages with few available resources, emerging fields). Moreover, research in translation studies has shown that – due to quality reasons – translators prefer to access multilingual corpora of texts, which have not been generated by a translation (comparable corpora). These comparable corpora allowed them to gather information about linguistic uses and terminology used in the technical field on which they were working. In spite of this obvious need, there are actually very few tools that can help the translator to explore comparable corpora and identify translation pairs.

The first part of the research carried out here was to create a prototype of such a tool. After reflecting on the state-of-the-art of alignment techniques based on comparable corpora, we have opted for a state-of-the-art method. This method does not require any pre-processing or specific linguistic resources and is more time-efficient than other more elaborate methods.

Once the terms are aligned, our prototype automatically generates terminological records, which have various pieces of information, which might help the translator. A consultation interface was developed to facilitate resource access.

While translation studies confirmed the appeal of comparable corpora to check translation hypotheses or better approach a technical field, we do not know how these corpora and their corresponding lexicons can be used as the only translation assistance tool (case in which there is no translation memory). This is the direction in which we take our research in Chapter 2.

2

User-Centered Evaluation of Lexicons Extracted from Comparable Corpora

2.1. Introduction

The aim of this chapter is to propose and experiment with an applicative evaluation protocol of the bilingual lexicons extracted from comparable corpora, intended for specialized translation. In this case, we rely on the prototype developed at LINGUA ET MACHINA, which we described in section 1.4.[1]

As far as we can tell, the lexicons coming from comparable corpora were assessed only in applicative terms within the context of cross-lingual information research and machine translation (MT).

In cross-lingual information research, [LI 11] increase the bilingual dictionary used by a search engine with translations extracted from comparable corpora. They show that the combination of the generalist resources and the lexicons extracted from the comparable corpus significantly improve the system's results (up to +0.016 points of Mean Average Precision (MAP).

In MT, [CAR 12] use comparable corpora to perform domain adaptation of MT systems. The inclusion of translations from comparable corpora in the translation system helps us to gain 2–3 BLEU points depending on the corpora.

1 The work presented is the result of work done within the context of the METRRICC ANR project in which we took part. Our participation in this set of work concerned the design of the protocol as well as a first experiment on it aiming to streamline the evaluation process. The evaluation itself was carried out by Dr. Planas from the Université Catholique de l'Ouest with a greater number of participants.

As for specialized (human) translation, we will also adopt a contrasting approach: starting from the beginning (the translator only has generalist bilingual resources), we will observe whether or not providing lexicons extracted from comparable corpora, in addition to the generalist resources, effectively enables him/her to improve the final quality of the translations. We will also use a second basis of comparison that will match the usual situation of the translator, in which he/she has at his/her disposal all kinds of specialized resources in addition to generalist dictionaries.

Once the translations are generated, then the question of evaluating their quality arises. While cross-lingual information research and MT have reference measures, human translation does not.

Therefore, we focused, in section 2.2, on the evaluation methodology used both in MT (section 2.2.1) and in human translation (section 2.2.2). While we would have liked, as an end goal, to evaluate human translation, it appeared more interesting to query the techniques used in MT, especially since they are much more operational than those found in translation studies.

In section 2.3, we will expose the assessment protocol that we have developed and describe its implementation as well as the results obtained. Section 2.4 looks at the results of our experiment and suggests new research paths to explore.

2.2. Translation quality evaluation methodologies

2.2.1. *Machine translation evaluation*

MT evaluation has two purposes. First, it analyzes, during the development of an MT system, the impact of a system modification on the quality of the translations. Second, the evaluation enables us to compare the systems between them, usually during a broad evaluation campaign. Each of these purposes has a matching evaluation technique.

When the evaluation is carried out during the system's development, the measures used are machine calculable measures based on reference translations; we then refer to *automatic evaluation* or *objective evaluation*. It is simple and cheap to implement these measures, although they are still perceived as practical substitutes to a much more costly evaluation which is considered to be better: human evaluation.

Human evaluation, also known as *subjective evaluation* is used in the *Statistical Workshop on Machine Translation* evaluation campaigns of the Association for Computational Linguistics (ACL) whose latest results are given by [KOE 06] and [CAL 07, CAL 08, CAL 09, CAL 10]. This evaluation requires judges to grade the quality of the translation. We can easily guess the cost of this in terms of time, organization and judge training; moreover, the results are hard to reproduce. However, the current consensus is in favor of human evaluation, which is considered to be better able to account for the quality of a translation.

In the following sections, we will look at the automatic evaluation techniques (section 2.2.1.1) and the human evaluation techniques (section 2.2.1.2).

2.2.1.1. *Automatic evaluation measures*

Automatic evaluation indirectly measures the quality of a translation: we do not assess the quality of the translation itself but whether it matches a reference translation produced by a professional translator. Instead of manipulating and comparing the linguistic parameters such as the preservation of meaning and the fluidity of the text, the evaluation measures use shallow or graphical information such as words or common word sequences between assessed translation and reference translation.

The best known and most widespread measure is BLEU from [PAP 02]. It relies on the following criteria:

– the number of word n-grams that the translation to be evaluated and the reference translation have in common, for n between 1 and 4;

– the (word number) size differences between translation to be evaluated and reference translation;

– the variation possibilities in the translation: same text can be translated in several different ways, the BLEU score can be calculated with several reference translations so as to allow more variation in the phrasing.

Following in BLEU's footsteps, other measurements have been suggested to improve the accuracy of the MT system evaluations. Among the alternatives, we can find:

NIST [DOD 02] – equivalent to BLEU, only the n-grams are weighted by their frequency (the most frequent n-grams are considered less informative) and the global precision is calculated using the arithmetic mean instead of the geometric mean.

Adaptation of the F-measure [TUR 03] – this measure was designed to be easily "interpreted"; it is borrowed from information retrieval. Recall and precision are, in this case, calculated from the number of n-grams that the translation to be evaluated and the reference translation have in common.

Meteor [BAN 05] – takes into account precision and recall calculated on word unigrams and word order. In addition to identical words, Meteor also considers similar words such as morphological variations or synonyms. One of the objectives of this measure is to allow researchers to carry out an assessment at the sentence level, when other measurements only work when the entire translation corpus is evaluated.

TER [SNO 06] – calculates the number of edit operations (insertions, deletions and substitutions) necessary to go from the evaluated translation to the reference translation.

These evaluation methods can themselves be meta-evaluated by calculating their correlation with human judgments. The metrics are evaluated over a translation corpus – in that case they are fairly reliable – or sentences. According to [CAL 09], automatic sentence translation evaluation is still an open problem: the best metrics are consistent with human judgments in 54% of cases, whereas the probability of a random agreement between automatic metrics and human judgment is 0.5.

It also seems difficult to identify an automatic evaluation technique which would provide more trustworthy results than another. For example, during the 2009 edition of the Workshop on Statistical Machine Translation [CAL 09], the measures which were the most correlated to human judgments were measures which combined several measures or measures based on the correspondences between semantic and syntactic structures. In the 2010 edition of the same workshop [CAL 10], the best measures were those which used surface information such as letter *n*-grams. Yet the data sets used in the 2009 and 2010 editions were quasi-identical.

The behavior stability of these "objective" measures faced with data can also be questioned: [CAL 09, CAL 10]'s results display serious variations in the performances of a simple measure depending on the language pair, the translation direction or the level of granularity of the evaluation considered.

Moreover, the objective evaluation measures have been criticized by [BLA 07], who explain that the latter are even less correlated to human judgments as the translation's quality increases. They also described an experiment in which MTs were postedited by humans. These translations were judged to be of a lesser quality than the translations generated by automatic systems, and this was based on measures such as BLEU and NIST. The authors use this experiment to remind us that these measures are not directly linked to the quality of the translations but that they only evaluate the resemblance to a reference dataset, which is moreover considered questionable, especially in translation.

2.2.1.2. *Human MT evaluation*

Human evaluation consists of presenting sentence translations to humans who must judge their quality. This method has evolved over the years. In 2006, [KOE 06] asked the judges to give translations two different grades on a scale of 1 to 5 (see Table 2.1): one concerns the adequacy between translation and original text (preservation of meaning) and the other concerns the fluency (good grammar). An interface is used to annotate the translations. Each judge sees the original text and annotates five translations at a time, which allows him/her to contrast the sentences and reach a better decision.

	Adequacy	Fluency
5	All meaning	Flawless English
4	Most meaning	Good English
3	Much meaning	Non-native English
2	Little meaning	Disfluent English
1	None	Incomprehensible

Table 2.1. *Match and fluidity evaluation scales used by [KOE 06]*

In 2007, [CAL 07] test two other methods:

Sentence classification: the judges have to rank the sentences starting from the worst translation to the best translation (with a possibility of ties).

Syntactic phrase classification: the idea is same as the sentence classification, except that it applies to the translation of phrases.

These two methods were added to limit the interpretation possibilities since it appeared that the adequacy and fluency scales left too much space for subjectivity. For example, it is difficult to assess the value of *much meaning* in the adequacy scale. Moreover, judges have a hard time grading adequacy and fluency separately. Inversely, the classification which brings the evaluation back to the level of a simple comparison is easier to apprehend and understand.

These methods were compared using inter- and intra-annotator agreement. The measure used is the $Kappa$ from [CAR 96] (see Appendix A1.6). As mentioned in Table 2.2, the classification method obtains a higher intra- and inter-annotator agreement. Moreover, it enables faster grading (Table 2.3). The phrase classification is itself more trustworthy and quicker than the sentence classification.

	inter-annotator agreement	intra-annotator agreement
Fluency	0.25	0.54
Adequacy	0.23	0.47
Sentence ranking	0.37	0.62
Phrase ranking	0.54	0.74

Table 2.2. *Intra- and inter-annotator agreement during the Workshop on Statistical Machine Translation in 2007 [CAL 07]*

In the 2008 edition of the workshop, [CAL 08] abandoned the evaluation method based on adequacy and fluency. Instead they suggested a simpler method in which the judges are presented with syntactic phrase translations and asked to decide if the translation is acceptable or not. The judges can also indicate that they are "unsure".

This method obtained the best level of agreement: 1.64 and 0.86 (respectively, for inter- and intra-annotators). Finally, in the 2009 and 2010 editions, only the translation classification method was retained.

	average time per element (secs.)
Fluency and adequacy	26
Sentence classification	20
Phrase classification	11

Table 2.3. *Annotation time during the Workshop on Statistical Machine Translation in 2007 – [CAL 07]*

The whole issue of human evaluation is centered around its subjectivity and lack of reproducibility since, as the inter-annotator agreement shows us, a single translation is not always assessed in the same way by the judges, which can lead to doubts over the level of trust we can have on these judgments. The solution is then to judge the translation based on a great number of judgments, which enables us to neutralize the individual differences. [BLA 07] mention that the judges have a tendency to become stricter as time goes by, and they also mention that training judges increases the level of agreement. Training consists in providing the judges with a list of instructions and a first mock evaluation. The divergences are then discussed to standardize the grading.

2.2.2. *Human translation evaluation*

In translation, the question of evaluation is a research field in itself. [WIL 04] refers to it as *Translation Quality Assessment* (TQA). TQA arises from translation criticism, an activity which consists of commenting on the literary quality of the translated text with or without referencing to the original text. This field of research started to develop during the 1970s when translation studies sought models with a dual objective: to give the translation industry the means to control the quality of its products and to enable the translation schools to assess their students. The translation evaluation is different from the MT evaluation on several levels:

– the level of expectations is higher: one assesses the translations from professionals, not their resemblance to a human translation;

– MT assesses translations in relation to other translations with the aim of ranking the translations so as to rank the systems that generated them; translation studies evaluate the translations in themselves, without comparing the professional translators with one another;

– MT uses a professional translation as reference, translation studies have no quality reference, the judge is the sole reference.

An overview of TQA can be found in the papers by [WIL 04] and [SEC 05]. [LAR 98] offers theoretic reflections on the method of translation evaluation. [WIL 04] draws the line between two types of models: the quantitative models and the non-quantitative models. The quantitative models (section 2.2.2.1) are more pragmatic, they must produce a quality score for any translation. These models generate evaluation grids which are used in the translation industry or in teaching. The non-quantitative models (section 2.2.2.2) are more theoretical approaches of the evaluation problem and focus mostly on the definition of what makes a "good" translation.

2.2.2.1. *Quantitative models*

Most of the quantitative models were designed by and for organizations that were looking for a way to assess the quality of their translations. The first TQA model was designed by the Canadian translation office in 1976. This model, called Sical (Canadian Language Quality Assessment System) – is described by [WIL 01] and [SEC 05]. It separates language mistakes (intelligibility, grammaticality and idiomatic expressions) and transfer mistakes (preservation of meaning). Each error is judged as major or minor, with its seriousness determined on the basis of the potential consequences of the mistake (for example, for the translation of a user manual: mistake which could cause a dangerous use). The global quality of the translation is estimated on the number and types of errors found in a randomly selected passage of 4,000 words (see Table 2.4).

		Maximum number of issues in a section of 4,000 words	
Rank	**Quality**	**Major issues**	**Minor issues**
A	Superior	0	0 to 6
B	Fully acceptable	0	7 to 12
C	Revisable	1	13 to 18
D	Unacceptable	1 and more	18 and more

Table 2.4. *Evaluation grid for the Sical model [LAR 98, WIL 04]*

Several variations of the Sical grid were proposed after it. Similarly, several evaluation grids were suggested by organizations such as American Translators Association (ATA), Society of Automotive Engineers (SAE) and Localization Industry Standards Association (LISA) or by the translation agency ITR.

All these evaluation grids follow the same pattern: they are a typology of translation errors, each mistake type is linked to a cost representing its seriousness. Some, such as SEPT – described in [LAR 98] – go so far as to list 675 types of mistakes. [LAR 98] points out rightly that all the models separate transfer mistakes (meaning or content) from language mistakes (form or expression) with a predominance of meaning on form. The same principle can be found in the earlier versions of human MT evaluation in which the judges were asked to grade adequacy (transfer mistakes) and fleuncy (language mistakes) separately.

Compared to the field of (computer-assisted translation) CAT, we can be surprised by the absence of validation or comparison process for the different models proposed. While there is a general awareness of the subjectivity of human judgments, nothing is done to quantify it. We could consider comparing these models on the basis of an inter-annotator agreement. And do the same for time costs. But apart from Sical, which is meant to take 1 h to evaluate a 4,000 word excerpt, no writer has mentioned the time that an evaluation takes depending on which grid is chosen.

These quantitative models have an operational aim and are rather criticized by the supporters of non-quantitative models, as we shall see in the following section.

2.2.2.2. *Non-quantitative models*

One of the main criticisms that supporters of the non-quantitative models have against evaluation grids used in the industry is the level of analysis of these grids. Indeed, most of the quantitative models remain at the level of words and sentences and rarely focus on the discursive level. Evaluation grids are monolithic, supposedly valid for all translations, without taking into account the text's function, the communication situation in which it was produced and the expectations of the client requesting the translation.

For example, [WIL 04] suggests going from a microtextual approach (based on the sentence, as are the quantitative modes) to a macrotextual approach which relies on the analysis and comparison of the argument structure of the source and target texts. [WIL 04] sequences each text into six argumental modules which are independent of its genre, type, function or field. In this theoretic context, a good translation is a translation which takes up each of the modules present in the source text and faithfully replicates their content and relations. The author believes that the absence of one of these modules is a major mistake, but does not provide any additional information.

[REI 71] suggests a functional approach to translation. She asserts that the evaluation criteria must depend on the text's function. To this end, she specifies four types of text:

Content-focused texts – these denote reference texts that favor the description of facts: press articles, scientific works and notices. The translator totally adapts the form of the text to the target language, he/she brings the text to the reader, first and foremost respecting the meaning of the source text.

Form-focused texts – these are texts with a poetic function, for example literary or artistic texts. The translator brings the reader to the text by first and foremost respecting the form of the source text, the translation has a greater freedom when it comes to the transfer of meaning.

Appeal-focused texts – these are conative texts meant to provoke a reaction in the reader: advertising and propaganda. In this case, the translation becomes a free adaptation: its first goal is to retain the effect of the text on the reader, there is no obligation to respect form or meaning.

Audio-medial texts – these are texts which are not transmitted in writing like theater plays and speeches. The translator has to adapt the text to its environment and to the way in which it will be pronounced: lip movement in dubbing and rhythm of songs. This last category is rather awkward because it is at a higher classification level than the other three (spoken vs. written): a text can be inciting and audiomedial (radio spot vs. poster advertisement), focused on form and being audiomedial (theater play vs. literary work), etc.

Just like the evaluation methods presented previously, Reiss distinguishes meaning and form and provides criteria on which to evaluate the translations. However, she does not provide any actual evaluation grid. She draws a line between linguistic elements such as semantic, lexical, grammatical and stylistic aspects of the extra-linguistic elements (communication situation, topic, time period, location, audience, speaker and affective challenges). Each criterion has more or less influence on the global quality of the translation, depending on the type of text translated. For example, in the case of content-focused texts, a complete match between semantic elements of the source and target texts is mandatory, whereas not respecting the stylistic equivalence is accepted and even recommended if it means that by adapting the source text into the target language there is a better transfer of meaning.

2.2.3. *Discussion*

We saw in this section several translation evaluation methods: automatic and human evaluation for MT; quantitative and non-quantitative approaches in translation studies. Translation studies do not offer a solution matching our goal: either the approaches are too theoretic or the models suggested are too complex to implement.

In MT the computer evaluation makes little sense. Even though we lose in reproducibility, we believe, as [BLA 07] does, that automatic evaluation is a very indirect evaluation of the quality of a translation and that it evaluates its resemblance to the reference more than the real quality of a translation as it could be perceived by humans.

Thus, we have taken our inspiration from human evaluation methods for MT and tried to manage, as best possible, the inherent subjectivity of this method. One of the solutions appears to be training evaluators and providing them with practice time.

Moreover, using several judges is a way to limit the impact of individual preferences. The use of inter-annotator agreement measures – like Kappa – enables us to quantify how trustworthy the judgments are and ensure that there is a sufficient level of agreement between the judges. Ideally, we should also multiply the number of translators and domains to gather more data and increase the evaluation's representative aspect.

Finally, since we work in a specialized field, the evaluation will have to focus on the quality of the translation of terms, domain-specific lexical units and any other lexical item whose use is different from common language. The concrete implementation of the protocol is described in the following section.

2.3. Design and experimentation of a user-centered evaluation

2.3.1. *Methodological aspects*

Implementing the evaluation protocol led to several questions:

Criteria and aim of the evaluation – what criteria should be chosen to determine the quality of a translation? Should we assess the quality of the translated text as a whole or only certain aspects?

Subject-matter expertise – knowing that there are no domain experts available, what reference can we use to evaluate the generated translations?

Basis for comparison – to what other resources should the comparable corpus lexicon be compared?

2.3.1.1. *Evaluation criteria and purpose*

The fact that the quality of translation is hard to evaluate was highlighted by the works mentioned in section 2.2. While there is a universal recognition of the two criteria of meaning and form, it is hard to refine the question any further. In the world of translation, there is no marking scheme or evaluation mode commonly agreed upon. For good reason, when compiling the various evaluation grids and non-quantitative pieces of work, we realize that the global quality of a translation depends on the complex interaction of a number of linguistic parameters (spelling, lexicon, semantics, styles and argumentative structure) as well as extra-linguistic parameters (place, period and audience). Moreover, their interaction and the weight of each parameter depends on the text's function and the expectations of the person ordering the translation. In the words of [LAR 98], we are faced with a "crazy magma of varying variables".[2]

2 "*fol magma de variables variables.*"

How can we then measure the impact of lexicons extracted from comparable corpora on the quality of a translation? Do we expect them to have a direct influence on the global quality of the translations or for them to only act upon certain parameters which in turn will influence the quality of the translation? What are the most important parameters in the case of a specialized translation?

In order to answer these questions, we shall stipulate that a specialized bilingual lexicon is meant to help the translator when he/she is stuck on a term or an expression specific to the text's field of specialty. There are two possible cases:

Decoding problem – it can be that the meaning of the term or the expression is opaque: the lexicon is enriched with information extracted from the corpus and provides access to a concordancer, with links to the similar entries and potentially can give a definition. All the information combines to enable the translator to understand the term's meaning.

Encoding problem – it can be that the translator understands the term but does not know how to translate it, i.e. does not know its equivalent in the target language: the lexicon then suggests candidate translations and each candidate translation has contextual information enabling the translator to make the right translation choice. In the case when a translator has a translation intuition which does not appear among the candidate translations, the terminology management software can allow him to search for this potential translation in the corpus from which the lexicon was extracted.

The bilingual specialized lexicons are thus meant to act on both metacriteria of quality: meaning transfer (decoding) and adequate form generation (encoding). There are many quality parameters mentioned by translation studies; however, specialized resources are only meant to act on a few of them, such as spelling, respecting terminology standards, idiomatics and correct interpretation of the source term. We cannot judge the added value of our specialized lexicons on the basis of the global quality of the translation, since it depends on other parameters on which our alignments have little or no influence: grammaticality, omissions/insertions, coherence, respecting the argumentative structure, localization, choice of register, etc.

Thus, we endeavor to only measure our bilingual lexica's ability to help the translator translate specialized terms or expressions which are problematic for him/her. To this end, we ask the translators to jot down the expression that they had a hard time translating as well as the translation they finally picked. The evaluation will cover the accuracy of the translation retained.

We will thus, no doubt, have to evaluate the translation of syntactic phrases, poly- or monolexical units, as [CAL 08] have done. They enable us to not only better target the evaluation, but also focus on subsegments of a sentence that will also have the consequence of reducing the annotation time and facilitate the judges' task, as was shown in [CAL 08].

Since the translation is carried out outside of any professional environment, we have not tried to establish an evaluation grid which, as the TQA grid does, would associate different costs to spelling mistakes, lack of idiomatic expressions, etc. We are only using general criteria of meaning (adequacy) and form (fluency). To this end, we will conform to the recommendations made by [REI 71], who recommends giving the priority to meaning rather than form when evaluating translations of texts focused on content.[3] We will use three categories to judge the quality of the translations (summarized in Table 2.5):

exact – The term chosen is the reference term or preferred expression used in the field, e.g. *distributional semantics* and *sémantique distributionnelle*;

accurate – this is not the reference term or expression and the phrasing could be awkward but the translator still has managed to give a semantic match and the meaning is preserved, e.g. *distributional semantics* and *sémantique distributionnaliste*;

false – the translation is incorrect: the translator has not understood the term and/or has not managed to provide a semantic match, e.g. *distributional semantics* and *sémantique distribuée*.

	adequacy	fluency
EXACT	+	+
ACCURATE	+	−
FALSE	−	−

Table 2.5. *Translation quality judgment criteria*

2.3.1.2. *Subject matter expertise*

Working with specialized texts adds an additional problem to the evaluation. Not only does the judge have to be fluent in the source and target language, but he must also be an expert in the speciality field of the texts to be translated. In the absence of an available expert, the solution chosen has to use specialized texts which exist in the source and target language and which were generated by an expert in the field. The target version of the texts will be our reference translation against which the generated translations will be benchmarked. Academic paper extracts are a perfect resource for this use. The fact that the author is an expert in the field ensures the legitimacy of the terminology choices. The papers are necessarily revised before publication, which ensures that any potential language mistakes were corrected. Finally, the reference is not a translation but a second version of the text generated by the same person but in a different language.

In addition to a reference translation, the judges could also use a terminology database which would enable them to validate cases in which the translator did not

3 The specialized texts match texted focused on content according to [REI 71]'s theory.

use the expected term but a variation or expression of equivalent meaning. The translations to be judged are always shown in context: the judge has access to the source and target sentences which contain the term as well as to the original documents.

2.3.1.3. *Basis for comparison*

Highlighting the added value of lexicons can be done by contrast: we compare the result of the translation of a same source text translated with different linguistic resources. These different situations in which the translators translate the same text due to different resources are called *translation situations*. We have determined three translation situations:

Minimum situation: in this situation, the translations are carried out with minimal resources, a kind of "survival kit" for the translator, i.e. a general language bilingual dictionary, a general language monolingual dictionary in the source language and a general language monolingual dictionary in the target language. In this case, we consider that the translations will also be of a minimum quality: this is the lower quality threshold.

Maximum situation: in this situation, the translations are carried out with a maximum of resources; we then consider that it is impossible to obtain better translations. In this case; the translator has access to bilingual and monolingual general language resources as well as various terminology resources.

Target situation: this situation is the evaluated situation; it matches the case in which translations are carried out due to the resource that is to be evaluated. In this case, the translators have the "survival kit" (general language resources) and a bilingual lexicon extracted from a specialized comparable corpus.

With this protocol based on different translation situations, we should avoid the *learning effect* which occurs when a single translator works on texts stemming from the same field in different translation situations. Indeed, when a translator translates a text with a given resource, he/she obviously has in mind some of the translations of the terms that were problematic. If the same translator than has to translate the same text again (or a text from the same specialty field) in a different situation, he/she will obviously reuse the translations learnt when he/she translated the text for the first time. The second translation situation is then given a favorable advantage. Thus, we should ensure that a translator never translates texts from the same domain in different translation situations.

The methodology choices have been argued and we will now describe, in the following section, our experiment of the protocol.

2.3.2. *Experimentation protocol*

This section describes the first experiment of the evaluation method. The data used is described in section 2.3.2.1, the evaluation's progress is presented in section 2.3.2.2.

2.3.2.1. *Data*

We have carried out the evaluation on one translation direction (from English to French) and on two topics: breast cancer (medical domain) and water science (environment domain).

2.3.2.1.1. Comparable corpora and extracted lexica

The corpus covering breast cancer contains approximately 400,000 words per language, and was handpicked from scientific publications gathered on the *Elsevier* portal[4] as well as from popular science websites meant for patients and their kin. There is a roughly equal distribution between scientific texts and popular science ones. The texts come from British and French sources.

The corpus covering the topic of water science contains two million words per language. It was crawled from the website of the French language journal *Sciences de l'eau*[5] and the English language journal *Water Science Technology*.[6] For the French language part, we obtained whole academic papers in PDF format (conversion was carried out, due to the Unix utility pdf2txt, followed by a few heuristics filtering headings and footers). As for the English part, all we could gather was the abstracts of the papers in (Hyper Text Markup Language) HTML format which were then converted into a text format.

We measured the corpora comparability using [LI 10]'s measure. The breast cancer corpus comparability is of 0.74 and the water science comparability is of 0.77. Corpus extracts are visible in the Appendix A2.1.

The lexicons were extracted according to the method described in Chapter 1, section 1.4. They can be found online.[7]

2.3.2.1.2. Texts to be translated

We selected eight English texts for which there existed a translation in French. The texts to be translated are the English texts; the French version is used to evaluate the translators' work. The texts are equally distributed along the topics and level of

4 http://www.elsevier.com/.

5 http://www.rse.inrs.ca/.

6 http://www.iwaponline.com/wst/.

7 http://80.82.238.151/Metricc/InterfaceValidation/ ; the user name is *test*, leave the "password" field empty. Use the drop-down menu "Glossary" to choose the topic.

specialization as we can see in Table 2.6. None of these texts appear in comparable corpora used to extract the lexica. Excerpts of these texts can be found in the Appendix A2.2.

	BREAST CANCER	WATER SCIENCE
scientific texts	3 paper abstracts 508 words portal *Elsevier*	3 paper abstracts 499 words journal *Sciences de l'eau*
popular science texts	1 web page 613 words *Canadian Breast Cancer Foundation* website [a]	1 web page 425 words *Lenntech* website on water treatment[b]

– http://www.cbcf.org/

– http://www.lenntech.com/

Table 2.6. *Size, origin, topic and degree of specialization of the texts to be translated*

The texts were chosen intuitively, respecting every single criterion: their topic had to match the lexicon's topic. The scientific texts are scientific publications and come from the same source as the texts in the acquisition corpus. The popular science texts come from a breast cancer prevention website published by the Canadian government (we have chosen a text explaining the pros and cons of screening) for the breast cancer topic. For the water science topic, the texts come from the website of a company selling water treatment solutions (the website has popular science pages explaining the activated carbon adsorption principle to potential clients).

2.3.2.1.3. Resources used in the translation situation

Minimum situation: the texts are translated without any specialized resource. The translator only has access to three online general language resources:

– the bilingual French/English[8] and English/French[9] Larousse dictionary;

– the monolingual French Larousse[10] dictionary;

– the monolingual English Cambridge[11] dictionary.

Target situation: in addition to the general language resources available in the minimum situation, the translator has access to lexicons extracted from specialized comparable corpora which he/she can access through the interface presented in

8 http://www.larousse.com/en/dictionaries/french-english.

9 http://www.larousse.com/en/dictionaries/english-french.

10 http://www.larousse.com/en/dictionaries/french/.

11 http://dictionary.cambridge.org/.

section 1.4.3. So, in addition to translation equivalence, the translator has access to terminology records. He/she can also check a translation hypothesis by searching the corpus.

Maximum situation: in addition to the general language resources of the minimum situation, the translator has full access to the Internet on which he/she can look up different specialized resources, concordancers, translation fora, etc. He/she can also use search engines to contextualize a term to be translated or to check an intuition. However, he/she is forbidden to look at sites from which the texts to be translated have been taken and from the acquisition corpora as well as the terminology database TERMIUM[12] used later on during the translation evaluation phase.

2.3.2.1.4. Translators and judges

With little human means (3 people) on which to experiment the protocol, we had to tweak the method a bit: there were collisions between the roles of organizer/translator and translator/judge. Translator 1, the author of this dissertation, also organized the evaluation. Her only experience in specialized translation is working on journalistic text translations in the last year of her English language and literature BA. Translators 2 and 3 were students in their last year of translation school. They also judged and ranked the translation (anonymization prevented the judges from knowing who generated which translation, and in what situation). All three share French as their mother tongue. None of the translators were familiar with the topic of water science or breast cancer.

2.3.2.2. *Evaluation progress*

The evaluation was carried out over two phases: a translation phase and an evaluation phase of the translation quality.

2.3.2.2.1. Translation phase

We have used a non-specialist translation person to translate in the minimum situation, which is meant to generate worse translations. The other two translators translated alternately in maximum and target situations. This alternatively enabled us to avoid the fact that a single translator worked on the texts on the same topic in different translation situations (the learning effect mentioned in section 2.3.1.3).

Each translator was given texts to be translated along with the following directions:

> *Translate each text according to the specified translation situation. Mention the time taken to translate each text. Once the translation has been done, list the terms or expressions that were problematic. Please mention which resources you used to find their translation and mention the translation that was finally chosen.*

---

12 http://www.termiumplus.gc.ca/.

Situation	BREAST CANCER texts	WATER SCIENCE texts
Minimum	Translator 1	Translator 1
Target	Translator 2	Translator 3
Maximum	Translator 3	Translator 2

Table 2.7. *Distribution of texts and translation situations among translators*

Each situation is precisely described to the translator as mentioned in section 2.3.2.1.3. The translation is made from the translator's second language to his/her mother tongue, in our case, from English into French. Once the texts are translated, all the problematic terms and the translation chosen by the translator are gathered.

We have only kept the problematic terms that were common to at least two translation situations for the evaluation (82% were common to the three situations) which led to a set of 148 problematic terms (87 for the breast cancer topic and 61 for the water science topic).

2.3.2.2.2. Translation quality evaluation phase

Two judges graded the quality of the translations of the terms. They were helped by a reference translation, which matched the term found in the target version of the text. Source term and reference translation are contextualized, i.e. presented in their original sentence. The judges also have access to the original source and target documents. Moreover, they can use the terminology database TERMIUM[13] in addition to the reference translation. The translations are anonymized and randomly mixed so that the judge cannot know under which situation the terms were translated. All this is provided in a table file, in which each set of translations is presented as in the excerpt 2.8.

Extract 2.1. Example of annotated translations

The judges carry out two evaluation tasks:

Ranking task: the judges rank the translations from the best to the worse (ties are allowed).

Judgment task: the judges also grade the quality of each translation separately according to the criteria defined above (exact, accurate and false).

In order to homogenize the evaluation as much as possible, detailed annotation directions and a few annotation examples on difficult cases were given to the judges. Given the small amount of data (only 148 set of problematic terms), we did not carry out a first pre-evaluation, which would have improved the homogeneity of the evaluation [BLA 07].

13 http://www.termiumplus.gc.ca/.

```
  #6 mammogram
VG-3 Research has shown that women who have regular mammograms
     are more likely to survive breast cancer.
  #7 mammographie
VG-3 La recherche indique que les femmes qui passent régulièrement des
     mammographies sont plus susceptibles de survivre au cancer.
```

ID	translation	rank	exact	acceptable
8	mammogramme	2	0	1
9	mammographie	1	1	0
10	mammographie	1	1	0

Table 2.8. *Example of annotated translations*

2.3.3. *Results*

The extracted lexicons were evaluated from the point of view of their usability (section 2.3.3.1) and the point of view of the quality of the translations they generate (section 2.3.3.2).

2.3.3.1. *Lexicons usability*

2.3.3.1.1. Translation speed

The estimated amount that a professional translator should be able to translate over an 8-hour day in a translation agency is between 2,000 and 2,500 words (250 to 313 words/hour) [SFT 09]. The results obtained show a rather quick translation time. In our experiments, the minimum situation was the one requiring the smallest translation time (503 words/hour). Since it should have been the most difficult situation, we could be led to believe that it would have required the most time (difficulty in deciding on a translation). One possible explanation could be that in this situation, the translator has fewer resources to check. As for the situations with specialized resources, the time spent is on par with the best times in a professional situation: 322 words/hour and 310 words/hour for the target and maximum situation, respectively, which is also surprising since students' translation speed is usually placed around 200 words/hour.

2.3.3.1.2. Use of resources

The translator noted the resources which they accessed to translate each problematic term:

General language resources: bilingual and monolingual general language dictionaries;

Specialized resources: lexicons extracted from comparable corpora in the target situation, the Internet for the maximum situation;

Intuition: using intuitive heuristics such as reusing the spelling of the term and modulating it to adapt to the target language's morphology, e.g. translating *sensitivity* by *sensitivité*.

A translation can be generated, due to several sources, for example, by translating a term word for word thanks to the general resource and then looking up evidence of the candidate translation in the specialized resource.

Figure 2.1 shows the number of times in which each resource was used depending on the translation situations. In the target and maximum situations, the translators did not use the general language resources much: the larger the specific resource, the bigger the role it played in the generation of the translation, and the less general resources or intuition were used. In the target situation, translators used intuition as much as the minimum situation, which could indicate that they were not completely satisfied with the resource.

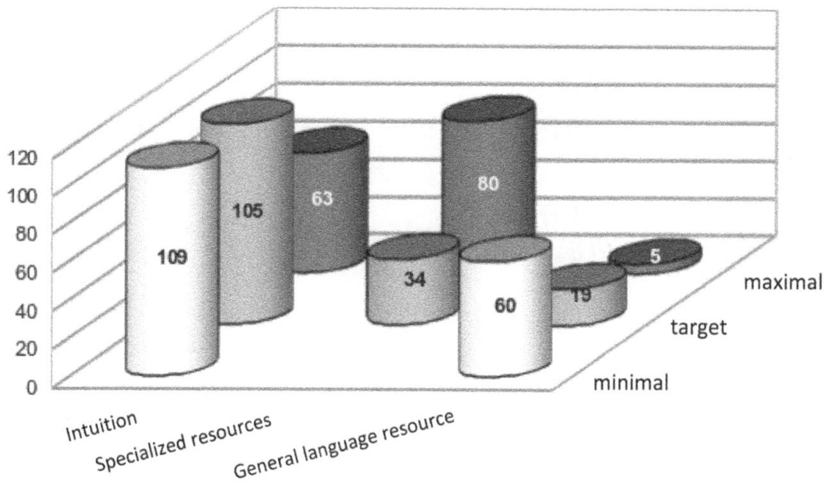

Figure 2.1. *Number of times in which each resource was used, depending on the translation situations*

2.3.3.1.3. Translators' impressions on the lexicons extracted from comparable corpora

The translation in a target situation was not easy. The specialized texts proved to be very hard to translate, and although the feedback on the interface was good, the lexicon content was strongly criticized. We could even say that at first, there was a strong rejection of it. Here is the verbatim email sent by one of the translators:

> *Basically, 75% of the technical words could not be found in the glossary, and of the 25% left, 99% had between 10 and 20 candidate translations*

> *but none of them were validated. So in the best of cases one was "more or less sure" but never totally certain. And in the worse case (which was rather frequent, unfortunately), one's decision had to be made "instinctively"*[14]

After discussing this, it appears that the translators expected to directly find the translation of a term when typing it into the query field. They were not sufficiently prepared to use a lexicon suggesting several candidate translations. We saw how they could implement strategies to get the most out of the bilingual lexicon, for example we suggested they use the information found in the terminology records (close terms, concordancer and collocations) and use the full-text search function to validate the translation ideas. This reaction to the lexicon could be partially explained by the fact that the translators were students and lacked experience.

2.3.3.2. *Quality of the generated translations*

2.3.3.2.1. Inter-annotator agreement

The inter-annotator agreement measure used is [CAR 96]'s Kappa. This measure takes into account the agreement observed $P(A)$ and the probability of a random agreement $P(E)$:

$$Kappa = \frac{P(A) - P(E)}{1 - P(E)}$$

In the case of the judgment task, we find a weak agreement (0.36) but a better agreement than [CAL 07] does (0.23 and 0.25) which judge whole sentences whereas we judge syntactic phrases. As for the ranking task, the agreement is strong (0.65). These results are consistent with those obtained by [CAL 07]: it is easier to annotate syntactic phrases than whole sentences and it is easier to rank translations than judge them as an absolute. Finally, we can point out that the agreement is stronger for the water science topic (0.42) than for the breast cancer topic (0.25).

2.3.3.2.2. Judgment task

The results of the judgment task are presented in Figure 2.2. We have evaluated the translations of the breast cancer topic and the water science topic separately.

In the case of the breast cancer topic, the proportion of translations judged to be wrong was almost equal in all three situations. The lexicons extracted from the

14 "En gros, 75 % des mots techniques ne figurent pas dans le glossaire, et sur les 25 % restants, 99 % ont entre 10 et 20 traductions candidates, mais aucune de validée. Du coup, dans le meilleur des cas on est "à peu près sûr", mais jamais totalement. Et dans le pire des cas (très fréquemment, malheureusement) on y va "à l'instinct".

comparable corpus (target situation) increase the number of translations judged to be exact compared to the minimum situation: 43% against 38%. The maximum situation is the one which generated the best translations (47% of accurate translations).

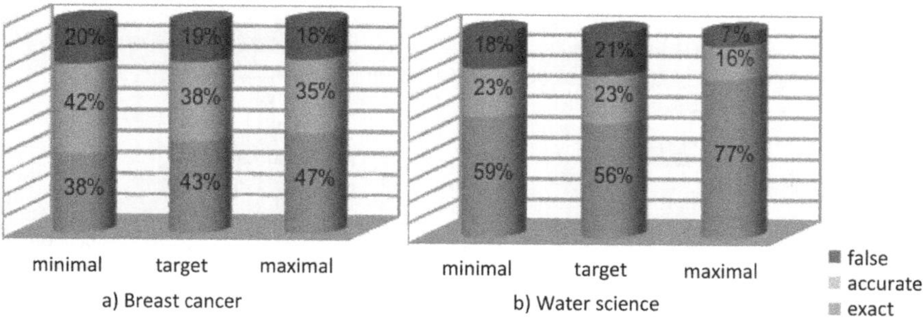

Figure 2.2. *Results of the judgment task*

In the case of the water science topic, the translations generated in the target situation (lexicon extracted from comparable corpora + general language dictionaries) are more often false than those translated in minimum situation (only with a general language dictionary): 25% versus 10%. This is not normal since both situations share a common base of general language resources. The translations generated in the target situation should be at least as good as those generated in the minimum situation. One possible explanation is that the translators which translated in a target situation mostly used general language resources and their intuition (as we can see in Figure 2.1), and did not use the specialized lexicon much; this may be because of their initial reaction of rejection.

2.3.3.2.3. Ranking task

The results of the ranking task are presented in Figure 2.3. We find results similar to those of the judgment task:

– When the translations of a single term are compared with one another, those generated in the maximum situation (general language dictionaries and Internet) are always the best, no matter the topic; this is even more visible with the water science topic.

– The translations carried out in the target situation are only better than those generated in the minimum situation in the case of the BREAST CANCER situation, but not in the case of the WATER SCIENCE topic.

2.3.3.3. *Lexicon coverage*

We observe that no matter the mode of assessment, the specialized lexicon only seems to present an interest compared to the minimal situation when using the breast cancer data. We can explain this with the fact that the vocabulary from the water science texts was not very well covered by the lexicon extracted from comparable corpora.

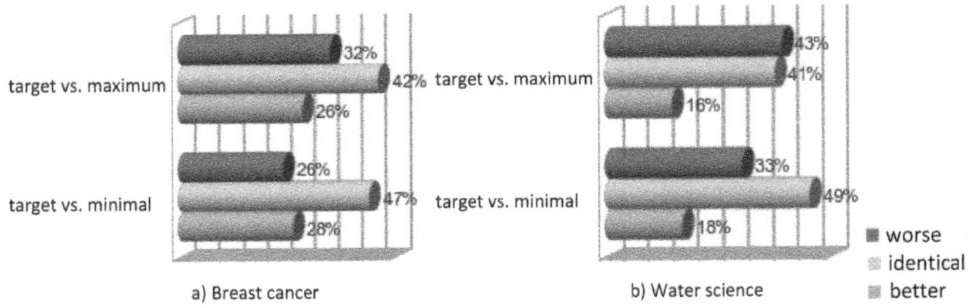

Figure 2.3. *Results of the ranking task*

The texts to be translated were intuitively handpicked, the only criterion being that their topic had to be the same as that of the comparable corpus. And the water science topic is much more general,[15] which may have led us to select texts with a different vocabulary from that of the comparable corpus. We can also note that the texts from the breast cancer corpus only come from French sources whereas part of the texts to be translated come from Canadian sources. This may have helped limit the coverage of the lexica. However, this issue was not raised by the translators.

For each topic, we calculated the overlap ratio between the vocabulary of the texts to be translated T and the vocabulary of the lexicon L:

$$coverage(L, T) = \frac{|L| \cap |T|}{|T|}$$

15 According to the website of the "*Sciences de l'eau*" journal, it is a multidisciplinary field covering seven great domains:

– hydrology, hydrogeology and water resource management;

– physicochemical quality of subterranean and surface water;

– hydrobiology, microbiology, toxicology and eco-toxicology;

– structure and operation of aquatic eco-system;

– the quality and processing of drinking water;

– the purification of residual water;

– the legal and socio-economic aspects of water management.

The results are given in Table 2.9. In the best case, even if the lexicon had all the correct translations, the translator would only find useful translations in 67% of the words of the texts to be translated for the "Breast cancer" topic and only 14% for the "Water science" topic. The breast cancer lexicon was extracted from a smaller and slightly less comparable corpus than the water science corpus but it covers more vocabulary than the water science lexicon.

	BREAST CANCER	WATER SCIENCE
texts to be translated (EN)	0.94	0.14
reference translations (FR)	0.67	0.78

Table 2.9. *Coverage of the texts to be translated (and their translations) by the extracted lexica*

2.3.3.4. *Reproducing the protocol on a wider scale*

The work presented until now belongs to work carried out within the context of the METRICC ANR project which we took part in. The objective of our participation was to suggest an evaluation protocol and carry out the first experiment on a small scale so as to hone the process. The large scale reproduction of the protocol was carried out by Dr. Emmanuel Planas [PLA 11] who teaches CAT at the Université Catholique de l'Ouest. We decided to present the results that Dr. Planas obtained because they are the logical prolongation of our work and contribute to clarify the question of the input of comparable corpora to specialized translation.

The protocol was reproduced with the data of the BREAST CANCER topic with a group of 20 translation students. Each translator translated a text in a single translation situation.

The groups of students attached to each translation situation were of a similar level. Let us point out that they are first year Masters students (M1) whereas in our experiment, we had someone who was studying translation for their BA (License) and two students who were in the second year of their Masters degree (M2). In the case of the evaluation, only the judgment task was carried out. A prior training session was carried out on the texts of the WATER SCIENCE topic, which guarantees a certain homogeneity in grading.

Figure 2.4 enables us to compare the results obtained by [PLA 11] with ours. The first striking point is that overall [PLA 11]'s translators are not as competent as ours (18% to 20% of false terms for us; 26% to 44% for [PLA 11]). This difference is normal since [PLA 11]'s translators are M1 translators and not M2 like ours were. [PLA 11] actually points out that the translation mistakes made in the maximum situation are mostly due to a lack of scientific knowledge and a lack of experience on the translators' part. In several cases, the translation is wrong because the translator blindly trusted an untrustworthy Internet source.

We can find the same relation between the situations: the maximum situation is the best, the minimum situation is the worst. The difference between the target situation and minimal situation is stronger for [PLA 11]: -7% of false translations when the translators use the lexicon extracted from comparable corpora (-1% in our case).

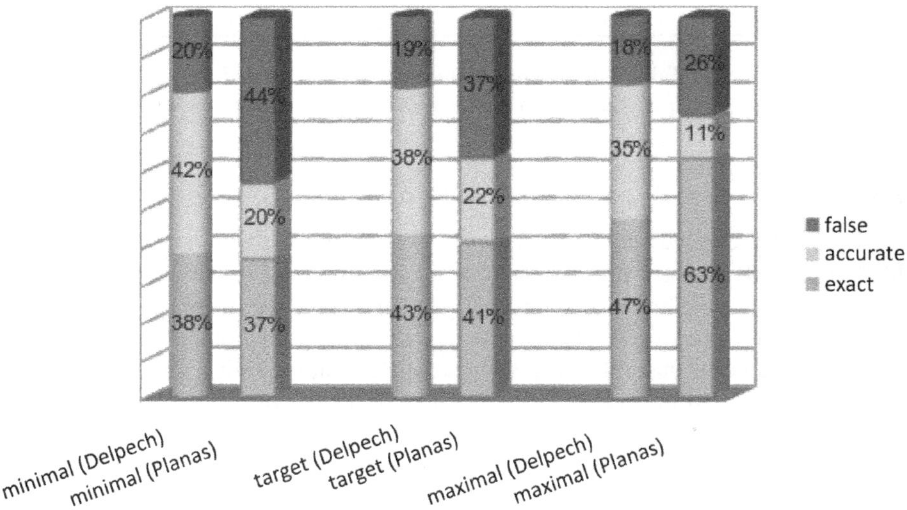

Figure 2.4. *Comparing the quality of translations obtained with the* BREAST CANCER *data: experiment by [PLA 11] vs. our experiment*

2.4. Discussion

It is difficult to draw broad conclusions on the use of lexicons extracted from comparable corpora lexicons based on our experiment: on the one hand, part of our data was badly built and on the other hand, we did not prove that the differences in quality observed were significant. [PLA 11]'s experiment, carried out only on the breast cancer data, mentions a stronger difference between the translations carried out only with generalist resources and the translations carried out with generalist resources and the lexicon extracted from the comparable corpus. However, the subjects of the experiment were translation students and not professionals. We know that students work differently from professionals [CAR 11]. At best, we can say that the lexicons extracted from comparable corpora can help inexperienced translators. A research perspective could be to reproduce the experiment with more solid data and professional translators.

Beyond the measurement of the usefulness of comparable corpora, these experiments revealed several obstacles to the use of comparable corpora in specialized translations.

First of all, we observed the importance of working within fine granularity thematics and the need to gather a corpus that is a close match to the texts to be translated.

Then we realized that the shape of the extracted lexicons is distracting for the translators and can even cause them to reject them. Presenting a list of 20 candidate translations is problematic ("99% have between 10 and 20 translations but none of them is validated"). After discussing this matter with the translators, it seems that a list of 3 or 4 translations is the maximum acceptable amount.

Finally, the mere listing of candidate translations, while it matches the concordancer, is insufficient: translators do not have enough hints to allow them to validate the translations (we are "more or less sure" but never totally... we choose "instinctively").

Due to these conclusions, here are five research directions to improve the management of comparable corpora:

Shaping and gathering needs: the lexicons extracted from comparable corpora represent a new type of resource which is less precise than the resources translators are used to. While they are acknowledged as useful in translation studies, it appears that this type of resource has not become a habit for translators and is not even part of their training. Thus, it would be beneficial to establish a dialogue between CAT tool developers, translation ergonomists and trainers so that comparable corpus analysis tools can effectively answer the needs of the translator and so that these tools can be taught during training sessions.

Corpus gathering: it is necessary for the corpus's comparability to be improved, whether this is, due to metrics, based on the vocabulary that the two corpora share [LI 11, LI 10] or by taking into account the discourse type when generating the corpus [MOR 07, GOE 09]. Matching the texts to be translated with the corpus texts must also be carried out in an optimal manner. Recent research has given rise to thematic crawlers [TAL 08, DE 11] and comparable corpora acquisition systems [KIL 11].

Contextualization of terms: it is essential to provide translators with the means to ensure their translation choices. Simple unaligned monolingual concordancers are insufficient. Candidate translations and source terms must be presented within contexts which are relevant to the translation. This research axis is currently being explored within the ANR project CRISTAL,[16] which focuses on knowledge-rich contexts for translation [MEY 01].

Tools: the translators' tools have to be adapted to allow them to correctly use the lexicons extracted from comparable corpora. Very few CAT tools were created to deal with this type of resource [SHA 06, BRO 11] and the corpus research functionalities are still limited. Moreover, very little bilingual lexicons exchange formats (TBX and XLIFF) and enable the translator to exchange lexicons extracted from comparable corpora [DEL 10].

Translation equivalences: in this case, we have to directly improve the quality of the extracted lexica. We saw that translators did not appreciate a long list of candidate translations, especially if in a great number of cases, none of them were useful. To improve the usability of the lexicons for technical translators, we should favor the precision of lexicons and potentially generate less candidate translation. In any case, we will focus on getting the correct translation to appear among the first candidates.

We chose to pursue our research within the context of translation equivalence research and more specifically, gave ourselves the goal of trying to obtain more specific lexica, even if the latter are smaller. The distributional method is a method used since the 90s, and despite the numerous research projects which tried to improve it, we saw in Chapter 1 that the results can be found between 13% and 65% of precision on the Top1 (Table 1.1). We should take into account at least 20 candidate translations to expect obtaining precision levels between 40% and 94% depending on the fields and language pairs. Moreover, the distributional approach requires a great amount of texts to obtain the best scores. However, using comparable corpora usually takes place when data is few and far between.

This is why we decided to follow other lexicon acquisition methods which are not specific to comparable corpora. These are methods aiming not only for the prior extraction of terms which are then aligned, but for the machine *generation* of translations from a source term. These methods have recently led to good results on comparable corpora [MOR 10, WEL 11, HAR 12]. We will draw an overview of them in the following chapter before suggesting an improvement on these methods in Chapter 4.

16 *Contextes RIches en connaissanceS pour la TrAduction terminoLogique* (Knowledge-rich contexts for terminology translation), www.projet-cristal.org.

3

Automatic Generation of Term Translations

3.1. Introduction

In this chapter, we present translation *generation* methods. Contrary to the approaches which try to *align* predefined terms on the base of distributional similarity, generation consists of generating a translation using a knowledge base of translation equivalences and of possible realizations in the target language.

One possible approach is to base ourselves on compositional semantics: the unit to be translated is decomposed in meaning-bearing sub-units, and these sub-units are translated and recomposed so as to create a term in the target language (section 3.2). A second type of approach is to rely on empirical knowledge (section 3.3). These approaches consider the unit to be translated more as a sequence of characters to be rewritten than as a linguistic unit. The translation is carried out thanks to translation models learned from examples of translation pairs.

3.2. Compositional approaches

In this section, we describe the expert approaches based on the compositionality principle. In this paradigm, the research focuses first and foremost on managing morphological, lexical, morphosyntactic and fertility variation phenomena. These approaches are used to translate the polylexical units, which are decomposed into words (section 3.2.2), as well as the morphologically complex monolexical units, which are decomposed into morphemes (section 3.2.3). In the second case, the difficulty lies in being able to deal with different morphological constructions in addition to cases of variation and fertility. Once the translations are generated, we have to check that they are possible in the target language. To this end, several methods of selection and filtering have been implemented (section 3.2.3).

3.2.1. *Compositional translation principle*

The compositionality principle can be stated as followed [KEE 85]:

> "*The meaning of the whole is a function of the meaning of the parts*".

This principle implies that it is possible to understand the meaning of an unknown expression, as long as the meaning of its components is known and that it is possible to interpret its structure. Basing ourselves on the compositionality principle to generate translations, we can suppose that it is possible to translate an unknown lexical unit as long as we can interpret its structure, translate each of its components and recombine them in the target language.

The compositional translation process can be formalized as follows:

$$\begin{aligned}\mathcal{CT}(\text{``ab''}) &= \mathcal{S}(\mathcal{R}(\mathcal{T}(\mathcal{D}(\text{``ab''}))))\\ &= \mathcal{S}(\mathcal{R}(\mathcal{T}(\{\text{a}, \text{b}\})))\\ &= \mathcal{S}(\mathcal{R}(\{\mathcal{T}(\text{a}) \times \mathcal{T}(\text{b})\}))\\ &= \mathcal{S}(\mathcal{R}(\{\text{A}, \text{B}\}))\\ &= \mathcal{S}(\{\text{A}, \text{B}\}, \{\text{B}, \text{A}\})\\ &= \text{``BA''}\end{aligned}$$

in which "ab" is a source term composed of *a* and *b*, "BA" is a target term composed of B and A and there is a bilingual resource linking *a* to A and *b* to B.

In practice, compositional translation ($\mathcal{CT}$) thus means:

1) decomposing the source term into "atomic" components ($\mathcal{D}$);

2) translating these components into the target language ($\mathcal{T}$);

3) recomposing the translated components in order to generate candidate translations ($\mathcal{R}$);

4) filtering the candidate translations with a selection function ($\mathcal{S}$) so as to only retain correct translations.

The first implementation happened at the end of the 1990s with the publication of [GRE 99]. The goal of this publication is first and foremost to show the attractiveness of the Web as a resource of natural language processing. However, it also demonstrates the relevance of the compositional approach to generate the translation of complex expressions. In the experiment, Grefenstette uses a reference lexicon built from a bilingual resource. He selects 724 German noun phrases and 1,140 Spanish noun phrases for this experiment, which are all meant to be translated into English. For each noun phrase to be translated, the author ensures that:

– it is possible to translate the noun phrase from the translation of its components (words);

– the bilingual resource has translations for the components;

– it is possible to build more than one candidate translation;

– the correct translation for the noun phrase is known.

By translating the German and Spanish noun phrases in a compositional manner, Grefenstette obtains 3,556 candidate translation in German and 6,186 in Spanish. The candidate translations are queried on the engine AltaVista, which provides for each query, its number of occurrences in the pages indexed by the engine. The candidate translation retained is the one with the greatest number of occurrences. By following this method, Grefenstette obtains respectively, 87% and 86% of correct translations for German and Spanish.

This version of compositional translation is very basic: we only carry out a word-to-word translation. This direct translation approach implies a strong parallelism between source language and target language and does not take into account various phenomena, which can happen during translation.

These phenomena are well-known and frequently listed in literature:

Morphosyntactic variation: source and target terms have different morphosyntactic structures, there might be a change of grammatical categories. For example, a noun can be translated as an adjective:

– *thérapie génique* (noun adjective) $\rightarrow$ *gene therapy* (noun noun);

– *anti-cancer* (noun) $\rightarrow$ *anti-cancéreux* (adjective).

Lexical variation: the source and target language use semantically close words, but they are not exact translations of one another:

– *traduction automatique* $\rightarrow$ *machine translation*;

– *mixed departmentalization* $\rightarrow$ *structuration mixte*.

Terminology variation: a source term can be translated by a target term with several variations, several translations are thus possible:

– *mixed departmentalization* $\rightarrow$ *départementalisation mixte, structuration mixte*;

– *oophorectomy* $\rightarrow$ *ablation des ovaires, ovariectomie*.

Fertility: the source and target terms are of different lengths:[1]

– *isothermal snowpack* → *manteau neigeux isotherme*;

– *oophorectomy* → *ablation des ovaires*.

In the following sections, we will show how these variation phenomena were dealt with in the works using the compositionality principle.

3.2.2. *Polylexical units compositional translation*

The compositional translation of polylexical units happens through a sequencing into words. Among the approaches presented, two of them follow [GRE 99] and suggest solutions to manage the lexical and/or morphological variation [ROB 06, MOR 10]. [LEO 08]'s contribution concerns the use of mixed documents when searching for candidate translations. [VIN 10]'s approach short-circuits the recombination phase of the components by using a "bag of equivalents".

3.2.2.1. *Lexical variation and multiple decomposition*

[ROB 06] improve [GRE 99]'s compositional translation on several aspects:

Multiple decomposition: for a term made of n lexical words, [ROB 06] generate 2^{n-1} possible decompositions, including the term itself. For example, the term "*système à base de connaissances*" can be decomposed in four ways: *système / base / connaissance*, *système à base / connaissance*, *système / base de connaissance* and *système à base de connaissance*. This multiple decomposition enables the machine translation system, to directly find the translations of the sub-parts of the term to be translated.

Lexical variation management: the translation of a word can be (1) its translation provided by a bilingual lexicon; (2) its synonym or a word which is semantically close, given by a thesaurus.

Generation of a thematic corpus on the fly: this enables the system to filter candidate translations over a greater number of target terms.

The method suggested the use of translation pairs (*seeds* or *graines*) to query a search engine and build a small comparable corpus from which source language and target language terms belonging to the same topic are extracted. The source terms are translated into the target language due to an improved compositional method: generating partial translations and taking into account translation synonyms. The candidate translations are filtered with the list of target terms. The use of words,

1 As defined by [ROB 06], we redefine this concept p. 111.

which are semantically close to the translations, has the effect of increasing the recall and lowering the precision: precision goes from 92% to 46% and recall goes from 53% to 65%. Noticing the strong precision obtained on the alignment carried out without using synonyms (92%), the authors suggest using these translation pairs as new seeds to start the gathering of a new corpus. Thus, [ROB 06] iteratively increase the number of translated terms while limiting the decrease in precision.

This method manages lexical variation issues to a certain extent, those of terminology variation. However, if one of the words in the terms is not translated by the bilingual dictionary, the source term will not be entirely translated. Moreover, this method does not manage cases in which the source term and target term do not have the same morphosyntactic structure. To rectify this, [MOR 10] suggest using morphological relations.

3.2.2.2. *Morphological relations*

During the compositional translation of a polylexical unit, it is possible that one of its components does not appear in the bilingual lexicon. In that case, either the translation fails or one can generate only a partial translation. [MOR 10]'s solution is to use the translation of a word belonging to the same morphological family as the missing component. For example, if when translating the French *bilan énergétique*, the translation of the adjective *énergétique* cannot be found in the lexicon, it is the translation of the noun from which it derives (*energy*), which is used to generate the candidates *energy balance* and *balance energy*.

[MOR 10] test this approach on relational adjectives.[2] The experiment consists of translating terms that include a relational adjective, and in the case where the translation of the adjective cannot be found in the bilingual lexicon, it is replaced by the translation of the noun from which it is derived. The experiment focuses on 1,578 French terms with the NOUN ADJECTIVE structure to translate into Japanese. Out of 1,578 terms, 829 contain a relational adjective (noted NOUN ADJR). The generated translations are filtered with a list of Japanese terms. French terms and Japanese terms were extracted from a comparable corpus.

With the simple compositional method, the authors obtain 69% precision on the terms NOUN ADJECTIVE and 63% on the terms NOUN ADJR but very few of the terms NOUN ADJR are translated: only eight out of 829. With the method based on morphological families, the authors translate 128 NOUN ADJR terms with an 88%

2 Relational adjectives are adjectives derived from nouns, which illustrate a relation between the noun they modify and the noun from which they derive. They are the syntactic equivalent of a noun complement or a relative clause explaining this relation: *la race chevaline* is *the equine race* → *la race de cheveaux* or *the race of equines*, i.e. *of horses*. They are opposed to qualifying adjectives which indicate a characteristic of the noun they modify, e.g. "a blue blook" [RIE 05].

precision. They compare the compositional approach based on morphology with the distributional approach. The latter provides a 15% precision on the Top10 and a 20% precision on the Top20, far from the results obtained with the compositional approach. This can be explained by the low frequency of terms (80% have a number of occurrences below 20) and fully justifies using the compositional approach to translate complex terms.

3.2.2.3. *Extracting translations from mixed documents*

[LEO 08] had the aim of translating polylexical units with a NOUN ADJECTIVE or NOUN OF NOUN structure from French to English. The translation of each element is obtained from a bilingual lexicon, the candidate translation is recombined following translation templates:

FR: $\mathtt{NOUN_1}$ $\mathtt{ADJECTIVE_1}$ $\rightarrow$ EN: $\mathtt{ADJECTIVE_1}$ $\mathtt{NOUN_1}$
FR: $\mathtt{NOUN_1}$ *de* $\mathtt{NOUN_2}$ $\rightarrow$ EN: $\mathtt{NOUN_2}$ $\mathtt{NOUN_1}$
FR: $\mathtt{NOUN_1}$ *de* $\mathtt{NOUN_2}$ $\rightarrow$ EN: $\mathtt{NOUN_1}$ *of* $\mathtt{NOUN_2}$

By applying the simple compositional method, [LEO 08] can generate translations for 72% of the units to be translated. The non-translated units at this point are either units in which one of the elements does not appear in the dictionary or units with the non-compositional meaning (e.g. *caisse claire* $\rightarrow$ *snare drum* which in French would be a *tambour piège*) or which present a lexical divergence. The solution used by [LEO 08] consists of obtaining extracts of texts in the target language, which are strongly susceptible of containing the translation of the unit to be translated. These text extracts are taken from bilingual documents, obtained by querying a search engine to look for the source unit in target language documents. The result page provided by the search engine thus contains mixed snippets[3] (in both languages).

[LEO 08] starts by searching the snippets for cognates,[4] of the word, which could not be translated with the bilingual dictionary. The term translations are generated using the cognates as translation. Thus, the author obtains 8% additional translations. In the case in which no satisfying cognate is found, [LEO 08] looks for the bigrams, which are the most frequent in the snippets. These bigrams are considered to be candidate translations and enable the translators to translate 2% additional translations. To select the best translation, several filters are applied to the candidate translations (the filters are detailed in section 3.2.4 on translation filtering).

3.2.2.4. *Bag of equivalents*

Most of the compositional translation techniques use syntactic templates to recompose the target words. This has the effect of increasing the expert's task who

3 Fragments of texts displayed until the title of each Web document in the results page provided by the engine.

4 For [LEO 08] two cognates are two words with the same four first letters.

must describe all the structure equivalences between the source and target languages. A more economic solution would be to generate all the possible permutations of the translated words and then to filter them with a target language corpus as [ROB 06] do. In the same vein, [VIN 10] suggest using a "bag of equivalents". [VIN 10] starts by acquiring word translation probabilities on a parallel corpus. A term to be translated is sequenced into words and for each word, a translation as well as the associated probability are added to a list of equivalents (the so-called "bag").

For example, if the term to be translated is *destruction of anti-personnel mines*, its Slovenian bag of equivalents is (*destruction* can be translated as *unievanje* or *unienje, personnel* is translated as *protipehoten, mine* is translated as *mina*):

Source term components	Bag of equivalents	
destruction	unievanje	0.86
	unienje	0.14
antipersonnel	protipehoten	1.00
mine	mina	1.00

This bag of equivalents is then compared to the target terms. The translation score of a target term is the average translation probability of the words in the bag of equivalents which are also found in the target term. If we use the translation of the English term *destruction of anti-personnel mines* into Slovenian again, the candidate translation *unievannje protipehotnih min* has a translation score of 0.95, and the candidate translation *unienje protipehotnih min* has a translation score of 0.71. The translation system has a precision level varying between 64% and 97% depending on the corpora (selecting the 300 best alignments), but these results should be tempered since source terms and target terms were extracted from a single parallel corpus, not a comparable corpus.

The disadvantage of the approach is that it requires a probabilistic lexicon previously acquired from a parallel corpus. Thus, it can only be applied in the case in which one has at his/her disposal a parallel corpus that is large enough to obtain a probabilistic lexicon, but is still too small to obtain a satisfying number of term pairs. The comparable corpus would be used to increase the number of translation pairs.

As was the case for the work by [ROB 06], [VIN 10]'s approach enables us to manage the lexical and syntactic divergences. It also enables us to manage terminology variation since a single source word can have several translations. The bag of equivalents techniques ignores the order of words and potential grammatical words: the terms *weapon confiscation* and *confiscation of weapon* both match the bag of equivalents *{weapon, confiscation}*. Finally, usage of the bag of equivalents lightens the translation process since it avoids having to generate all the translation permutation of each of the words in the complex term.[5]

3.2.2.5. *Hybridization with distributional method*

The basic compositional method used by [MOR 12] consists of (1) identifying the lexical words of the complex term, (2) translating each of these lexical words in the target language (a same word can have several possible translations), (3) generating all the possible combinations of translated words and (4) selecting the combinations which can be found among the complex terms previously extracted from the target corpus. These translations are then ranked by frequency. In this state, if one of the components cannot be translated, the translation of the whole term fails.

[MOR 12] suggest to rely on the distributional method to deal with cases in which translation fails because one of the elements could not be translated. For a complex term made of two components $c1$ and $c2$ (e.g. *antécédent familial*):

– If the component c_1 (*antécédent*) cannot be translated:

- its context vector is gathered in the source corpus:
$\overrightarrow{\text{antécédent}} = \{(famille, 332), (familial, 73), (cancer, 68)...\}$

- its vector is translated into the target language thanks to a bilingual dictionary:
$\overrightarrow{t(\text{antécédent})} = \{(family, 332), (familial, 73), (cancer, 68)...\}$

– If the component c_2 (*familial*) can be translated by the bilingual dictionary, one gathers the context vectors of each of these translations. For example, *familial* can be translated in English as *familial* and *family*, so two target context vectors are gathered:

- $\overrightarrow{\text{familial}} = \{(risk, 37), (cancer, 68)...\}$

- $\overrightarrow{\text{family}} = \{(history, 372), (mutation, 50), (cancer, 24)...\}$

Following this step, the source term *antécédent familial* can be represented in two ways in the target language:

1) $\overrightarrow{t(\text{antécédent})} + \overrightarrow{\text{familial}}$

2) $\overrightarrow{t(\text{antécédent})} + \overrightarrow{\text{family}}$

5 The number of translations generated is of $\prod_{i=1}^{n} l_i p!$ in which l_i is the number of possible translations for each of the lexical words in the complex term and p is the number of lexical words creating the complex term [MOR 10].

These two representations are compared to the ones of the target terms previously extracted from the corpus. For example, the English term *family history* is linked to two vectors: $\overrightarrow{\text{family}} + \overrightarrow{\text{history}}$ in which:

- $\overrightarrow{\text{family}} = \{(history, 372), (mutation, 50), (cancer, 24)...\}$
- $\overrightarrow{\text{history}} = \{(family, 37), (cancer, 68)...\}$

To obtain the translation score between *antécédent familial* and *family history*, the authors calculate, for each possible coupling between the source term components and the target term components, the geometric mean of the similarities of the coupled component vectors:

1) $\sqrt{sim(\overrightarrow{t(\text{antécédent})}, \overrightarrow{\text{family}}) \times sim(\overrightarrow{\text{familial}}, \overrightarrow{\text{history}})}$

2) $\sqrt{sim(\overrightarrow{t(\text{antécédent})}, \overrightarrow{\text{history}}) \times sim(\overrightarrow{\text{familial}}, \overrightarrow{\text{family}})}$

3) $\sqrt{sim(\overrightarrow{t(\text{antécédent})}, \overrightarrow{\text{family}}) \times sim(\overrightarrow{\text{family}}, \overrightarrow{\text{history}})}$

4) $\sqrt{sim(\overrightarrow{t(\text{antécédent})}, \overrightarrow{\text{history}}) \times sim(\overrightarrow{\text{family}}, \overrightarrow{\text{family}})}$

Thus, the authors obtain four different scores for the *antécédent familial* ↔ *family history*.

These scores are calculated for each pair of *(source term, target term)* in the corpus. The candidate translations are finally ranked by diminishing scores.

The results obtained show that the hybrid method increases the number of translated source terms, even if this implies a decrease in precision. For the translation from French to English, the basic compositional method can only translate 140 out of 836 terms (16.7%), and its precision is of 73.2% on the Top1 and 79.1% on the Top5. With the hybrid method, the system generates translations for 514 source terms (61.1%), and the precision level is of 42.1% on the Top1 and 55.4% on the Top5.

3.2.3. *Monolexical units compositional translation*

The monolexical units compositional translation can only translate morphologically complex units. Therefore, these approaches generate few translations, but they are usually of a very high quality. Three morphological word formation processes are approached: prefixation, neoclassical compounding (based on Greek or Latin and combining forms such as "hydro" and "logy" to form "hydrology") and word compounding (based on the combination of words such as "wall" and "paper" that form "wallpaper").

3.2.3.1. *Translation of words formed by means of prefixation*

[CAR 05, CAR 09a]'s publications describe a machine translation system for neologisms formed by means of prefixation. The system relies on Lexeme Formation Rules, LFR (*Règles de Construction des Lexèmes*). An LFR describes a word derivation process as well as the change in meaning which it causes. In the ITALIAN part of the Table 3.1, we can see the illustration of an LFR describing the derivation of a verb X of meaning X' into a verb riX of meaning *reiterativity* (X'). More specifically, this LFR can describe the derivation of the verb *costruire* (build) into *rebuild* (reiterate the action of building). A bilingual LFR establishes a match between two LFR of different languages, as is shown in Table 3.1.

	ITALIAN		FRENCH	
	INPUT	OUTPUT	INPUT	OUTPUT
G	X	riX	Y	reY
SX	cat:v	cat:v	cat:v	cat:v
S	X'(...)	reiterativity (X'(...))	Y'(...)	reiterativity (Y'(...))

Table 3.1. *Example of bilingual LFR – adapted from [CAR 09a]*

In [CAR 05], the translation process is applied to prefixed verb and prefixed deverbal noun neologisms and is carried out over three stages:

1) Search for prefixed words in a corpus which relate to the Italian side of a bilingual LFR and whose lexical base is present in the bilingual dictionary.

2) Translation of the lexical base through the bilingual dictionary.

3) Generating the translation with the French side of the LFR.

The first stage generates noise: 15% of the verbs and 2% of the nouns are not genuinely prefixed words.[6] The data from the first step are manually cleaned, and only the words that are genuinely built are translated. The translations are considered correct at 97% for verbs and 91% for nouns. The other translations are considered uncertain, no translation is judged false.

[CAR 09a] adapts the LFR method to the translation of prefixed relational adjectives. In spite of the morphosyntactic similarities between Italian and French, the generation of relational adjectives in Italian is freer and more productive than in French. There are thus many Italian relational adjectives, which do not have a matching relational adjective in French, e.g. *gattesco* meaning "cat-like", *creditizione* meaning "relating to credit". To manage this, [CAR 09a] suggest that relational adjectives share their LFR with the noun from which they are derived. Thus, an

6 For example, *to delay* is not caused by the prefixing of the verb *lay* with the prefix 'de' and does not mean 'the contrary of lay'.

Italian adjective could be translated by a French noun as long as the correspondence between adjective and noun is established. This is very similar to what [MOR 10] do. In addition to a bilingual lexicon, this translation method also relies on two monolingual resources (French and Italian), which allow them to link relational adjectives and the nouns from which they derive.

The translation starts with the decomposition of the prefixed adjective into *prefix + adjective*, then the system looks for the adjective's translation in the bilingual dictionary and attempts to build the adjective up again in the target language:

1) *anticostituzionale* is sequenced into *anti-* and *costituzionale*

2) *costituzionale* is translated by *constitutionnel*

3) The adjective *anticonstitutionel* is built again from *anti-* and *constitutionnel*

If the Italian adjective cannot be directly translated into French, the system follows this procedure:

1) Find the Italian noun from which the adjective is derived: *costituzionale* → *costituzion*

2) Translate this noun into French: *costituzion* → *constitution*

3) Prefix the noun: *constitution* → *anticonstitution*

Following this procedure, *anticonstituzionale* is translated by *anticonstitution*. In the end, if it is possible to find, from the French word, the matching relational adjective, we can translated *anticonstituzionale* by *anticonstitutionel*:

1) Replace the noun by the adjective: *constitution* → *"constitutionnel"*

2) Prefix the adjective: *"constitutionnel"* → *"anticonstitutionel"*

Of the 1,783 prefixed relational adjectives, this method enabled the translation system to find 88% of correct translations through a French relational adjective and 12% of correct translations through a noun. The author does not mention any evaluation of the linguistical quality of the neologism generated.

3.2.3.2. *Translation of words formed by means of neoclassical compounding*

A neoclassical compound is a word made by combining forms of Greek or Latin origin. These combining forms are bound morphemes, i.e. they cannot be used on their own as words. For example, the term *vagotomy* is made of the combining form *vago*, from the Latin *vagus*, and of *tomy*, from the Greek *tomê*. None of these forms can operate autonomously: *vago* and *tomy* are not English words.

[HAR 12] distinguishes between two types of combining forms:

ICF: the initial combining forms, such as *cardio-, patho-,* which appear at the beginning of a compound.

FCF: the final combining forms, such as *-logy, -cide,* which appear at the end of a compound.

Translated neoclassical compounds take the form: *ICF+(FCF|word),* i.e. one or several ICF followed by a FCF or a word, for example: *histo/patho/logy, cardio/vascular, photo/bio/reactor.* The bilingual lexicon generation process is carried out as follows:

1) Extraction of source and target neoclassical compounds from the comparable corpus, i.e. any adjective or noun which contains an ICF or an FCF.

- e.g. *neurology* is extracted from the source corpus and *neurologie* is extracted from the target corpus

2) Identification of the source compound structure, which must match the form *ICF+(FCF|word).*[7]

- *neurology* is sequenced into *neuro+logy*

3) Translation of the compound: the ICF and FCF are translated via a bilingual lexicon of combining forms, and the identified words are translated via a general language bilingual dictionary. For each element, several candidate translations are generated when several translations are possible.

- *neuro* is translated by *neuro* and *névro*

- *logy* is translated by *logie*

4) The recombination step is easy: the order of the target elements is the same as the order of the source elements, thus, *histopathology* can only be translated as *histopathologie* in French and not as *pathohistologie.*

- there are two candidate translations: *neurologie* and *névrologie*

5) Finally, the candidate translation is retained if it appears in the target classical compound list extracted from the corpus.

- the candidate translation retained is *névrologie*

The method is applied to four languages: from English to French, German and Spanish. The bilingual lexicon of combining forms was hand-built. The French entries

7 Those who do not match this form are not translated.

were taken from [BÉC 92] then translated into English, German and French. Precision ranged from 96% to 97%. The recall varied between 30% and 37%. Using English as a pivotal language, [HAR 12] also generate French–German, Spanish–French and German–Spanish lexicons with a precision varying between 97% and 100%. Recall varies between 18% and 35%.

[WEL 11] suggest a similar method to translate neoclassical compounds except that the structure of the compounds is slightly different: *R1 trans? R2 suffix?*, i.e.:

R1 A type 1 combining form - equivalent to the ICF in [HAR 12].

trans? A transitional element such as *o* or *i* which can be found for example in *Kalorimetrie*. These elements enable the translation system to deal with allomorphy: for example, the combining form */hydr/* can be realized in the form *hydr-* as in (*hydration*) or *hydro-* as in (*hydrology*).

R2 A type 2 combining form - equivalent to the FCF in [HAR 12].

suffix? An optional suffix.

The method is tested on two language pairs (German–French and German–English) in both translation directions. When the candidate translations are filtered on the terms extracted from the corpus, precision varies between 97% and 99%.[8] As for the candidate translations not found in the corpus, it appears that between 50% and 78% of them are correct translations. There is no information provided for the recall.

3.2.3.3. *Translation of word compounds*

Compound words are simply words which can be sequenced into other words. Unlike neoclassical compounds, compound words can be sequenced into elements, which can be used on their own. They are different from polylexical units in that these words are not separated by spaces. For example, the German noun *Bleiisotope* is made from the word *Blei* ("lead") and the word *Isotope* ("isotope"). This process is very common in German and in Germanic languages in general.

[WEL 11] have actually focused on the case of German noun compounds. [WEL 11] only focused on the NOUN_1 NOUN_2 structure, which is translated in French by the NOUN PREP NOUN structure and in English by the NOUN NOUN structure or the NOUN PREP NOUN structure. Note that these structural equivalences make it possible to generate fertile translations (more words in the target than in the source term). For example:

1) *Korrosionsschultz* is sequenced into *Korrosion* and *schultz*. We can see here that the sequencing takes into account the linking element *s* in *Korrosionsschultz*.

8 Precision is not directly mentioned in the article, we calculate it from the Table 8 in the paper of [WEL 11]: in $\frac{correct}{TL-terms}$

2) *Korrosion* is translated in English by *corrosion,* and *schultz* is translated by *protection* thanks to a general language bilingual dictionary.

3) All the terms whose syntactic structure is either NOUN NOUN or NOUN PREP NOUN are identified in the list of terms extracted from the target corpus, which enables the translation system to find the translations *corrosion protection* and *protection against corrosion.*

The method was not wholly evaluated. Only the number of translations obtained was evaluated, not their accuracy. In a primary set of 2,000 German nouns (which are not necessarily noun compounds), the results obtained are:

– For the translation into French:

- 86 nouns were translated through other methods (bilingual dictionaries, classical compound method and graphical variation search).

- Of the 1914 words remaining, 152 (8%) were translated by decomposition.

– For the translation into English:

- 636 nouns were translated with other methods.

- Of the remaining 1364 nouns, 248 (18%) were translated by decomposition.

The difference in results between the two languages can be explained by the size of the dictionaries used (30,000 entries for the German–French dictionary and 820,000 entries for the German–English one).

Another approach to translating word compounds consists of going through pivotal languages as [GAR 08] do. Their aim is to translate word compounds from a source language SL to a target language TL using several bilingual dictionaries and associating the target language terms to a translation in a third language which is used as a pivot language (PL).

The translation is carried out as follows:

1) Decomposition of the compound to be translated:

- *ekurudhë* is decomposed into *hekur* and *udhë.*

2) Generation of a gloss (a sort of literal translation) in the target language by translating each of the words:

- *{hekur, udhë}* becomes *{iron, path}.*

3) The same decomposition and gloss generation in the target language is applied to the PL entries of the bilingual dictionaries, for example:

- *eisenbahn* → *{eisen, bahn}*→ *{iron, path}*;

- *ferrovia* → *{ferro, via}*→ *{iron, path}*;

- *järnvag* → *{järn, vag}*→ *{iron, path}*.

4) For each PL entry whose gloss is identical to the one generated for the source language, the matching translation is selected (the element order can be inverted to cover the cases in which the order of the elements is not kept from one language to the next):

- *eisenbahn* → *railroad*;

- *ferrovia* → *railroad*;

- *järnvag* → *railway*.

5) The candidate translations are ranked according to the score: $\frac{freq(g,e_c)}{freq(g)}$ in which $freq(g, e_c)$ is the number of times in which the compound word was translated by e using the gloss g and $freq(g)$ the number of times in which the gloss g was generated from the dictionaries' entries:

- *ekurudhë* → *railroad*.

The point of going through a pivot language is that it enables us to manage lexical divergence cases. In the example, we see how it enabled the translation to find the translation for the Albanian compound word *erkurudhë* to the English *railway* when one of the two elements composing it was not directly translatable into English (*rail* is not the translation of *hekur* which means "iron"). Even if it is not highlighted in the article, this method also enables us to manage cases in which one of the two terms does not have a compositional meaning: *Krankenhaus*, literally meaning sick house, can be translated as *hospital* by going through the pivot translation *Sjukhus*, meaning sick house. However, one of the disadvantages is that it requires translation examples in several languages ([GAR 08] work with between 10 and 50 languages). The authors can generate a candidate translation for 13.20 % of the compounds. After ranking, they obtain a precision of 19.4% on the Top1 and 36.3% on the Top10.

3.2.4. *Candidate translation filtering*

Once the translations have been generated, it is usual for the source term to be associated to several candidate translations. It is also possible that the translation process generated agrammatical terms in the target language. We thus have to filter these translations. We have found three filtering methods in the state-of-the-art: (1) looking for an attestation of the generated translation in the target corpus; (2) contexts similarity (applying the distributional method) and (3) supervised learning.

3.2.4.1. *Looking for an attestation*

This method consists of looking for the attestation of the generated translation in the target corpus. It is the method used for example by [MOR 10, HAR 12] and [WEL 11] who work with comparable corpora: potential target terms are first extracted from the target part of the corpus and then the generated translations are filtered from this list of target terms. In this case, it is possible that a potential translation is rejected because it is not extracted by the term extractor even if it is found in the corpus. [GRE 99, CAR 09b, LEO 08] use a search engine as well as the number of hits from the engine to check that the generated translations do indeed exist in the target language.

We should be wary when using the internet: the amount of data is such that it is perfectly possible to find word attestations that would be either impossible or incorrect in the target language (spelling mistakes, lexical creation games...). This is why authors generally also rely on the frequency of these attestations. [GRE 99], for example, retains the most frequent translation. [LEO 08] uses a series of statistical filters like the ratio of frequencies obtained from the Web. A translation will only be retained if its frequency is at least higher to the $1/10{,}000^{th}$ than the frequency of the source term. The idea is that the source term and its translation must have comparable frequencies, the ratio of 1/10,000 is explained by the fact that English (target language) is much more present than French (source language) on the internet.

A second risk is that the Web contains a wide variety of texts; these texts belong to different subject fields, language registers or serve various communicative goals. Even if a generated translation is attested on the Web, we have to check that it appears in similar contexts as the original term, at least when it comes to the subject field. For example, if one translates *chemin de fer* (literally "iron path" but meaning "railway") in French by *iron path* in English, this word association finds 26,600 results in Google at the point of writing. However, it is not at all the translation of *chemin de fer* but the title of a music album. The solution is then to carry out a comparison of the appearance contexts of the source and target texts with the distributional method presented in Chapter 1.

3.2.4.2. *Filtering based on context similarities*

This filtering method uses the same principle as the distributional method: the closer the contexts, the more probable it is that the source and target terms are translations of one another.

[LEO 08] compares what he calls the *mondes lexicaux* (lexical worlds) of the source term and its candidate translation. The lexical world of a term is built by querying this term on a search engine and obtaining, from the 1,000 first result snippets, the 50 words and 50 adjectives which are the most common. Just like the distributional approach, in order to be comparable, the lexical worlds are translated via a bilingual dictionary. The similarity between the lexical world of the source term (S) and the lexical world of the candidate translation (T) is given by the Jaccard index:

$$Similarity(S,T) = \frac{|M(S) \cap M(T)|}{|M(S) \cup M(T)|} \qquad [3.1]$$

in which $M(X)$ represents the set of words from the lexical world of X. Only the translation pairs with a similarity above a given threshold are retained.

[BAL 04] proceed in a different manner. They use a comparable corpus built from the Web and from translation pairs belonging to a single field. The source terms are used as the queries in a search engine to build the source corpus, and the target terms are used as queries in a search engine to build the target corpus. The alignment is made between the terms extracted from the source corpus and the terms extracted from the target corpus. Only the terms belonging to the same domain as the original translation pairs are kept. The level of belonging to the domain is based on the Jaccard index (in this case, $M(X)$ is the documents recalled by the engine in which the term X appears).

[GAR 08] also tested the input of the context similarity to rank the candidate translations. Their experiments covered the German–Swedish couple based on the parallel corpus Europarl (15 and 21 millions words, respectively) and not the Web. The impact of this strategy is weak: the precision on the Top1 goes from 19.6% to 20.1% and from 38.8% to 39.1% on the Top10.

3.2.4.3. *Supervised learning filtering*

[BAL 04] translate noun compounds from Japanese to English by following the compositional rule. The recomposition of the term in the target language is ensured by translation templates. A translation template of the type [N_2^E in N_1^E] in which N_i^E is an English noun which is the translation of the Japanese word of rank *i*. Morphological variations can be used to match the translation of the Japanese noun and the translation template. For example, in *kaNkei·kaizeN*, *kaNkei* can be translated as *relation, connection, relationship* and *kaizeN* can be translated by *improvement, betterment*. The generated candidate translations are: *relation improvement, betterment of relationship, improvement connection, relational betterment* among which the translation *relational betterment* was generated using the morphological similarity between *relation* and *relational.*

A first filtering technique is based on a Corpus-based Translation Quality score (CTQ). For a translation generated with the template t and containing the words w_1 and w_2, the CTQ score takes into account:

– $p(w_1, w_2, t)$: the probability of finding w_1 and w_2 in the template t

– $p(w_1, t)$: the probability of finding w_1 in the template t.

– $p(w_2, t)$: the probability of finding w_2 in the template t.

These probabilities are calculated over a target language corpus. This score thus corresponds to a language model. The CTQ score is obtained with:

$$CTQ(w_1, w_2, t) = \alpha \cdot p(w_1, w_2, t) + \beta \cdot p(w_1, t) \cdot p(w_2, t) \quad [3.2]$$

in which α and β are weighting coefficients ($0 \geq \alpha, \beta \geq 1$ and $\alpha + \beta = 1$).

In a second experiment, [BAL 04] rank the candidate translations with a model learned on translation examples: a positive example is a correct translation pair; a negative example is a wrong translation pair. Each example is linked to three types of features:

– *Features coming from the corpus*: this is the CTQ score as well as various occurrence and co-occurence frequencies of the translation template and words included in the translation (eight features in all).

– *Features coming from the bilingual dictionaries*: this is mainly the translation probabilities (six features in all).

– *Features based on the templates*: these are two traits which take into account the type of template and the component element which acts as its head (two features in all).

The authors use the Support Vector Machine (SVM) algorithm to learn to model. This algorithm outputs continuous values between +1 and -1, indicating if the translation belongs to the positive class (correct translation) or the negative class (incorrect translation). This value is used to rank the candidate translations.

In this way, [BAL 04] obtain 43% of correct translations in the direction Japanese $\rightarrow$ English and 51% of correct translations in the direction English $\rightarrow$ Japanese, while the selection based uniquely on the CTQ score obtains 37% in the direction Japanese $\rightarrow$ English and 42% in the direction English $\rightarrow$ Japanese.

In this last sub-section, we have seen that the selection of candidate translations can be driven by Web data, comparable corpora or translation examples found in a bilingual dictionary. We will now look at approaches in which the generation itself comes from rules stemming from translation examples.

3.3. Data-driven approaches

The approaches described below are called "data-driven" for just like the data-driven approaches of MT, they rely on the analysis of a great volume of translation examples. We describe two types of approach: analogy-based translation [LAN 09] and rewriting rules learning [CLA 09] which can be associated with morphological family learning [CLA 11].

3.3.1. *Analogy-based translation*

[LEP 03] tells us that analogy is an old concept, first presented by the Greek philosopher Aristotle as follows: "*A is to B as C is to D*". Analogy is introduced in linguistics by Saussure who defines it as the "*operation through which, given the two forms of a same word, and only one form of a second word, we create the missing form*".[9] For example, this is the reasoning through which we find the progressive form of *ring* from the example *sing* → *singing*. To do this, we solve the analogical equation:

$$[sing : singing = ring : x]$$

whose solution is:

$$\Rightarrow x = ringing$$

Analogy is thus a proportion relation between four elements which can be written:

$$[x : y = z : t]$$

and explained by x *is to* y *as* z *is to* t. An analogical equation is an analogy in which the fourth term is missing:

$$[x : y = z :?]$$

According to [LEP 03], formal analogy (i.e. which applies to a chain of characters) was used successfully in NLP in the domain of MT (paradigm of the example-based translation) and in text-to-speech (transformation of a chain of graphemes into phonemes).

The works of [LAN 09] suggest using analogy to translate monolexical terms belonging to the medical field. Analogy-based translation is carried out from a set of source terms I, a set of target terms O and the translation relations between these terms. For example, let us start from a set of source words *{constitution, profession, constitutionnel, professionnel}*, a set of target words *{constitution, profession, constitutional, professional}* and the translation relations *{(constitution, constitution),*

9 "*opération par laquelle, étant données deux formes d'un même mot, et seulement une forme d'un second mot, on crée la forme manquante*"

(profession, profession), (constitutionnel, constitutional)}. We attempt to establish the missing translation relation between the source word $professionnel$ and the target word $professional.$

The analogy-based translation procedure of a source word i is:

1) Gather the set of triplets (x, y, z) so that x,y and z generate an analogy with i, in the example: *(constitution, profession, constitutionnel)* for $professionnel.$

2) Translate these triplets, in our example we get *(constitution, profession, constitutional)*.

3) Select the set of target words *{*o_1,o_2..o_n*}* which create an analogy with the triplets obtained in step 2; in our example we obtain $professional.$

4) Select the right translation among *{*o_1,o_2...o_n*}*; a single solution in our example: $professional.$

Steps 1. and 3. create analogy equations that [LAN 09] solve as follows:

1) Let there be the following equation: $[x\ : y = z\ :?]$

- e.g. *[constitution: profession = constitutionnel: ?]*

2) Carry out several random combinations of y and z while keeping the letter order:

- e.g. *constiprofesstuiontion*, *pcronosftietsutsiiononnel*, etc.

3) For each combination, establish its complement in relation to$x$:

- e.g. *constiprofesstuiontion* *constitution* $\rightarrow$ *professionnel, prosfestnionel, etc.*

- e.g. *pcronosftietsutsiiononnel* *constitution* $\rightarrow$ *porfiesonnel, professionnel, etc.*

4) The complement(s) obtained represent the possible solutions of the analogical equation.

We should note that the analogical approach is confronted with computing cost issues, especially with the combination of character chains (resolving the analogical equation, step 2) and with processing of all the triplets which create the analogy of the word to be translated (analogy-based translation, steps 1 and 3). Moreover, analogy-based translation generates several candidate translations for a single source term which then have to be filtered in a third step. [LAN 09] carry out the selection of the best candidate translation by machine learning. To this end, they use a binary classifier based on the perceptron algorithm called "voted-perceptron" [FRE 99]. The ranking model is learned from analogy relation examples aligned in a similar way as in the equation [3.3] in which the analogical relation r is aligned to the analogical relation r', x being the translation of x', y the translation of y' so forth.

$$(r, r') = ([x : y = z : t], [x' : y' = z' : t']) \qquad [3.3]$$

The machine learning features are the analogy degree, the number of times in which a form is generated, the length ratio between t and t' and the translation likelihood score (calculated from the n-grams learned on the corpus). An experiment is carried out on 1,000 terms from the MLS and on six languages: English, Spanish, Finnish, French, Russian and Swedish. The results go from 53.6% of accurate translations for the direction Finnish $\rightarrow$ English to 64.3% of accurate translations for the direction Spanish $\rightarrow$ English.

3.3.2. *Rewriting rules learning*

[CLA 09] tries to translate monolexical medical terms. He notices that they are generally built from the Greek and Latin roots present in many languages and that the morphological derivation rules are also regular from one language to the next, which provides him with translation pairs with close spelling, e.g. *ophtalmorragie* $\rightarrow$ *ophthalmorragia* and *leucorragie* $\rightarrow$ *leukorrhagia*. The spelling variations are judged to be sufficiently regular to learn the rewriting rules, i.e. the rules which apply to one or several sub-chains of the term to be translated and generate the equivalent of this sub-chain in the target language. For example, if we apply the rewriting rules *leuco* $\rightarrow$ *leuko, rragie* $\rightarrow$ *rrhagia* to *leucorragie*, we obtain *leukorrhagia*.

The rewriting rules are learnt with a list of translation pairs. The process is identical to that of statistical machine translation, only it is based on a sequence of letters instead of words. We find here the three modules of a statistical machine translation system: (1) alignment; (2) translation model learning (rewriting rules) and (3) language model learning.

The translation pairs are aligned at the letters-level with the DPalign tool[10] which has the advantage of being able to align sequences not written with the same alphabet. The rewriting rules are inferred from these alignments. Every time that, in a translation pair example, two aligned letters are not identical, the system generates every rule that can possibly rewrite the source string as the target string. For example, for the difference *e/a* in the pair (*leucorragie, leukorrhagia*), the system generates several rules: *e* $\rightarrow$ *e, ie* $\rightarrow$ *ia, gie* $\rightarrow$ *gia*, etc. The best rule is chosen on the basis of the ratio between the number of times in which the rule entry matches a sub-chain in a source word and the number of times in which the rule can be entirely applied to a pair of words.

10 http://search.cpan.org/ cjfields/BioPerl-1.6.1/Bio/Tools/dpAlign.pm

As for the language model, it matches the n-gram probabilities[11] of letters learned on the target part of the translation pairs.

To translate a term, all the possible rewriting rules are applied to it, which generates several translation candidates. The most probable translation is selected with the language model:

$$P(w) = \prod_{i=1}^{m} P(l_i | l_{i-n+1}, ..., l_{i-1}) \quad [3.4]$$

in which $P(l_i | l_{i-n+1}, ..., l_{i-1})$ is the probability of finding the i^{st} letter of the word knowing the n letters before it.

[CLA 09] obtains 85.4% of correct translations in the direction French → English and 84.8 % in the direction English → French, based on 5,400 examples taken from UMLS [LIN 93]. While the technique has been tested on other language couples, the results decrease depending on the morphological and graphical similarities between the languages: from 87.9% for the direction Portuguese → Spanish, to 57.5% for the direction English → Russian.

3.3.3. *Dealing with morphological variation*

To finish, we will mention the work of [CLA 11] whose translation technique is based on a decomposition of the term to be translated into *morphs*: "we distinguish morphs, elementary linguistic signs (segments), from morphemes, equivalence classes with identical signified and close significants" [CLA 11]. This work can be compared to the compositional approaches described in section 3.2.3 which translates the monolexical units by going through morphological decomposition. However, contrary to the knowledge-based approaches, the system suggested by [CLA 11] learns the translation equivalences between morphs from examples. It is also able to deal with fertility cases.

Starting from a database of medical term translation examples (8,000 pairs extracted from the UMLS), [CLA 11] learn the alignment probabilities between character chains by adapting [DEM 77]'s maximization expectation algorithm. This algorithm enables the authors to obtain alignments with an empty character chain (case of fertile translations) but does not take into account distortion (case in which the order of the aligned elements is different).

The maximization-expectation algorithm operates in two phases which are repeated until convergence is reached:

11 A n-gramme is a sequence of n elements, in this case letters.

– *Expectation (initialization)*: the expectation phase counts the possible alignments between the character sub-chains of the source term and the character sub-chains of the target term. These character sub-chains are what [CLA 11] refers to as morphs. These accounts are stored in a morph alignment table written γ

– *Maximization (initialization)*: the maximization phase calculated the alignment probabilities of the morphs by standardizing the counts of γ, these probabilities are stored in a table written δ:

$$\delta(s,t) = \frac{\gamma(s,t)}{\sum_x \gamma(s,x)}$$

where s is a source morph and t is a target morph.

– *Expectation (iteration 1)*: the probabilities stored in δ are reused to weigh the alignment accounts, a new γ table is generated.

– *Maximization (iteration 1)*: once again, the accounts are standardized to generate a new version of the δ table.

... iterations follow each other until they have reached the end criteria ...

– *End*: the iterations cease when there are no more or very little differences left between the δ obtained in iteration i and the δ table obtained in iteration $i + 1$.

One of the limits of this approach is that it does not take into account the allomorphic variation, i.e. the fact that a single morpheme can be realized under different forms. This variation leads to a scattering of the alignment probabilities. If we take the example of the translation from Japanese to French, which is the case that [CLA 11] deals with, we know that in French the meaning of "bactérie" ("bacteria") can be realized as *batérie*, *bactéri-* as in *bactéricide* or even *bactério-* as in *bactériologique*. Yet, these three morphs will each be aligned separately with their Japanese match kin:[12]

SOURCE	TARGET	PROBABILITY
kin	bactérie	0.4
kin	bactério	0.3
kin	bactéri	0.2

The calculation of alignment probabilities of the maximization phase is thus modified to take into account all the morphological equivalents:

$$\delta(s,t) = \frac{\sum_{m \in M} \gamma(s,m)}{\sum_x \gamma(s,x)}$$

12 We use the roman script equivalent to kanji (romaji).

in which M is the set of morphs associated to t, i.e. in our example, if $t = bactérie$, $M = \{bactérie, bactéri, bactério\}$.

As described in the algorithm 1, this set of morphs M is obtained by applying rewriting rules to t which have themselves been learned from the previous iteration's alignments: if two morphs are aligned with a same kanji in the table γ and the length of their longest common sub-chain ($plscc$) is above a certain threshold, then the authors consider that they belong to the same morpheme. For example, *dermo* and *dermato* are aligned with the same kanji and share the sub-chain *derm*. From this pair of morphs, the authors can deduce the rewriting rule $r = plscc(m_1, m_2) \ominus ato \oplus o$, i.e. "rewriting the suffix ato into o". Applying this rule to the morph *hemato*, enables the translator to identify it as a variant of *hemo* and vice-versa. This system of rewriting rules uses formal analogies between morphs, as in our example: $dermato : dermo = hémato : hémo$. In their experiments, [CLA 11] only take into account analogies of degree 3: the rewriting rules which are learned are of the shape of *prefix* $\oplus$ *base* $\oplus$ *suffix*.

Algorithm 1 Maximization phase modified to take into account morphological variations

Require: γ
for all sub-chain s s.t. $\gamma(s, \cdot)$ **do**
  for all m_1, m_2 s.t. $\gamma(s, m_1) > 0$ and $\gamma(s, m_2) > 0$ and $plscc(m_1, m_2) > threshold$ **do**
    build the prefixing and suffixing rule r from m_1 and m_2
    increment the score of r
  end for
  for all sub-chain t s.t. $\gamma(s, t) > 0$ **do**
    build the set M of morphs associated to t using the n' most frequent rewriting rules stemming from the previous iteration
    calculate $\delta(s, t)$
  end for
end for
return δ

Very little detail is given on the way to translate French medical terms into Japanese, apart from the fact that the morph translation probabilities in δ are used in a Viterbi-type algorithm [VIT 67]. Of the 128 terms to translate, 92 found a translation (71.8%). Of these 92 translations, 58 matches those of the ULMS (63%). If the authors take into account the translations that appeared in on-line medical resources, the number of correct translations rises to 82 (89.1%).

3.4. Evaluation of term translator generation methods

The translation generation is evaluated in a similar way to the distributional approach, only it is important to evaluate the generating power of the methods, i.e. their ability to generate at least one candidate translation for each source term, no matter how exact the translation is. This information is provided by coverage, written C, which is calculated by:

$$C = \frac{|ST|}{|S|} \qquad [3.5]$$

$$ST = \{s : |\mathcal{T}(s)| > 1\}$$

where S is the set of source terms and $\mathcal{T}(s)$ is the set of translations generated by the system for the source term s.

The precision shows, for the source terms for which the system has generated a translation, the proportion of those which have been matched with at least one correct translation. Just like several translations can be generated, precision can be calculated for the N best translations:

$$P_N = \frac{|SR_N|}{|ST|} \qquad [3.6]$$

$$SR_N = \{s : \mathcal{T}_N(s) \cap \mathcal{R}(s) \neq \emptyset\}$$

where $\mathcal{T}_N(s)$ is the set of the first N translations of s and $\mathcal{R}(s)$ is the set of reference translations for s. As translation generation offers a good precision, it is the precision for the Top1 which is used in most cases ($N = 1$). Sometimes, precision is calculated over the set of candidate translations suggested by the system ($N = |T(s)|$).

The recall shows the fraction of source terms for which the system has generated at least one exact translation among the N best translations:

$$R_N = C \times P_N = \frac{|SR_N|}{|S|} \qquad [3.7]$$

Finally, F1-measure enables us to show the compromise between precision and recall:

$$F1 = 2 \times \frac{P \times R}{P + R} \qquad [3.8]$$

Some authors take into account two levels of accuracy for translation. The first level is called the *reference* level, i.e. a translation which exists in a linguistic reference resource (for example, UMLS in the medical field) or which is validated by an expert as being the canonical translation. However, there are many cases in which a candidate translation generated by the system, even though it does not match the definition of a reference translation, is still acceptable and usable. This concept of *acceptable* translation is referred to as *silver-standard* by [BAL 04], as *acceptable* translation by [LEO 08] and as *uncertain* translation by [CAR 05].

Tables 3.2 and 3.3 summarize the results obtained by the compositional translation techniques and data-driven approaches. C is the coverage P, R and F1 match precision, recall and F1-measure when only taking into account the reference translations on the Top1 (except in the case of [HAR 12] and [WEL 11] who consider the set of all the translations of a source term - results marked with a star). P_A, R_A, $F1_A$ are the cover, precision, recall and F1-measure when taking into account the reference translations and acceptable translations (still Top1). The PLU and MLU acronyms refer to polylexical and monolexical units, respectively. The GL acronym means general language.

Results obtained cannot be compared for the experiments rely on different sets of data, but we can observe that globally, while the translation generation methods do not have the ability of suggesting translations for all the source terms that are presented to them, we find more precise translations than under the distributional approach. With translation generation methods, precision varies between 19% and 94% on the Top1, whereas with the distributional approach, precision varies between 13% and 65% on the Top1 and 30% to 89% on the Top10.

The main issue of translation generation is its coverage. Many terms cannot be translated with this method, especially with compositional approaches which tend to focus on a very specific type of structure (for example, 8% of translations generated in the case of German noun compounds of [WEL 11]). The data-driven approaches globally show the best results: 54% to 85% of precision on the Top1 with 72% to 100 % coverage against 19% to 94% precision on the Top1 with 8% to 100% coverage for compositional approaches. However, the latter require very large amounts of specialized data: at least 5,400 pairs of aligned medical terms for [CLA 09] and up to 19,800 for [LAN 09]. On the contrary, compositional approaches "only" require bilingual dictionaries (which are usually easily available) and a few translation templates.

REFERENCE	FILTERING METHOD	LANGUAGES	ELEMENTS TO BE TRANSLATED NB.	TYPE	DOMAIN	TRANSLATION RESOURCES SIZE	TYPE	RESULTS C	P	R	F1	P_A	R_A	$F1_A$
[GRE 99]	Web + frequencies	DE → EN ES → EN	724 1140	PLU	GL	36.7k	GL dictionary		.87 .86					
[ROB 06]	Web + context similarity	FR → JA	194	PLU	AI/NLP	50k 50k 96k	GL dictionary scientific dictionary JA thesaurus, GL	1	.81	.82	.81			
[BAL 04]	binary classifier	EN → JA JA → EN	750 750	PLU	press	550k	GL dictionary	.92 .98	.51 .44	.47 .42	.49 .43	.78 .84	.72 .82	.75 .83
[MOR 10]	contextual similarity score (800k word corpus)	FR → JA	829	PLU	medical	173k	GL, medical, technical dictionary		.88					
[MOR 12]	frequency (530k word corpus)	EN → FR	836	PLU	medical	246k	GL dictionary	.17	.73	.27				
	frequency (220k words)	EN → DE	964	PLU	medical	171k	GL dictionary	.09	.89	.16				
	contextual similarity score (530k word corpus)	EN → FR	836	PLU	medical	246k	GL dictionary + context vectors	.61	.42	.50				
	corpus extracted terms (220k words)	EN → DE	964	PLU	medical	171k	GL dictionary + context vectors	.53	.44	.48				
[LEO 08]	Web + frequencies + contexts	FR→ EN	1075	PLU	GL		GL dictionary	.83	.89	.74	.81	.94	.78	.85
[CAR 05]	none	IT → FR	115	prefixed words	press		GL dictionary + LFR	1	.94	.94	.94	1	1	1
[CAR 09b]	Web + frequencies	IT → FR	30376	prefixed words	press		GL dictionary + LFR			.42 to .94				
[HAR 12]	corpus extracted terms	EN → FR EN → DE EN → ES	1068 3538 2126	classical compounds	environment	146k + 83 70k + 61 62k + 58	GL dictionary + classical roots	.37 .36 .3	.98* .96* .97*	.36* .35* .29*	.53* .51* .45*			
[WEL 11]	corpus extracted terms	DE → EN EN → DE	364 315	neoclassical compounds	environment		neoclassical roots		.99* .97*					
		DE → EN DE → FR	1364 1914	word c	environment	820k 30k	GL dictionary	.18 .08						
[GAR 08]	probability	SQ, BG, CS, FA, DE, HU, RU, SK, SV[13] → EN	10273	word compounds	GL		GL dictionary	.13	.19	.03	.05			

Table 3.2. *Results of the state-of-the-art – translation generation methods based on compositionality*

REFERENCE	FILTERING METHOD	LANGUAGES	ELEMENTS TO TRANSLATE NB.	TYPE	DOMAIN	RESOURCES FOR TRANSLATION SIZE	TYPE	RESULTS C	P	R	F1	P_A	R_A	$F1_A$
[CLA 09]	probability	FR → EN	1000	MLU	medical	5.4k	medical dictionary	1	.85	.85	.85			
		EN → FR	1000			5.4k		1	.85	.85	.85			
		PT → ES	1000			5.4k	UMLS	1	.88	.88	.88			
		EN → RU	1000			5.4k		1	.58	.58	.58			
[LAN 09]	binary classifier	FR → EN	1000	PLU,MLU	medical	17.3k	UMLS	1	.57	.19	.29			
		SP → EN	1000			19k		1	.63	.23	.33			
		FI → EN	1000			19.8k		1	.54	.21	.3			
[CLA 11]	probability	FR → JA	128	PLU,MLU	medical	6.4k	UMLS	.72	.63	.45	.53	.89	.64	.74

Table 3.3. *Results of the state-of-the-art – data-driven translation generation methods*

3.5. Research perspectives

We have noticed in the previous chapter that translators found lexicons extracted through distributional methods to be difficult to use (too many candidate translations, a level of precision that is too low). The latter prefer having few translations but for them to be more trustworthy. After this state-of-the-art on the translation generation methods, we can state that this approach seems to be better adapted to the extraction of lexicons meant for specialized human translation.

We have shown there are two ways in which to generate translations. On the one hand, compositional translation methods can be described as an "expert" or "knowledge-based" approach, based on general language dictionaries and a linguistic analysis of the term to be translated. On the other hand, data-driven methods use specialized bilingual resources as translation examples. Table 3.4 synthesizes the strengths and weaknesses of the distributional, compositional and data-driven approaches.

	DISTRIBUTIONAL	GENERATION	
		COMPOSITIONAL	DATA-DRIVEN
Precision	-	+	+
Coverage	+	-	-
Independent from the frequency of the terms to be translated	-	+	+
Operates without examples	+	+	-

Table 3.4. *Comparison of machine acquisition methods for bilingual lexica*

We choose to continue our research in the context of compositional translation for several reasons:

– Compared to the distributional approach, compositional translation is less dependent on the size of the corpus. Indeed, once the translation is generated, a single occurrence in the target corpus can be enough to validate the translation, whereas the distributional approach requires source and target terms to be sufficiently frequent to obtain representative context vectors. Moreover, we know, thanks to the work of [MOR 10] that the compositional method provides better results than the distributional method when it comes to translating terms with a compositional meaning.

– Concerning the empirical approaches, the latter require that there exist specialized lexicons or bilingual terminologies. It is not a surprise if such approaches seem to be restricted to the medical field and all use the same resource (UMLS). These approaches do not enable us to approach a new domain without going through the work of constituting a specialized bilingual lexicon of a large size (at least 5,400 entries). They are thus limited to the domains in which there already exists a minimum of available resources. However, our goal is to be able to jump start the acquisition of bilingual lexicons when there are no or very little specialized resources.

The main limit of compositional translation is its coverage: only certain lexical units can be translated. These units must be complex, i.e. able to be cut up into sub-units. This is the case of polylexical units or even monolexical units stemming from a morphological construction process. Moreover, their equivalent in the target language must also be divisible, and there must be a bijection between the components in the source term and the components in the target term (Figure 3.1).

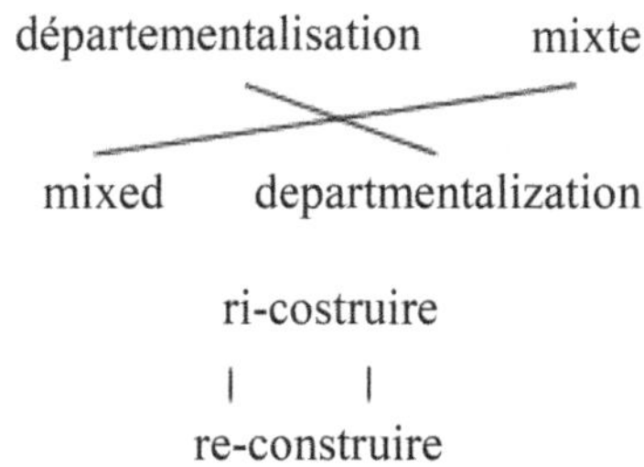

Figure 3.1. *Examples of alignments identifiable with compositional translation*

Translation pairs in which one of the elements is not complex or whose components' meaning is too far will not be translated in this manner. An example of such an impossible translation is the alignment between the English term 'snorkelling' (which cannot be decomposed into morphemes) and its French equivalent '*palmes-tuba-masque*' (literally 'fins-snorkel-mask') which can be decomposed into three morphemes: *palmes* ('fins'), *tuba* ('snorkel') and *masque* ('mask').

In spite of this, compositional translation remains an advantage to identify the translations of specialized lexical units since it is known that "complex words form more than 60% of the new terms found in techno-scientific domains" [NAM 07].

Most of the compositional translation difficulties have been studied – with more or less success - by the previous works:

– The non-parallel nature of syntactic structures is easily dealt with by compositional methods due to the permutations of the translated components, to the "bag of equivalents" approach or the translation templates.

– Morphological divergences can be dealt with by using a word or lexical base belonging to the same morphological family as the component to be translated - see for example the use of relational adjectives in [MOR 10] and [CAR 09a].

– The lexical divergence is managed with the inclusion of synonyms or semantically close words by [ROB 06] or by taking into account all the translations suggested by a probability lexicon [VIN 10].

The question of fertility is the least studied these days. Only [WEL 11] and [CLA 11] mention it explicitly. Each focuses on a specific case. [WEL 11] focus on the equivalence between noun compounds and noun phrases (e.g. Elektronenmikroskop ↔ electron microscope). [CLA 11] establish parallels between neoclassical combining forms and words that are graphically close (e.g. bacteri- ↔ bacteria).

Moreover, the processing of monolexical units by the compositional approach lacks genericity. Each author is focusing on a specific type of word formation process (prefixation, neoclassical compounding and word compounding). Yet, a word can be the result of several word formation processes: post-oophorectomy, clinico-pathologic, histologically, etc.

Finally, filtering the candidate translations is often based on a single criterion (attestation of the form, frequency and contextual similarity), and there is no study (outside machine learning) which try to combine these criteria.

These three points (fertility, independence from the morphological structure of the source term and combination of criteria for filtering) are research axes that we have chosen to approach in this dissertation. Our research has led us to develop a variation of the compositional translation method which we have called *morpho-compositional*. The context of our research as well as the work hypotheses are presented in the following chapter.

PART 2

Contributions to Compositional Translation

4

Morph-Compositional Translation: Methodological Framework

4.1. Introduction

The aim of this chapter is to present the methodological framework of our research. The first section 4.2 defines our translation method as well as the notions used. In section 4.3, we endeavor to highlight our contributions. The evaluation methodology is presented in section 4.4. A conclusion to the chapter is given in section 4.5.

4.2. Morpho-compositional translation method

We place ourselves within the context of monolexical unit compositional translation, and wish to offer an approach inspired by the work of [CAR 09b, WEL 11, HAR 12] which would be generic enough to deal with various types of word formation processes as well as with cases in which the monolexical unit can be translated by a polylexical unit. Moreover, we also wish to offer a ranking method for the generated translation that takes into account various criteria and not just its frequency or the similarity of distribution between it and the source term.

The suggested translation method, which we call *morpho-compositional method* can be broken down into five stages:

1) *Decomposing* the source term into morphemes or "morpheme-like" elements:

- *post-menopausal* is sequenced into *post* and *menopausal*.

2) *Translate*, with a bilingual dictionary, each of the elements into the target language; the translation can also call upon *morphological variants* or *synonyms*:

- *post* can be translated as *post* or *après*;

- *menopausal* can be translated as *ménopause*.

3) *Recomposing* the translated elements so as to generate a candidate term in the target language, which can be made of one or several words:

- *post* and *ménopause* can be recomposed in four ways: *postménopause, ménopausepost* (one word) and *post ménopause, ménopause post* (two words);

- *après* and *ménopause* can also be recomposed in four ways: *aprèsménopause, ménopauseaprès, après ménopause, ménopause après*.

4) *Searching for an attestation* of the candidate terms in a target language corpus:

- only *postménopause, post ménopause, après (la) ménopause* and *ménopause après* can be attested in a corpus.

5) *Ranking* the candidates extracted from the corpus based on a score obtained by combining several criteria:

a) *postménopause*;

b) *après la ménopause*;

c) *post ménopause*;

d) *ménopause après*.

From now on in this book, we use the term *translation generation* to refer to stages 1 to 4 and the term *translation ranking* to refer to stage 5.

The method we suggest does not rely on translation templates and does not rely on prior knowledge of the morphological structure of the target term. Stages 1, 2 and 3 generate all possible translation hypotheses. After stage 3, we thus have a large number of candidate translations, and some of them are "miscreations" (e.g. *ménopauseaprès*). Stages 4 and 5 serve to limit the number of candidate translations by only selecting the translations attested in a target language (stage 4) and then ranking them from the most likely to the least likely (stage 5).

Moreover, our method allows bound morphemes to be translated by free morphemes. In our example, it is the translation of the prefix *post* by the preposition *après*. This type of translational equivalence has never been used in compositional translation as far as we know.

4.2.1. *Scientific positioning*

Free and bound morpheme equivalences have already been used by [CLA 11] in the context of data-driven approaches. In this work, they establish morphological families, such as {*bactério-, bactéri-, bactérie*}, which are aligned with the same kanji and can be used in translation. [CLA 11] also mention that several generated translations are paraphrases, which show the advantage of the bound morpheme ↔ free morpheme equivalence to generate fertile translations.

In the same way, [DÉL 09] generates paraphrases to help the understanding of medical texts, especially of neoclassical compounds. She works with monolingual comparable corpora, i.e. two corpora of texts belonging to the same speciality field and dealing with the same topic (e.g. tobacco, cancer and diabetes) but with one of them containing texts aimed at specialists (scientific corpus) and one with texts for a non-specialist audience (popular science corpus). Neoclassical compounds are extracted from the scientific corpus, and their paraphrases are then generated using the morpho-semantic analyzer DÉRIF [NAM 05] which is able to generate glosses of morphologically complex words (for example, in French, *gastrite* ('gastritis') is paraphrased as *inflammation de l'estomac* ('stomach inflammation')). The glosses are then turned into word patterns and projected into the vulgarized corpus: the word sequences matching the pattern are considered to be paraphrases.

To generate a gloss, DÉRIF works in two steps. First, a hierarchical decomposition of the morphologically complex word is generated, and the morphological processes contributing to the word's creation are identified. For example, in French, *gastralgie* (gastralgia) is decomposed into:[1]

```
[ [ gastr N* ] [ algia N* ] NOUN ]
```

and "*prétraitement*" (*preprocessing*) can be decomposed in two ways:

(1) `[ pré [[traiter VERB] ment NOUN] NOUN]` [pre [[process] ing]]
(2) `[ [ pré [traiter VERB ] VERB] ment NOUN] [[pre [process]] ing]`

Second, basing itself on compositional theory,[2] DÉRIF generates a pseudo-definition (or gloss) from the results of the morphologically complex word analysis. Thus, *gastralgie* is paraphrased into *douleur (du – liée au) estomac* (pain

1 The decompositions were obtained from the on-line version of DÉRIF: http://www.cnrtl.fr/outils/DeriF/requete.php.

2 "*Les théories en morphologie lexicale permettent de déduire la définition d'un mot morphologiquement complexe en fonction de celui de ses constituants. Donc, un système implémentant une telle approche théorique (comme DériF, see 4) est à même de calculer la pseudo-définition de mots inconnus à partir des procédés morphologiques mis en oeuvre*". [NAM 05] (Lexical morphology theories enable one to deduce the definition of a morphologically complex word depending on that of its complements. Thus, a system implementing such a theoretical approach (like DériF, see 4) is able to calculate the pseudo-definition of unknown words from implemented morphological processes).

in/linked to the stomach) and *prétraitement* can be glosed as *(Période-Temps) qui précède le traitement – (Period – Time) which precedes the processing* – (decomposition 1) or as *(Action – résultat de) prétraiter – (Action – result of the action) of preprocessing* – (decomposition 2). In the case of *gastralgie*, DÉRIF is able to create a link between a neoclassical combining form and its lexical equivalent in French: *gastr* was linked to *estomac* (stomach) and *algie* to *douleur* (pain). DÉRIF deals both with the classical compounds like *gastralgie* and also the words obtained by the affixation of a neoclassical combining form, such as *hepatic,* which is paraphrased as *in relation with the liver.*

In the field of cross-lingual information retrieval, [SCH 06] created the MORPHOSAURUS system based not on words, but on what [SCH 06] call "subwords" which they define as "the minimal meaning-bearing constituent of a domain-specific term" – i.e. specialized morphemes. The MORPHOSAURUS system relies on a multilingual lexicon in which each "subword" is linked to a sematic identifier, no matter what language it is in. For example, *nephr-, ren-, rein* and *riñon,* which mean *kidney,* are all linked to the same identifier. [SCH 06] distinguish between several types of "subwords" depending on how they combine with other "subwords":

Stems: roots which carry the word's main semantic content and which approximately match neoclassical combining forms or un-decomposable words (*hepat, diaphys, head*).

Prefixesem: elements placed in front of a stem (*de-, re-*).

Proper prefixesem: prefixes which cannot be prefixed themselves (*peri-, down-*).

Infixes: transitional elements (*o* in *gastrointestinal*).

Suffixes: elements placed after a stem (*-a, -tomy*).

Proper suffixes: suffixes which cannot be suffixed themselves (verb endings *-ing, -ieron*).

Invariants: elements which match words and cannot be used as "subwords" since they could generate ambiguities in the decomposition phase (*ion, gene*).

Certain derivational and flexional suffixes, such as *-ation, -s* as well as auxiliaries and modal verbs are not taken into account.

We can see that over the three previously mentioned bodies of research, two have used morphology theories: [CLA 11] rely on [MEL 06] and [NAM 05] rely on [COR 87]. As for [SCH 06], they manipulate notions inspired by morphology which they have adapted to their aims: the "subwords" globally match morphemes except for the "Invariant" category and the fact that certain suffixes and grammatical morphemes are ignored by the MORPHOSAURUS system.

Literature establishes several analyses of the morphological processes, and this diversity in points of view is also visible in a great variety in terminology:

– [MEL 06], for example, distinguishes between *morphemes*, an element of meaning (signifier) and *morphs*, linguistic segments, which are a possible realization of a morpheme (signified). For example, the morpheme *plural* matches the morphs /-z/, /-s/, /-ɪz/, /-ən/, in English (as in *girls, bricks, boxes, oxen*).

– [MAR 85] only uses the term *moneme* which matches not a unit of meaning but a "meaning effect matching a formal difference". The monemes can be identified by substituting them: the substitution test consists of replacing one element in the spoken chain by another and observing whether this replacement generates a change in meaning. A moneme matches both the phonic realization and the observed meaning effect. In English, there is thus a single moneme "*plural*" with the form /-z/, /-s/, /-ɪz/ or /-ən/.

– Finally, traditional French grammar [RIE 05] only distinguishes one element, the *morpheme* which is both a unit of meaning and of form.[3] A morpheme can present several graphical or oral variations called *allomorphs*: for example, the root of the French verb *aller* presents four allomorphs: *all-, i-, v-, aill-*. It is usually the most frequent or most representative variation which is used to refer to the morpheme. In English, there is a morpheme /-z/ whose meaning is *plural* and which has three allomorphs: /-s/, /-ɪz/ and /-ən/.

In the case of our research, we have decided to adopt the position of [SCH 06], i.e. the fact that the elements on which we base our translations can sometimes match morphemes and sometimes get close to them without totally matching them. We have thus defined several categories based both on linguistic criteria and graphical criteria. We have chosen to focus on elements with a referential meaning, or elements which have a strong potential to change the meaning of a word.

4.2.2. *Definitions and terminology*

4.2.2.1. *Polylexical units*

Any unit made of several lexical words. This category includes the "classical" polylexical units *breast cancer, clinical trial*, but also all kinds of phrases or idioms: *post-menopause, acting on cancer, two-dimensional, etc.*

3 "*le morphème est généralement considéré comme l'unité minimale porteuse de sens obtenue par segmentation des énoncés. Il s'agit donc d'un segment préconstruit associant une forme et un sens, mais qui ne peut plus se décomposer en segments de même type*" p. 533, (a morpheme is usually considered to be the base meaning-conveying unit obtained by sequencing utterances. It is thus a pre-built segment associating a form and a meaning, which cannot be decomposed into segments of the same type).

4.2.2.2. *Monolexical unit*

A unit made of a single word: *cancer, breast, post, menopause*.

4.2.2.3. *Word*

Words match a sequence of characters made up of at least one letter and possibly figures or hyphens: e.g. *anti-p21, bio-rad, cancer, vasomotor, gastric*, etc. These graphic criteria mean that we are not counting as words the linguistic categories, such as locutions or even word compounds whose components are separated by spaces ('letter box' for example). These elements belong to the polylexical unit category. Words are *self-sufficient* units: they can appear in an isolated manner in texts, i.e. surrounded by characters other than a figure, a letter or a hyphen. We can distinguish *complex words* and *simple words*.

4.2.2.4. *Complex word*

A complex word is a decomposable word which has several sub-elements called morphemes, e.g. *anti-p21* → *anti+p21, bio-rads* → *bio+rads, vasomotor* → *vaso+motor*. Complex words are words translated with our method. We only deal with complex words, which are lexical words, i.e. which belong to the grammatical categories NOUN, ADJECTIVE, VERB and ADVERB.

4.2.2.5. *Morpheme*

A morpheme is an element which cannot be decomposed into sub-elements. These are approximately the morphemes which have been defined according to grammatical tradition, since they cannot be decomposed and match meaning elements: *anti-* meaning *opposite to*, *-bio-* meaning *relating to life*, *-vaso-* meaning *canal, vessel, motor* meaning *which generates or transmits movement, cancer, gastric*. We distinguish between free morphemes (simple words) and bound ones.

4.2.2.6. *Simple word or free morpheme*

A simple word is a word which cannot be decomposed into sub-elements: *cancer, gastric, p21, rad, motor*. In our analyses, we will only retain lexical words. As a word, it can operate self-sufficiently in the texts. This property is distinguished from *bound morphemes*. A simple word can be combined with other morphemes to generate a complex word (*motor* in *vasomotor*, *p21* in *anti-p21*).

4.2.2.7. *Bound morpheme*

A bound morpheme, just like a simple word, cannot be decomposed into sub-elements. Contrary to the simple word, it cannot appear autonomously in texts, e.g.: *anti-* meaning *against*, *-bio-* meaning *relating to life*, *-vaso-* meaning *canal, vessel*. They match the following linguistic categories: *combining forms, prefixes, suffixes*. We thus eliminate other categories, such as infixes (*um* in *kum'ain*, which means "speaking of the one who is eating" in Tagalog), circumfixes (*ge...t* in *gesagt* which means "said" in German), or interfixes (*o* in the French *gastrointestinal*).

4.2.2.8. *Prefix*

A prefix is a bound morpheme which is always at the beginning of a complex word: e.g. *anti-* in *anti-p21*. In the languages studied, several prefixes can agglutinate at the beginning of a word (*anti-reelection*) but we do not take this possibility into account.[4]

4.2.2.9. *Combining forms*

Combining forms are elements from Greek or Latin originally used in the generation of neoclassical compounds. We find them under different names in literature: suppletive bases, archeoconstituents, neo-latin components, classical bases, suppletive primitives, etc. ([NAM 03, quoted by [GRA 04]]). [MAR 79] uses the French term "confixe" (which is not to be confused with its false friend "confix" in English which is a synonym of circumfix). The linguistic works by [BAU 83, MAR 79, RIE 05] have highlighted the fact that certain combining forms always appear in initial positions (*poly-*, *mono-*), and others always appear in final position (*-cide*, *-vore*), and other indifferently appear in either position (*-graph-*, *-phil-*). We do not draw the distinction: in our analysis, combining forms can appear in any position.[5] However, as the border between speciality language and general language is porous, we have also been flexible in our categories. Some elements with Greek or Latin origins which can be found in initial position, but which are commonly used in the general language, have been considered to be prefixes (e.g. *multi-*, *poly-*). Other elements were allocated to both categories (e.g. *méta-/-méta-*, *micro-/-micro-*).

Since we are not analyzing interfixes,[6] many of the combining forms considered directly integrate the interfix: we consider for example *-chondri-*, *-chondr-* and *-chondro-* as three combining forms whereas from a linguistic point of view, it is the combining form *-chondr-* interfixed with *-i-* or *-o-* or without an interfix.

Combining forms can be combined together and/or with a simple word to create a complex word. To this lexical base, we can add prefixes and suffixes.

4.2.2.10. *Suffix*

A suffix is a bound morpheme, which is always placed at the end of a complex word, e.g. *-ly* in *histologically*. In the languages on which we experimented morpho-compositional translation (French, English and German), suffixes are mainly used for derivation (*incorporate* → *incorporation*). Flexional prefixes are not taken

---

4 To simplify the morphological sequencing algorithm writing, we have not implemented any rules analyzing words with several prefixes (this case does not appear in our data).

5 Contrary to [HAR 12] who distinguishes "Initial Combining Forms (ICFs) *and* Final Combining Forms (FCFs) 74.

6 Contrary to [WEL 11] who sequence *Kalorimetrie* into *Kalor, i* and *metrie*.

into account since we work with the lemmatized forms of words in which the inflexion phenomena have been neutralized.

As for derivation, we have limited ourselves to a small set of suffixes. These suffixes were chosen because we consider them to be translated by a free morpheme in the target language, a phenomenon that we wish to look at in more detail. These are the *-ability, -able* meaning *'capable', -hood* meaning *'state', -like, -ly* denoting *manner,* and *-wise* denoting *meaning*. Thus, the majority of the suffixes have not been taken into account. For example, a word such as *gastric* will not be sequenced into *gastr* and *ic* whereas from a purely linguistic point of view, it is indeed made of two morphemes.

4.2.2.11. *Notations*

The occurrence of a word or a set of words in a text is noted with double speech marked, such as "breathless". The signified or the translation (gloss) of a word is given in single speech marks 'without breath'.

Prefixes are followed by a hyphen, *anti-*; combining forms are surrounded by hyphens, *-gastr-*; suffixes are preceded by a hyphen, *-able*; and words have no hyphen, *cancer*.

In a complex word, the boundaries between morphemes are shown with a plus sign, e.g. *-gastro-+intestinal, anti-+p21, -histo-+logical+-ly*. In a polylexical unit, the boundaries between words are shown by a space, *contre le p21, manière -histo-+logique*.

Translation is shown by an arrow going from the source term to the target term: *-histo-+logical+-ly* → *-histo-+logique+-ment*.

4.2.3. *Underlying assumptions*

Morpho-compositional translation relies on the following assumptions.

4.2.3.1. *Compositional meaning*

We theorize that complex words have a compositional meaning which can be computed from the meaning of the morphemes which make them up: *anti-+tarte* has the meaning of *against tarter*.

This is a relatively realistic assumption. It is for example the one which the analyzer DÉRIF relies on. There are a few counter-examples such as the case in which the meaning of a word is figurative (*rose des vents*). However, these counter-examples are mostly found in general language, and this is a reasonable assumption to consider that in the technical language, using metaphors or images is uncommon.

4.2.3.2. *Compositional translation*

We make the assumption that there is a parallelism between the source and target languages: if a source term has a compositional meaning, then its translation also has a compositional meaning, and additionally, there is a bijection between the source morphemes and target morphemes: $anti\text{-}_1\text{-}+abortion_2 \rightarrow anti\text{-}_1+avortement_2$, $contre_1$ *(l')* $avortement_2$.

This seems a realistic assumption in the case of neoclassical compounds and prefixed words; and as [NAM 07] and [CAR 09b] pointed out, these word formation processes are relatively similar for Western European languages such as English, German, Spanish, French and Italian. On the contrary, this may be less self-evident in the case of word compounds (see for example the work of [GAR 08] which actually deals with these non-matching cases) and suffixed words.

4.2.3.3. *Fertility*

The combination of morphemes into words is specific to each language. A single-word source term can thus be translated by a multi-word target term: *minefield* → *champ (de) mines, cytotoxic* → *toxique (pour les) cellules.*

4.2.3.4. *Distortion*

We consider that the order of the morphemes is not necessarily kept from one language to another: *pathophysiological* → *physiopathologique, tumor-margin* → *marge tumorale*. This hypothesis separates us from [HAR 12] and [CAR 09b].

4.2.3.5. *Lexical divergence*

The target morpheme cannot be the exact translation of the source morpheme: *information-giving* → *offrir des informations, post-conception* → *après-fécondation.*

4.2.3.6. *Morphological variation*

The part-of-speech of a word is not necessarily kept during translation: *antitumor* (NOUN) → *antitumoral* (ADJECTIVE); *post-operative* (ADJECTIVE) → *aprés (l') intervention* (PREPOSITIONAL PHRASE).

4.2.4. *Advantages of the proposed approach for processing comparable corpora*

Taking into account the phenomena of fertility, distortion, lexical divergence and morphological variation helps us to use the specificities of comparable corpora to our advantage. The target part of comparable corpora is made from spontaneously generated texts, they are not influenced by any source text and thus do not suffer from loan or "calque". Therefore, the target terms present in the corpus have fewer chances of having a similar structure to that of the source term, hence the advantage in trying to generate translations whose morpho-syntactic and lexical structure is relatively far from the source term's structure. Sometimes, it even happens that only the generation of a variation will enable one to find the translation: *anthracycline-containing* can only be translated with a fertile variation (*contenant de l'anthracycline* and not **anthracycline-contenant*). Moreover, we know that translation pairs are much less frequent in comparable corpora than in parallel corpora. Even if in the target language there is a translation with an identical structure to the source term structure, it is possible that this canonical translation cannot be found in the target corpus. So identifying variations is also a way to increase the number of translation pairs extracted without penalizing the quality of the final lexicon.

Finally, the variations, in particular the fertile variations and morphological variations, are particularly useful for specialized translation. On the one hand, depending on the sentence structure in which the translator inserts his translation, it might be more idiomatic to use a fertile or morphological variation. On the other hand, it happens frequently that a fertile variation matches a popular version of a scientific term (*ovariectomy* $\rightarrow$ *ovariectomie* vs. *ablation des ovaires*), which is useful when the translator translates popular science texts. Moreover, fertile variations are close to paraphrase and help the translator understand the meaning of the source term in his/her mother tongue.

4.3. Issues addressed and contributions

The method we have suggested enables us to approach different issues: fertile translation generation, covering multiple modes of morphological construction and ranking candidate translations. We will now detail each of these issues and highlight our contributions.

4.3.1. *Generating fertile translations*

The notion of fertility was introduced by [BRO 90] in their work on word alignment. Within this context, a *word*'s fertility is defined as "the number of French words that an English word produces in a given alignment".

In their 1993 article, [BRO 93] present five word alignment models. The first model only acquires transfer probabilities, i.e. for each source word f and each target word e, the probability that a human translator would translate e by f is estimated to be $t(f|e)$. In addition to this, the second model also estimates distortion probabilities, i.e. $d(i|j)$: the probability that a target word in the position i corresponds to a source word in the position j. The notion of fertility appears in the third model (IBM3). In addition to transfer and distortion probabilities, this model also estimates the fertility probabilities, i.e. "the number of French *[target]* words to which e is connected in a randomly selected alignment is a random variable, ϕ_e, that we call the fertility of e." [BRO 93].

Thus for [BRO 93], fertility is a figure indicating the number of target words which can potentially translate a source word. In Table 4.1, we see that there is a 0.342 probability for the English word *nodding* to be translated by a set of four French words, and a probability of 0.293 that it may be translated by a set of three French words, etc.

e =*nodding*

ϕ	$n(\phi\|e)$
4	0.342
3	0.293
2	0.167
1	0.163
0	0.023

Table 4.1. *Fertility probability of nodding – adapted from [BRO 93]*

In their work on the acquisition of complex term translations, [DAI 05] and [ROB 06] describe fertility as the case in which the source term and target term have different lengths, and they "define the length of a MWT as the number of content words it contains":

> "fertility: source and target MWTs *[Multi-Word Terms]* can be of different lengths"

The example given by [ROB 06] is that of the translation of the French term *table de vérité* (truth table) by the Japanese term *shinri·chi·hyo* which means *truth value table* in which the component *chi* which means 'value' does not have a match in the source term.

In our work, we have focused on the case in which the target language uses more lexical words than the source language to express the same idea. In this specific case, we will talk of *fertile translations*.

Fertile translation – Let there be two disjoint sets S and C in which S is a set of source terms and C is a set of target terms. Let there be the translation relation $T \subseteq S \times C$ and the function $l(x)$ indicating the number of lexical words of the term x. The set of fertile translations F is defined as $\{(s, c)|(s, c) \in T \text{ and } l(c) > l(s)\}$.

The fertility relation F is anti-symmetrical: $sFc \Rightarrow \neg cFs$. For example, the translation equivalence between *truth table* (two lexical words) and *shinri·chi·hyo* (three lexical words) is a fertile translation when it is translated from English to

Japanese but not when translated from Japanese to English. The translation of *growth rate* by *taux de croissance* is not considered fertile as the number of lexical words remains the same. Let us mention that we have limited our field of study to the cases in which $l(s) = 1$ and $l(c) \geq 1$, i.e. the translation of a monolexical unit to a mono- or poly-lexical unit (*post-menopause* → *post-ménopause, après (la) ménopause*).

During a study of fertile translations found in the terminology database TERMIUM,[7] we have found two types of fertility: *semantic fertility* and *surface fertility*.

4.3.1.1. *Semantic fertility*

In the case of semantic fertility, the target term contains more morphemes than the source term. These additional morphemes can be the source of additional words in the target term.

This is the case for the translation of *express option* by *option voie rapide* ('express lane option') in French, in which the French language adds the notion of *voie*, i.e. *lane*, which is implied in the English expression. This is also the case for the translation of *snorkeling* by *plongé avec tuba* for which the English has a morpheme allowing it to directly refer to diving with a snorkel whereas in French, to obtain an expression with a similar meaning, we have to combine the morpheme *plongée* with the morpheme *tuba* due to the preposition *avec*.

It does not automatically entail that there is a higher number of words in the target language: *clavicule*, a word made of a single morpheme in French is translated by *collarbone* in English, a word made of two morphemes (*collar+bone*). It is impossible to deal with semantic fertility with the compositional method for the latter requires a bijection between source-term morphemes and target-term morphemes. Such cases can only be dealt with distributional methods or by using a pivot language [GAR 08] or by leveraging non-mixed documents [LEO 08].

4.3.1.2. *Surface fertility*

In the case of surface fertility, source language and target language operate an identical semantic sequencing, source and target terms contain the same number of morphemes and each source morpheme has its target equivalent (and vice versa). The languages only vary in the way in which they combine the morphemes to create words:

Surface fertile translation: let there be a fertile translation sFc, $M(s)$ the set of morphemes of the term s, $M(c)$ the set of morphemes of the term c and $\mathcal{T}$ a function of the translation. sFc is surface fertile is for any $m_c \in M(c)$ there is a unique $m_s \in M(s)$ so that $\mathcal{T}(m_s) = m_c$.

7 http://www.termiumplus.gc.ca/tpv2alpha/alpha-fra.html – last accessed 23/03/2011.

The first case of surface fertility is the one in which a compound word is translated by a phrase, for example the translation of *mouthwash* in *bain de bouche*. The morphemes used in both languages are free morphemes. The fertility is caused by the fact that the target language chooses to create a phrase rather than to agglutinate the words to create a word compound. The semantic relation between the words 'bain' and 'bouche' is given by the word order in English when it is indicated by the preposition *de* in French.

A second fertility case is the one in which a bound morpheme is translated by a free morpheme, *unhindered* $\rightarrow$ *sans entraves*. Fertility in this case is created by the fact that the bound morpheme *un-* is translated in French by the free morpheme *sans* which is realized as a word.

Compositional translation can generate surface fertile translations. The translation of word compounds into target language phrases has been dealt with by [WEL 11] in the case of German compound nouns. The variation between bound morpheme $\rightarrow$ free morpheme has not been investigated in the context of compositional translation. In data-driven approaches, only [CLA 11] suggest learning to gather the variations of a single morpheme which they then link to their translation (*{bactérie, bactério-, bactéri-}* $\rightarrow$ kin). However, they only focus on the neoclassical compounds, which omit cases such as *unhindered*$\rightarrow$ *sans entraves*.

Beyond the question of fertility, the proposed translation generation method will not be limited to the small morphological structures as is the case in [CAR 09b]'s work (only prefixed words), [HAR 12]'s work (only neoclassical compounds) and [WEL 11]'s work (noun and neoclassical compounds). The following section provides a detailed list of the morphological structures that we will endeavor to deal with.

4.3.2. *Dealing with diverse morphological structures*

Contrary to other compositional approaches based on morphological decomposition, the translation method which we present tries not to limit itself to a small set of structural equivalences between source and target language (prefixed $\rightarrow$ prefixed, word compound $\rightarrow$ phrase, neoclassical compound $\rightarrow$ neoclassical compound).

The entry is a morphologically complex word. This word can be built by prefixation "*pretreatment*", neoclassical compounding "*densitometry*", suffixation "*childless*", word compounding "*anastrozole-associated*" or any combination of these four word formation processes. The output of the translation system is a list of n words which can be morphologically complex or not. For example, *postoophorectomy* can be translated as *postovariectomie, après l'ovariectomie* or *après l'ablation des ovaires*.

We now describe the four word formation processes and illustrate them with examples of English → French translations taken from the terminology database TERMIUM[8] and the bilingual concordancer LINGUEE.[9]

4.3.2.1. *Word compounding composition*

A word compound is the result of a juxtaposition of two or several words. Sometimes, a hyphen emphasizes the border between the words, and sometimes they are glued to one another.[10] With time and use, it is usual for the compositional meaning of compound words to lose its transparency to speakers. For example, the French term for "sprinkle" is "*saupoudrer*" which is made from *sau*, an old variation of *sel* (salt) and *poudrer* (to powder).[11] We then talk about *demotivation*. One of the difficulties in popular compound translation is that they are generally composed to become a new meaning unit and may very well not have a compositional meaning, such as for example, *a lounge chair* is not necessarily a "chair which is in your lounge" but more of an armchair [RIE 05]. These compounds can be translated in a fertile manner when the target language does not concatenate compound translations:

– *life+span → durée de vie*;

– *word+coiner → forgeur de mots*;

– *mal+entendant → hearing impaired.*

4.3.2.2. *Neoclassical compounding*

Neoclassical compounds [NAM 07, RIE 05] also called "*mots confixés*" [MAR 85] are words which have undergone a similar process to the word compounding, only the components are bound morphemes matching the original Greek or Latin elements (aka combining forms). [RIE 05] also welcome as neoclassical compounds the words made with a combining form and a word from the more common vocabulary of a language (e.g. *biomass*).

This word formation process is often used in techno-scientific domains, and among them they hold almost half of the neologisms recorded in medical texts [LOV 98, quoted by [NAM 05]]. Moreover, the neoclassical compound formation rules are very similar in all the European languages, which make their machine translation easier [IAC 03, quoted by [NAM 05]].

---

8 http://www.termiumplus.gc.ca/.

9 http://www.linguee.com/.

10 Linguistic theories also include in word compounds the groups of word which show strong integration (e.g. you cannot integrate another element: * *an Allen green key* versus *a green Allen key*) and have syntactic autonomy. Since we are only focusing on the translation of monolexical units (i.e. made of a single word), we will set aside this type of word compound.

11 http://www.cnrtl.fr/etymologie/saupoudrer.

Sometimes, certain neoclassical compounds – which are originally earmarked for a technical domain – slide into common use due to the popularization of certain concepts. [COS 07] mention the case of the combining form *-tele-*, whose meaning is "at a distance" and which can be found in words such as *television, telescope, telepathy*. Once they become common in everyday language, some combining forms can become free, such as the form *-bio-* has in French, where it has become an adjective meaning 'organic' (e.g. '*alimentation bio*' → 'organic food'). Due to their high productivity, other combining forms become common prefixes: *anti-* in *antidote, antifreeze*; *arch- archbishop, archduke*. The porosity between specialized and general language can make the classification of these morphemes borrowed from classical languages a bit difficult. Finally, let us mention that neoclassical compounds, as free lexical bases, are subject to prefixing and suffixing (*bibliographically, anelectrolytic*).

The neoclassical compounds can generate fertile translations when the combining form is translated into the target language either by a word derived from the same classical root: *dermoreaction* → *réaction dermique* (skin reaction); or by a word of the same meaning belonging to general language: *ludothérapie* → *play therapy* (ludotherapy). A fertile translation can be the popular variation of a technical term: *bunioniectomy* → *bunionectomie, ablation des oignons* (bunion removal).

4.3.2.3. *Prefixation*

Prefixation joins bound morphemes called *prefixes* to a free lexical base (simple or complex word). The prefix is usually of the same part-of-speech as the base. The prefix is always located in front of the lexical base and operates a semantic change:

– *pre-+adolescence* means "before adolescence";

– *anti-+perspiring* means "which (fights) against perspiration".

Fertile translation can happen when the prefix is translated by a word of the same meaning in a target language: *unbleached* → *non blanchi* or when it exists as a free form in the target language: *nonabortive* → *non abortif*. In some cases, the generation of a fertile variation can enable the translator to find a paraphrase of the source term in the target language: *pretreatment* → *avant le traitement*.

4.3.2.4. *Suffixation*

Suffixation joins bound morphemes called *suffixes* to free lexical bases (simple or complex word). The suffix is always located after the lexical base. Suffixing commonly has the effect of changing the part-of-speech in addition to causing a semantic change:

– *physiological+-ly* means "from a physiological point of view";

– *breath+-able* means "which can be breathed".

As was the case for prefixation, a fertile translation can happen when the prefix is translated by a word of similar meaning in the target language: *wingless* → *sans ailes*. The generation of fertile translations can also enable the translator to find paraphrases in the target language: *extremely* → *de façon extrême* (in an extreme fashion).

4.3.3. *Candidate translations ranking*

As for the candidate translations ranking, we have mentioned the fact the existing methods were usually based on a single criterion (number of attestations, context similarity, etc). One of the contributions of our work is to explore new ranking criteria which we will try to combine. We will experiment with criteria such as the frequency of the target term, the similarity between its context and the source term context, the translation probability between the part of the discourse of the source term and the part(s) of the discourse of the target term, etc. Among the criteria combination methods, we will notably try out machine learning algorithms, and more specifically learning-to-rank algorithms [LIU 11].

In compositional translation, [BAL 04] are the only ones to combine several criteria to order translations. To this end, they train a SVM classifier from exact and false translation examples. Each example is associated with a feature vector listing various criteria linked to the source term, to the target term or to the translation itself, and are as many hints to the accuracy of the translation. An example is positive if the target term matches the reference translation, negative if the target term is not the reference translation. The classifier outputs a continous value between -1 and +1 which is used to rank the candidate translations.

This approach is based on the prediction of an "accuracy" or "quality" score from a *(source term, target term)* pair, and is the equivalent of the *point-wise* approaches used in the learning-to-rank paradigm.

Learning-to-rank is a type of machine learning mostly used in information retrieval where it is used to rank documents according to how relevant they are to a given query. The parallel with the candidate translation ranking issue is obvious: we try to rank the target terms according to how accurate they are as a translation of a given source term.

As far as we know, the learning-to-rank algorithms are not commonly used to rank translations. We can cite the paper by [SOK 12] which mentions statistical machine translation work aiming to improve the ranking of different translation hypotheses using learning-to-rank algorithms. Their first results are encouraging: they show that their ranking model obtains up to +0.4 BLEU. However, the work remains in the exploratory phase: [SOK 12] claim that the experiment conditions (lack of integration to the decoding module, small number of features) do not enable them to properly evaluate the added-value of their approaches.

[LIU 09] distinguishes three types of learning-to-rank algorithm:

– The *point-wise* approaches learn to associate a *(query, document) pair* to, for example:

- either a class, such as *relevant, rather relevant, irrelevant*, the ranking task is then seen as a classification issue.

- or a relevance score, in which case the ranking task is seen as a regression issue.

– The *pair-wise* approaches try to learn preferences: given a triplet *(query, document 1, document 2)*, they indicate whether the document 1 is more relevant than the document 2 to answer the query. The final ranking of the documents is not given directly for the *pair-wise* and *point-wise* approaches: it is deduced from the relevance score or categories (*point-wise*) or from the preferences (*pair-wise*).

– As for the *list-wise* approaches, they directly learn the best way to permute documents when answering a query, so that the documents are ranked from the most to the least relevant. The processed data is directly given in the form *(query, {document 1, document 2... document n})*.

Figure 4.1 is taken from [LIU 09] and provides a historical overview of the learning-to-rank approaches. According to [LIU 07, LIU 09] and [CAO 07], it appears that the list-wise approaches, which are the most recent, are also the most efficient, at least when it comes to information retrieval. For example, [LIU 09] tested several learning-to-rank algorithms on reference information retrieval datasets. The evaluation measures used are the MAP and NDCG.[12] The various experiments show that the list-wise approaches provide the best results whatever the evaluation measure (NDCG at rank 1, 3 and 10 and MAP).

In the next part of our work, we will thus rely on the list-wise approach to try and rank the generated translations.

4.4. Evaluation methodology

The evaluation of the generated translations will be carried out from two references: an *a priori* reference and an *a posteriori* reference. This distinction was first introduced by [OZD 06] in the context of word alignment in parallel corpora:

> "On the whole, we can distinguish two ways of proceeding to build reference data. The first is to manually annotate a sample of data independently of the output provided by the alignment system *[...]*. The result is a reference which we call *a priori* reference. The second is to

12 MAP and NDCG are presented in Appendix A1.

directly judge the output provided by the system that we are trying to evaluate *[...]*. We then talk of *a posteriori* reference."

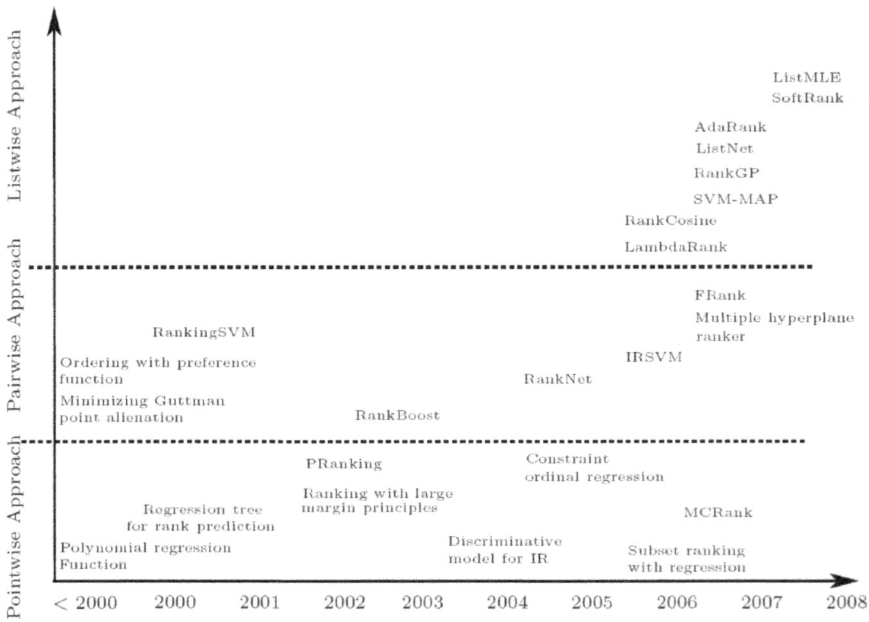

Figure 4.1. *Historical view of the approaches in learning translation ranking – from [LIU 09]*

Our method will be experimented on the BREAST CANCER medical corpus described in sections 2.3.2.1.1 and 5.2. For these two references, we will start from a single set of source terms (S) whose translation is not given by our general language bilingual dictionary. The *a priori* reference (R) will be built by projection of the medical meta-thesaurus UMLS in our corpus. The *a posteriori* reference (P) will be built by the manual annotation of the translations generated by our system. We will use these annotated outputs as examples for ranking model learning (T) from which we will subtract the translations belonging to the *a priori* reference which will be used for the evaluation of the ranking (E). The ranking will thus only be evaluated on translations belonging to the *a priori* reference and for which the system has suggested at least one translation.

To summarize, we are manipulating five sets, illustrated in Figure 4.2.

Evaluation of the translation generation:

– S matches the source terms to be translated;

– R matches the *a priori* reference;

– P matches the *a posteriori* reference, $R \cap P \neq \emptyset$.

Evaluation of the translation ranking:

– T matches the ranking model learning data: $T = P \setminus R$;

– E matches the ranking model evaluation data: $E = P \cap R$.

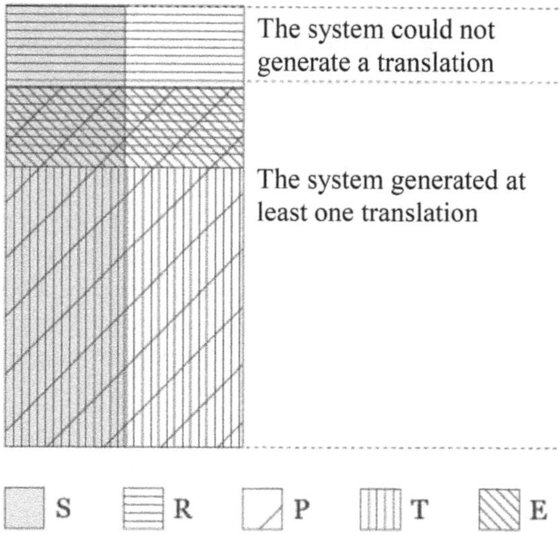

Figure 4.2. *Set of data used for the evaluation*

The main difference between the *a priori* and *a posteriori* references is that the source terms present in the *a priori* reference all have an identified translation in the target corpus, whereas for the *a posteriori* reference, the source terms are simply terms found in the source text and whose translation is not provided by our general language bilingual dictionary: we do not know if their translation can be found in the target texts.

4.4.1. *A priori reference*

The main advantage of *a priori* references is that they are often built from known linguistic resources often used within a research domain: they enable us to compare one system to other systems. A second advantage of the *a priori* reference is that it enables the evaluation of the recall and analysis of the silence cases, which cannot be done with an *a posteriori* reference (the source terms do not necessarily have an equivalent in the target corpus).

However, this type of reference only offers a fragmentary view of the system's performances. This is all the more genuine in the domain of translation, where we know that it is hard to list all the possible translations of a term and that the use of a translation can only be evaluated versus a given applicative context. A striking example is that of the evaluation carried out by [CLA 11]: when they only based themselves on the translations found in the UMLS, they obtained a precision of 63%; however, if they took as correct the translations not found in the UMLS but attested in on-line medical dictionaries, they obtained a precision of 89%. We have observed exactly the same phenomenon in our outputs: even though the UMLS translations are sometimes very free, a good number of our correct translations generated by our system were not mentioned in the UMLS.

The *a priori* evaluation also gives a biased view of the lexicons which will be extracted once the algorithm is implemented into a piece of CAT software:

– On the one hand, the fact that the evaluation is only based on the cases in which the translation can effectively be found in the target corpus, helps the algorithm. There are many more false translations in the *a posteriori* reference since for some terms even if a correct translation is generated, it will never be selected since it does not appear in the corpus (any other translation generated and found in the corpus will automatically be false).

– On the other hand, the reference is not exhaustive: by offering a strict reference, it sets aside generated translations which would be correct even if they are not present in the reference.

4.4.2. *A posteriori reference*

The *a posteriori* reference has the main advantage of providing a better estimate of the performances that can be expected from the system in use. It provides answers to questions such as: how many source terms actually receive a translation? What is the quality of these translations? In the end, how many source terms can expect to receive at least one correct translation?

The linguistic units to be translated are not *terms* from the domain in a proper sense[13] but simply words present in the source corpus and whose translation does not exist in the general language bilingual dictionary (or whose translation suggested by the dictionary cannot be found in the target corpus). The *a posteriori* evaluation is carried out with the view to enrich the general bilingual resources due to specialized translations taken from comparable corpora, which matches our applicative context, whereas the *a priori* reference is more adapted to the evaluation of bilingual terminology extraction tools.

13 As in denominating the concept of the domain.

As we have explained in section 1.2.3, the translator's needs cannot be limited to the technical terms but must include any formulation whose translation he/she does not know. For example, *aromatherapy* can be considered to be a term from the medical field; however, this term is also often used in everyday language, and it would be unusual for a translator not to know how to translate it. On the contrary, the expression *patient-centred* would probably not find itself in a terminology list[14] but its translation can be problematic since the compound nouns with a NOUN-PAST PARTICIPLE structure do not exist in French, we will have to distance ourselves from the source language and make sure that the suggested translation matches the domain's linguistic uses.

4.5. Conclusion

This chapter has enabled us to present the methodological framework of our research. We have presented the bases of our translation method and positioned ourselves with regards to similar work. We have detailed the addressed issues by highlighting our contributions. Finally, we have detailed and defended our evaluation methodology. The next chapter presents the data on which we experimented our translation method.

14 It appears neither in the UMLS nor in the TERMIUM.

5

Experimental Data

5.1. Introduction

In this chapter, we present the data used to test the translation method presented in the previous chapter. We have applied our method to the translation from English to French and English to German. First, we present the comparable corpora used [5.2], then the source terms selected to test the translation method [5.3] as well as the data used for the evaluation of the translation generation [5.4] and the translation ranking training and evaluation datasets [5.5]. Finally, we present the linguistic resources on which our translation system relies [5.6].

Data extracts can be found in Appendix 2. The German corpus, the morpheme translation table and the reference lexicons are freely available under LGPL-LR license.[1]

5.2. Comparable corpora

We have used specialized texts from the medical domain dealing with breast cancer. We define a specialized text in the same way that [BOW 02] does, that is as a text generated by an expert in the domain and meant for other experts (scientific discourse) or for a wider audience (popular science discourse).

The texts were manually gathered from academic portals and information websites meant for patients suffering from breast cancer and their relations. The English texts come from British sources, the French texts from French sources and the German texts from German sources. The English and French texts all deal with female breast cancer (texts dealing with male breast cancer were deleted). We have

1 http://www.lina.univ-nantes.fr/?Linguistic-resources-from-the,1676.html.

found many more popular articles on breast cancer in English than in French (there are many associations supporting it in the United Kingdom). This explains the imbalance between the academic corpus and the popular corpus in French (1.45 times more words for the academic corpus, see Table 5.1). It was very difficult to find files for the German corpus, especially academic papers. Thus, we have mainly used academic abstracts for the academic part, which explains the great number of files in this part of the corpus (Table 5.2). We have also used academic texts dealing with male breast cancer.

Once these texts were gathered and converted to a text format, they were lemmatized and POS tagged by the linguistic analyzer XELDA.[2]

	EN	FR	DE
Academic	198,244 (48 %)	267,180 (59 %)	197,187 (49 %)
Popular	218,336 (52 %)	184,504 (41 %)	201,760 (51 %)
Total	416,580	451,684	398,947

Table 5.1. *Composition and size of the corpora in terms of number of occurrences*

	EN	FR	DE
Academic	70	78	103
Popular	272	217	162
Total	342	295	265

Table 5.2. *Composition and size of the corpora in terms of number of files*

We have also evaluated the corpora comparability (Table 5.3) using the measurements of [LI 10] presented in section 1.3.4.1. This measurement indicates the expectation of finding the translation of a source term in the target corpus (and vice versa). It is based on the projection of a bilingual dictionary onto the corpus (we used the bilingual dictionary described in section 5.6.1).

	EN-FR	EN-DE
academic	0.71	0.42
popular	0.69	0.46
ALL	0.74	0.45

Table 5.3. *Corpora comparability given the* XELDA *analyzer dictionary*

According to [LI 10]'s measurement, the comparability of the corpora is rather low. To establish a comparison, [LI 10] carried out experiments with corpora whose

2 http://www.temis.com.

comparability ranged from 0.882 to 0.916. The dictionary used in that case was generated from various online resources and totals 75,845 translation pairs (our dictionary has 59,495 or 69,285 pairs depending on the languages).

Furthermore, the English–German corpus is much less comparable than the English–French corpus, which shows that we will have more difficulties to extract translation pairs from it. This lower comparability is explained by the fact that it was hard to find German-language files, which led to adding texts that were not key to the domain, and thus contained peripheral vocabulary.

5.3. Source terms

The terms to be translated were extracted from the English corpus in a semi-supervised manner, according to the following process:

1) We established a small list of bound morphemes belonging to the English language and automatically extracted from the English corpus all the words that contained these morphemes, or at least, all the words that had a substring of characters matching a bound morpheme. For example, we extracted the words *postchemotherapy* and *poster* because they contained the substring *post.*

2) These words extracted from the corpus were manually separated: those that were not true morphologically complex words (mistakes during the extraction, such as *poster*) were eliminated; those that were genuinely morphologically complex were kept and separated into morphemes: *postchemotherapy* was separated into *post, chemo* and *therapy.*

3) If the morphological separation in phase (2) highlighted new bound morphemes, the process was restarted in (1), during which the new morphemes were presented to the corpus so as to bring back more morphologically complex words.

We also added words containing hyphens (e.g. *ER-positive*) as well as words resulting from the concatenation of two or more words (e.g. *mouthwash*). These compound words were manually approved. We thus obtained a list of 2,025 morphologically complex English words. From this list, we excluded in each language pair all the English words which had a translation in our general language bilingual dictionary and whose translation could be found in the target corpus. In the end, we obtained a list of 1,839 complex words to be translated into French (S^{FR}), and a list of 1,824 words to be translated into German (S^{DE}).

81% of the source terms correspond to a word compound or a prefixed and/or suffixed word compound. The terms with a neoclassical combining form only account for 19% of the source terms (Table 5.4). Fifty-eight percent of the source terms contain at least one bound morpheme (prefix or combining form or suffix). The majority of the source terms are composed of only two morphemes, and the maximum number of morphemes is four (Table 5.5).

Morphological structure	S^{FR}	S^{DE}	Example
Word compound	42%	42%	*acute phase*
Prefix + lexical base	28%	28%	*non-differential*
Neoclassical compound	17%	17%	*oncogenesis*
Lexical base + suffix	9%	8%	*sleeveless*
Prefix + lexical base + suffix	2%	2%	*abnormally*
Neoclassical compound + suffix	1%	1%	*chemotherapeutically*
Prefix + neoclassical compound	1%	2%	*pro-angiogenic*

Table 5.4. *Morphological structures of source terms*

	S^{FR}	S^{DE}
2 morphemes	88 %	88 %
3 morphemes	11 %	11 %
4 morphemes	1 %	1 %

Table 5.5. *Size of the source terms (number of morphemes)*

5.4. Reference data for translation generation evaluation

5.4.1. *A priori reference*

To build our *a priori* reference, we used the UMLS (Unified Medical Language System) [LIN 93], a medical domain metathesaurus. This metathesaurus gathers concepts whose terms belong to more than 60 controlled vocabularies and classifications used in biomedicine (MeSH, SNOMEDCT, MeDRA, etc.). The 2000 edition of the metathesaurus contained approximately 730,000 concepts and 1.5 million terms in 17 languages.[3]

This metathesaurus is often used as a reference for the machine translation of terms, especially when evaluating data-driven methods since it also provides training examples [LAN 08, LAN 09, CLA 09, CLA 11].

To create our *a priori* reference, we followed these steps:

1) extraction, for each source term s of S^{FR} and S^{DE}, of the French and German terms, respectively, which were associated with the same concept as s in the UMLS;

2) manual cleaning of extracted target terms;

3) search for attested target terms in the target corpus.

3 http://www.nlm.nih.gov/mesh/umlsforelis.html - last accessed on 12/02/2012.

1) Extraction of the source term → target term associations from the UMLS

The English terms (as well as their French and German translations) were extracted from the MRCONSO.RRF.aa and MRCONSO.RRF.ab files of the UMLS. The content of these files consists of 18 columns separated by a pipe character (see extract 5.1).

Extract 5.1. Content of files MRCONSO.RRF.* from the UMLS meta-thesaurus

```
C0001418|ENG|P|L0001418|PF|S0010818|N|A7568548||C2852||NCI|PT|C2852|Adenocarcino
ma|0|N|256|
C0001418|ENG|S|L9068756|PF|S11315684|Y|A17310266|2839509015|443961001||SNOMEDCT|
PT|443961001|Malignant␣adenomatous␣neoplasm|9|N|2304|
C0001418|ENG|P|L0001418|VO|S0585881|Y|A0640520|||SNMI|PT|M-81403|Adenocarcinoma
␣NOS|9|N||
C0001418|ENG|S|L0680539|VO|S0940401|Y|A0996143||M0000355|D000230|MSH|PM|D000230|
Malignant␣Adenomas|0|N|256|
C0001418|ENG|S|L2775107|PF|S3623578|Y|A16362919|573026011|189582009||SNOMEDCT|OF
|189582009|[M]Adenocarcinoma␣NOS␣(morphologic␣abnormality)|9|O||
C0001418|FRE|P|L3246449|PF|S3773563|N|A11067791|||10001141|MDRFRE|LT|10001141|Ad
\'enocarcinome|3|N||
C0001418|FRE|S|L5705743|PF|S6538780|Y|A9155521||M0000355|D000230|MSHFRE|EN|D0002
30|Carcinome␣glandulaire|3|N||
C0001418|FRE|S|L6175020|PF|S7052488|Y|A11051669|||10001141|MDRFRE|LT|10001166|Ad
\'enocarcinome␣SAI|3|N||
C0001418|GER|P|L1229669|PF|S1471615|N|A10139059|||10001141|MDRGER|LT|10001141|Ad
enokarzinom|3|N||
C0001418|GER|S|L1226879|PF|S1468825|Y|A1419477||||WHOGER|PT|1289|ADENOCARCINOM␣N
NB|2|N||
```

The concept identifier is given in the 1st column, the language is given in the 2nd column and the term in the 15th column. In this extract, we can see that the concept "C0001418" is associated with the following terms:

– English: *adenocarcinoma, malignant adenomatous neoplasm, malignant adenomas, [m]adenocarcinoma NOS (morphologic abnormality)*;

– French: *adénocarcinome SAI, carcinome glandulaire*;

– German: *Adenokarzinom, adenocarcinom N NB.*

This extraction step provided us with a list of 261 English terms associated with 771 German terms and a list of 259 English terms associated with 768 French terms.

2) Manual cleaning of extracted target terms

One of the difficulties in using this resource is that it is a thesaurus and not a purpose-built translation resource. Thus, as we can see in the example, the terms associated with a concept are rather varied linguistic forms which match the concept but sometimes are not exact translations of one another. This particularity means that some work does not use the UMLS concepts directly but the links established within each controlled vocabulary which constitutes the UMLS. For example, [LAN 08] create three resources: first resource from the MesH translation links, second resource from those of the MedRA and third resource from the SNOMED CT.

In spite of this, we wished to use the concept identifiers because we focused on non-canonical translations. This choice allowed us to obtain relatively free translation equivalences. For example, for the English term *discomfort*, we obtain the German terms *unwohlsein* (unease) and *fuehlt sich nicht wohl* (does not feel comfortable). For *self-image*, we obtain in French *perception de soi, autoperception* (self-perception).

However, we noticed that some translations extracted from the UMLS had a meaning that was very far from the source term's meaning. For example, *epirubicin-vinorelbine* is associated with *épirubicine*, even though "épirubicine" and "vinorelbine" are two different drugs; the first drug being an anthracycline (inhibiting RNA and DNA synthesis) and the second drug an antimitosis drug (inhibiting cell division).[4] The term *epirubicin-vinorelbine* is used to refer to a treatment which combines both the drugs.[5] Thus, we examined all the suggested target terms and eliminated those which, after querying the necessary resources,[6] appeared to present a meaning that was too far from the source term. When in doubt, we decided to leave a potentially wrong target term rather than take it out.

We also observed that the UMLS provided both singular and plural forms for some target terms (*polyamine* → *polyamine, polyamines*) and sometimes a form mentioning the term's feminine variant (*intolerant* → *intolérant(e)*). These forms were also manually corrected and/or eliminated.

After manual verification, our equivalence list contained 261 English terms associated with 767 German terms (4 target terms discarded) and 259 English terms associated with 732 French terms (26 target terms discarded).

3) Searching for attested target terms in the target corpus

In this third and last stage, we looked for the attestations of the target terms in the target language texts. To help match them, the terms were normalized on the UMLS entry side as well as on the corpus side: lowercasing, hyphen deletion and lemmatization. All the unattested target terms were discarded from the reference as well as the source terms for which none of the target terms listed by the UMLS were attested in the corpus.

---

4 Source : http://en.wikipedia.org/wiki/Epirubicin and http://en.wikipedia.org/wiki/Vinorelbine.

5 Source: http://www.ncbi.nlm.nih.gov/pubmed/?term=epirubicin-vinorelbine.

6 Collaborative encyclopedic entries with interlingual links: http://en.wikipedia.org/.
Bilingual concordancer: http://www.linguee.fr/.
Specialized English monolingual contexts: http://www.ncbi.nlm.nih.gov/pubmed/.
English medical dictionary: http://medical-dictionary.thefreedictionary.com/.

Thus, we obtained a list of 126 English terms aligned with 163 French terms (R^{FR}) and 90 English terms aligned with 104 German terms (R^{DE}).

Table 5.6 summarizes the different stages of the *a priori* reference construction.

	EN→ FR	EN→ DE
(1) translations found in the UMLS	261 → 771	259 → 768
(2) translations after manual cleaning	261 → 767	259 → 732
(3) translations attested in the target corpus (R)	126 → 163	90 → 104

Table 5.6. *Stages of the* a priori *reference construction*

5.4.2. *A posteriori reference*

To build the *a posteriori* reference, we had translators annotate the system's outputs.[7] Part of the translations were annotated by several annotators so as to compute the inter-annotator agreement (a random selection of 100 translations for each language was annotated by at least two annotators). The agreement measure used is the $Kappa$ index of [CAR 96] (see Appendix A1.6). We obtain a $Kappa$ of 0.71 for English–French and of 0.77 for English–German. In case of a disagreement between two annotators, the annotation carried out by the most consensual annotator[8] is retained.

Four values were used in annotation, each corresponding to a usage "cost" for the translator: *exact*, *accurate*, *close* and *false*. Table 5.7 summarizes the annotation criteria. In any case, the target term can be longer than the source term (fertile translations).

VALUE	Meaning	Translation operations
Exact	$=$	0 or adaptation to the type of discourse
Accurate	$=$	Morphosyntactic transformation
Close	$\simeq$	Potential complementary research
False	$\neq$	Other mandatory research

Table 5.7. *Values for translation annotations*

5.4.2.1. *Exact*

The target term corresponds to the exact translation of the source term, i.e. it is the "canonical" specialized term, or a popular equivalent:

7 The English outputs were annotated by a student in the second year of her Masters (M2) at (Higher Education Institute of Translation and Interpreting) ISIT, the author of this book and a third fluent English speaker. The German outputs were annotated by a translator and two ISIT students (M2).

8 I.e. the one with the best average $Kappa$.

– there is *semantic equality* (neither addition or loss of meaning) → the target term provides the translator with the meaning of the source term;

– the translator can use the target term *as is*.

Examples:

– *pathophysiological* → *physiopathologique*;

– *cardiotoxicity* → *toxicité cardiaque, toxicité pour le cœur*;

– *tumour margin* → *marge tumorale*.

5.4.2.2. *Acceptable*

The target term corresponds to a morphosyntactic variant of the exact translation:

– there is *semantic equality* (neither addition or loss of meaning) → the target term provides the translator with the meaning of the source term;

– the translator will have to carry out a *morphosyntactic transformation* to recreate the exact translation.

Examples:

– *dosimetry* → *dosimétrique* (exact translation: *dosimétrie*);

– *cytoprotection* → *protéger les cellules* (exact translation: *protection des cellules, cytoprotection*);

– *œstrogene-sensitive*→ *sensibilité à l'œstrogène* (exact translation: *sensible à l'œstrogène*).

5.4.2.3. *Close*

The target term does not correspond to the canonical term nor does it correspond to a popular equivalent or a morphosyntactic variant but it is still useful in translation:

– there is *semantic proximity* (intersection or inclusion of meaning) → the target term provides the translator with elements to understand the source term;

– the translator will *potentially* have to carry out *additional research* to find the translation of the source term.

Examples:

– *desirability* → *désir*;

– *high-dose* → *dose un peu plus élevée*.

5.4.2.4. *False*

The target term is useless in translation:

– there is *no semantic proximity* → the target term does not provide any elements for the translator to understand the source term;

– the translator will have to find the translation by *other means*.

Examples:

– *immunoscore* → *immunomarquer*;

– *risk-reducing* → *risque de réduction.*

In the end, P^{FR}, the *a posteriori* reference for English–French, is composed of 730 English source terms associated with 2,129 candidate translations, which have been manually annotated. P^{DE}, the *a posteriori* reference for English–German, is composed of 654 English source terms associated with 2,016 candidate translations, which have been manually annotated.[9]

5.5. Translation ranking training and evaluation data

Our training data (T) corresponds to the source terms (and their candidate translations generated by the system and then annotated) which do not belong to the *a priori* reference ($T = P \setminus R$). It contains 647 English terms associated with 1,970 candidate translations in French and 588 English terms associated with 1,829 candidate translations in German.

Our evaluation data (E) corresponds to the source terms (and their candidate translations generated by the system and then annotated) which belong to the *a priori* reference ($E = P \cap R$). It contains 83 English terms associated with 159 candidate translations in French and 66 English terms associated with 187 candidate translations in German.

5.6. Linguistic resources

5.6.1. *General language bilingual dictionary*

The general language bilingual dictionary used by the translation generator is the dictionary provided with the linguistic analyzer XELDA (version 2.8.1). This dictionary has 37,655 English entries aligned with 59,495 French translations and 69,285 German translations.

9 The figures of 730 and 654 correspond to the number of source terms for which the system generated at least one candidate in French and German, respectively.

5.6.2. *Thesaurus*

The thesaurus used by the generator is also the one provided with the linguistic analyzer XELDA (version 2.8.1). It has 5,064 entries associated with 7,596 synonyms in English; 2,387 entries associated with 3,169 synonyms in French and 4,209 entries associated with 4,883 synonyms in German.

5.6.3. *Bound morphemes translation table*

To our knowledge, there is no existing bilingual dictionary of bound morphemes. Creating such a resource, and ensuring it is almost exhaustive, goes beyond the remit of this work. Therefore, we limited ourselves to describing in a file the possible translations of the bound morphemes found in the source terms.[10] These translations can be bound or free morphemes. For example, the combining form *-phyto-* can be translated in French by "*-phyto-*" or "*plante*". To create this resource, translators used specialized monolingual morphological dictionaries found on the Internet[11] and an encyclopedic dictionary [DRO 06].

This resource indicates the nature of each English bound morpheme (prefix, combining form and suffix) and the list of translations as well as their morphological type (prefix, combining form, suffix and word). In most cases, the translation is of the same morphological type as the source morpheme, e.g. a prefix is translated by a prefix, a combining form is translated by a combining form and a suffix is translated by a suffix. The only exception is the English suffix *-less* which can only be translated by private prefixes *ab-* or *a-*.

Allomorphs and interfixed forms are considered to be independent entries. For example, the English combining form derived from the Greek *-plasis-* ("action of making and modeling") is found under three entries: *-plasia-*, *-plasty-* and *-plasy-*. The combining form *-patho-* has three possible matching translations in German: *-path-*, *-pathie-* and *-patho-*.

The extract in Table 5.8 provides a glimpse of these translation tables. The combining forms are followed by the ":c" symbol, suffixes are marked by the ":s" symbol, prefixes are marked by the ":p" symbol and words are marked by the ":w" symbol. The entire resource can be found in Appendix A2.3.3.

10 The English–French table was drawn up by the author, the English–German table was drawn up by a translator.

11 http://medical-dictionary.thefreedictionary.com/, http://georges.dolisi.free.fr/Terminologie/Menu/terminologie__medicale_menu.htm.

EN	DE	FR
patho:c	behandlung:w, krankheit:w, leiden:w, path:c, pathie:c, patho:c	maladie:w, path:c, pathie:c, patho:c, souffrance:w
phyto:c	pflanze:w, pflanzen:w, phyt:c, phyto:c	bourgeon:w, excroissance:w, phyt:c, phyto:c, plante:w, végétal:w
plasia:c	plasie:c, plastisch:c, plastischer:w, umformbarkeit:w, verformung:w	modeler:w, plase:c, plasie:c, plasique:c
plasty:c	plasie:c, plastisch:c, plastischer:w, umformbarkeit:w, verformung:w	plastie:c, plastique:c, plastique:w, réparation:w
plasy :c	plasie:c, plastisch:c, plastischer:w, umformbarkeit:w, verformung:w	
less:s	a:p, ab:p, abs:p, los:s, nicht:w, ohne:w	a:p, ab:p, aucun:w, privé:w, sans:w

Table 5.8. *Extract from the English → French morpheme translation table*

Tables 5.9 and 5.10 indicate the size of the translation tables. All in all, the latter has 242 English entries that are associated with 1,001 French translations and 1,081 German translations.

	# EN entries	# FR translations				
		Prefixes	Combining forms	Suffixes	Words	Total
Prefixes	50	97	0	0	163	260
Combining forms	185	0	410	0	310	720
Suffixes	7	2	0	6	13	21
Total	242	99	410	6	486	1001

Table 5.9. *Size of the English–French bound morpheme translation tables (number of entries and translations)*

5.6.4. *Lexicon for word decomposition*

In the case of word decomposition, we use a lexicon of bound morphemes and a lexicon of free morphemes. The bound morpheme lexicon is simply created from the entries of the morpheme translation table.

	# EN entries	# DE translations				
		Prefixes	Combining forms	Suffixes	Words	Total
Prefixes	50	87	0	0	194	281
Combining forms	185	0	385	0	382	767
Suffixes	7	3	0	13	17	33
Total	250	90	385	13	593	1081

Table 5.10. *Size of the English–German bound morpheme translation tables (number of entries and translations)*

The free morpheme lexicon is composed of the general language bilingual dictionary entries, the thesaurus entries and the attested words in the English corpus. Tokenization and lemmatization were carried out by the XELDA analyzer. Where possible, we have separated words found in the resources into other words to obtain a maximum of entries in our single morpheme lexicon. For example, if the word "*ataxia-telangiectasia*" was found in the corpus, we added three words to our lexicon: *ataxia-telangiectasia, ataxia* and *telangiectasia*. Algorithm 2 describes this process.

Algorithm 2 Extraction of a list of single morphemes

Require: C (corpus words), D (dictionary entries)
  $words \leftarrow \emptyset$
  for all $word\_a$ **in** $C \cup D$ **do**
    $words$.add($word\_a$)
    for all $word\_b$ **in** split_on_hyphens_and_spaces($word\_a$) **do**
      $words$.add($word\_b$)
    end for
  end for
  return $words$

5.6.5. *Morphological families*

We automatically acquired families of morphologically-related words using the stemming algorithm from [POR 80]. This algorithm, originally meant for information retrieval, identifies the stem of a word by applying suffix stripping rules. For example, the words *elaborately, elaborate* and *elaboration* are all based on the stem *elabor*: thus we consider that they belong to the same morphological family.

To extract morphological families, we stemmed all the words of the corpora in each language as well as the bilingual dictionary entries and the thesaurus entries which had first been separated with 2 algorithm. We obtained 5,835 English morphological families (an average of 2.51 words per family), 7,049 French morphological families (an average of 2.45 words per family) and 7,348 German morphological families (an average of 2.15 words per family).

The resulting algorithm sometimes generates mistakes. For example, the words *ironically*, *ironical* and *iron* are all linked to the same stem, *iron*. Moreover, words such as *individualistic*, *individualist*, *individualisation*, *individualised* and *individualise* are allocated to two different families when they should belong to the same one. We evaluated the quality of the morphological families. To this end, we extracted 50 morphological families for each language, which were automatically acquired and observed:

– *The rate of false positives:* percentage of word pairs classified in a single family when they do not belong to the same one, e.g. classifying *iron* and *ironically* in the same family.

– *The rate of false negatives:* percentage of word pairs which are not classified in the same family when they belong to a single family, e.g. classifying *individualisation* and *individualised* in two separate families.

Results show that the stemmer tends to miss morphological ties rather than generate mistaken ones, except in German, where it appears to obtain good results.[12] The details of the evaluation as well as the morphological families extracts are given in Appendix A2.3.4.

	EN	FR	DE
False positives	0.19%	0.08%	0.02%
False negatives	14.77%	15.45%	0%

Table 5.11. *Evaluation of morphological families*

5.6.6. *Dictionary of cognates*

To increase the translation possibilities, we extracted cognate pairs from the corpus, and used them as a corpus-specific specialized bilingual dictionary. We used [HAU 11] to identify the cognates: this is a classifier – LibSVM by [CHA 11] – trained on translation pairs extracted from bilingual dictionaries. Its the features are the following:

– edit distance [LEV 66];

– longest prefix in common;

– number of bigrams in common;

12 In German, part of the pairs was taken out of the evaluation since we were unable to determine whether the words belonged to the same family or not.

– length of the source term;

– length of the target term;

– difference between the length of the source term and the length of the target term.

To build the training set, we used four dictionaries, which can be found on the FREE DICTIONARIES PROJECT website:[13]

– Universal dictionary (maintained by the DICTS.INFO project);

– Wiktionary (maintained by the WIKTIONARY.ORG project);

– Omegawiki (maintained by the OMEGAWIKI.ORG project);

– Wikipedia (maintained by the WIKIPEDIA.ORG project).

We extracted all the pairs *(source term* and *target term)* from these four dictionaries, for which the edit distance between the source and target terms is less than or equal to four. If the source and target terms were translations, they would be a positive example; if not, they would be a negative example. We selected as many positive examples as negative examples so that the model is unbiased toward both classes (COGNATE vs. NON-COGNATE). We obtained 42,404 examples for English–French and 14,798 examples for English–German.

The training was carried out with the data-mining library WEKA [HAL 09], which offers a package for LibSVM. We learned two models: first model to identify the English–French cognates and the other model to identify the English–German cognates. The average error rate obtained by 10-fold cross-validation is of 3.49% for the English–French cognate identification and of 6.93% for the English–German cognate identification.

We created the specialized dictionary thanks to Algorithm 3. For each word in the source corpus, we retained any target term as translation as long as its edit distance is less than or equal to four and its SVM classifier confirms that it is a cognate. If several target terms match these criteria, we retained the one with the shortest edit distance with the source word. The corpus words were previously separated with Algorithm 2 .

In the end, we obtained 6,708 English–French and 6,391 English–German translation pairs.

13 http: //www.dicts.info/uddl.php.

5.7. Summary

This chapter has enabled us to present the data used to test the translation method presented in Chapter 4: comparable corpora, source terms, reference lexica, training data and linguistic resources. In the next chapter, we will describe the results obtained with translation generation.

Algorithm 3 Extraction of a dictionary of cognates from a comparable corpus

Require: C_s (source corpus), C_t (target corpus), $Classifier$ (Cognate classifier)
  $Dictionary \leftarrow \emptyset$
  for all w_s **in** C_s **do**
    $translation \leftarrow \emptyset$
    $score \leftarrow 4$
    for all w_t **in** C_t **do**
      ed =edit_distance(w_s, w_t)
      if $ed \leq score$ **and** $Classifier$.isCognate(w_s, w_t) **then**
        $translation \leftarrow w_t$
        $score = ed$
      end if
    end for
    if $translation \neq \emptyset$ **then**
      $Dictionnary$.add($w_s, translation$)
    end if
  end for
  return $Dictionary$

6

Formalization and Evaluation of Candidate Translation Generation

6.1. Introduction

In this chapter, we present the implementation of the translation generation method described in Chapter 4 (stages 1 to 4). The aim of this method is to be able to translate various types of morphologically complex words and generate fertile translations.

We will start by detailing the translation generation algorithm (section 6.2). Then, we will present the evaluation of the results of the morphological splitting module in section 6.3. Section 6.4 evaluates the quality of the generated translations. We describe the various experiments whose goal was to highlight the influence of data and generation strategies. Finally, we discuss the limits of our work as well as the research prospects in section 6.5.

6.2. Translation generation algorithm

The translation method presented in Chapter 5 is implemented due to Algorithm 4. This algorithm takes as input a monolexical source term ($source\_term$) and outputs zero, one or more mono- or poly- lexical units in the target language ($translations$).

The algorithm relies on the resources described in Chapter 5, which we have thus named:

– $Trans$ is a translation resource linking source language elements with target language elements: a morpheme translation table, general language bilingual dictionary and dictionary of cognates.

Algorithm 4 Translation generation

```
Require: source_term, target_corpus

  translations ← ∅
  for all {c_1, ...c_i} in D(source_term) do                         ▷ 1. Decomposition
      for all {t_1, ...t_j} in T(c_1) × ... T(c_i) do                  ▷ 2. Translation
          if i ≠ j then
              continue
          end if
          for all {w_1, ...w_k} in R ({t_1, ...t_j}) do                ▷ 3. Recomposition
              for all match in S({w_1, ...w_k}, target_corpus) do      ▷ 4. Selection
                  add match to translations
              end for
          end for
      end for
  end for
  return translations

  function D(source_term)
      decompositions ← ∅
      for all {m_1, ...m_i} in SPLIT(source_term) do          ▷ 1.1 Morphological splitting
          for all {c_1, ...c_j} in CONCATENATE ({m_1, ...m_i}) do      ▷ 1.2 Concatenation
              add {c_1, ...c_j} to decompositions
          end for
      end for
      return decompositions
  end function

  function R({t_1, ...t_i})
      recompositions ← ∅
      for all {t_1, ...t_i} in PERMUTATE ({t_1, ...t_i}) do               ▷ 3.1 Permutation
          for all {w_1, ...w_j} in CONCATENATE ({t_1, ...t_i}) do         ▷ 3.2 Concatenation
              if FILTER ({w_1, ...w_j}) then                               ▷ 3.3 Filtering
                  add {w_1, ...w_j} to recompositions
              end if
          end for
      end for
      return recompositions
  end function
```

– Var^{src}, resp. Var^{tgt}, is a resource which can manage source language variation (src), respectively target language variation (tgt): morphological families, thesaurus.

– $Corpus^{src}$ is a tokenized, lemmatized and POS-tagged source language corpus.

– $Comp^{src}_{type}$, resp. $Comp^{tgt}_{type}$, is a list of source, respectively target, language elements in which $type$ stands for $pref$ in the case of prefixes, $comb$ in the case of combining forms, $suff$ in the case of suffixes, and $word$ in the case of words (these lists correspond to the $Trans$ and Var^{src} resource entries and to the words extracted from the source language corpus).

– $Stop^{tgt}$ is a list of stop words in the target language.

To clarify, we add a translation example to the description of the algorithm. In this case, it is the translation of the English term *cytotoxic* into French, using the following toy data set ($src = en$ and $tgt = fr$):

$Comp^{en}_{comb}$ = {-cyto-}
$Comp^{en}_{word}$ = {cytotoxic, cytotoxicity, toxic}
$Comp^{fr}_{comb}$ = {-cyto-}
$Comp^{fr}_{word}$ = {cellule, toxique}
$Trans$ = {
{-cyto- → -cyto-, cellule},
{toxic → toxique},
{cytotoxicity → cytotoxicité}
}
Var^{en} = {cytoxic → cytoxicity}
$Stop^{fr}$ = {pour, le}
$Corpus^{fr}$ = "le/DET cytotoxicité/N être/AUX le/DET propriété/N de/PREP ce/DET qui/PRO être/AUX toxique/A pour/PREP le/DET cellule/N ./PUN"

Table 6.1. *Toy dataset for the translation of* cytotoxic *into* toxique pour les cellules *and* cytotoxicité

As a compositional translation method, the translation generation function can be decomposed into four sub-functions which are applied sequentially:

– Decomposition $\mathcal{D}$ (section 6.2.1).

– Translation $\mathcal{T}$ (section 6.2.2).

– Recomposition $\mathcal{R}$ (section 6.2.3).

– Selection $\mathcal{S}$ (section 6.2.4).

The translation of *cytotoxic* is thus given by a composition of functions, and each is applied to the result provided by the previous one:

$$Translation(\text{"cytotoxic"}) = \mathcal{S}(\mathcal{R}(\mathcal{T}(\mathcal{D}(\text{"cytotoxic"}))))$$

6.2.1. *Decomposition*

The decomposition function $\mathcal{D}$ can itself be decomposed into two functions called SPLIT (morphological splitting) and CONCATENATE (morpheme concatenation):

$\mathcal{D}$("cytotoxic"")
= CONCATENATE(SPLIT("cytotoxic""))

6.2.1.1. *Morphological decomposition (*SPLIT*)*

This step decomposes the source term into morphemes using Algorithm 5. The split is carried out by matching the items in the resources $Comp^{src}$, $Comp^{src}_{comb}$, $Comp^{src}_{suff}$, $Comp^{src}_{word}$ with the string of characters representing the source term. Length constraints are also taken into account ($\mathcal{L}0$, $\mathcal{L}1$, $\mathcal{L}2$). For example, string $string[1 : n]$, containing n characters, can be split into a lexical base $string[1 : i]$ and a suffix $string[i + 1 : n]$ if $string[i + 1 : n] \in Comp^{src}_{suff}$ and $string[1 : i] \geq \mathcal{L}2$. The parameters of the length constraints used by Algorithm 5 were set empirically ($\mathcal{L}0 = 5$, $\mathcal{L}1 = 4$, $\mathcal{L}2 = 4$).

A source term is first split into an optional prefix + lexical base $_1$, which is then split into lexical base $_2$ + an optional suffix. Finally, lexical base$_2$ is split into one or more combining forms or words. When several splits are possible, only the ones with the greatest number of components are retained.

CONCATENATE(SPLIT("cytotoxic""))
= CONCATENATE({cyto, toxic})

6.2.1.2. *Morpheme concatenation (*CONCATENATE*)*

The CONCATENATE function generates all the possible concatenations for morphemes resulting from the morphological split. For example, if the source term *abc* was split into three morphemes {a,b,c}, then there are four ways to concatenate these morphemes: {abc}, {a,bc}, {ab,c}, {a,b,c}. For a source term being split into n morphemes, there are 2^{n-1} possible concatenations.

CONCATENATE({cyto, toxic})
= {cyto, toxic}, {cytotoxic}

Morpheme concatenation increases the chances of finding translations. Let us take an example: say we want to translate the term *non-cytotoxic* and our resources have translations for *non*, *cyto* and *cytotoxic* but not for *toxic*. If we only base ourselves on the output of the morphological split, i.e. on *{non-,-cyto-,toxic}*, the translation of *non-cytotoxic* fails as there is no translation for *toxic*. However, if we use concatenation as an intermediate step, we also obtain the split *{non-,cytotoxic}*. Since our resources have translations for *non* and *cytotoxic*, we can translate the source term.

Algorithm 5 SPLIT: Morphological splitting

Require: $source\_term, Comp_{pref}, Comp_{comb}, Comp_{suff}, Comp_{word}$
$\mathcal{L}0 = 5$; $\mathcal{L}1 = 4$; $\mathcal{L}2 = 4$;

```
lemmas_splits ← [ ]          ▷ Splitting on the hyphens and then splitting each sub-element
for all lemma in SPLIT_ON_HYPHENS(source_term) do
    prefix = GET_PREFIX(lemma)                              ▷ Extracting optional prefix
    base = REMOVE_PREFIX(prefix, lemma)
    suffix = GET_SUFFIX(base)                               ▷ Extracting optional suffix
    base = REMOVE_SUFFIX(lemma, suffix)
    splits ← ∅                       ▷ Several possible decompositions for the lexical base
    for all (c1, ...cn) in GET_COMPONENTS(base) do          ▷ (c1, ...cn) is the list of
components in the lexical base
        add (prefix, c1, ..., cn, suffix) to splits
    end for
    add splits to lemmas_splits
end for
                                         ▷ Combining all the splits of each sub-element
splits = {(s1, ..., sn)|s1 ∈ lemmas_splits[1], ..., sn ∈ lemmas_splits[n]}
                      ▷ Returning all the combinations with the greatest number of morphemes
return {split|split ∈ splits, length(split) = max ({length(split)|split ∈ splits}) }

function GET_PREFIX(lemma)
    for all pref in sorted by descending length (Comp_pref) do
        base = REMOVE_PREFIX(prefix, lemma)
        if lemma = pref or (lemma starts with pref and length(base) ≥ L0 and (base ∈
Comp_words or base can be decomposed into words or combining forms)) then
            return pref
        end if
    end for
end function

function GET_COMPONENTS(base)
    C = {w|w ∈ Comp_words and length(w) ≥ L2} ∪ Comp_comb
    return splits = {(c1, ..., cn)|ci ∈ C for all 1 ≤ i ≤ n, and c1 + ... + cn = base}
end function

function GET_SUFFIX(lemma)
    for all suff in sorted by descending length (Comp_suff) do
        base = REMOVE_SUFFIX(lemma, suffix)
        if lemma ends with suff and length(base) > length(suff) and length(base) ≥ L1
then
            return suff
        end if
    end for
end function
```

In the case in which we would still have had the translation *toxic* → *toxique*, concatenation enables us to generate several possible translations and thus potentially interesting variants for the translator. For example, if the dictionary has translations for *non-*→*non*, *-cyto-*→*cellule*, *toxic*→*toxique* and *cytotoxic*→*cytotoxique*, then we can both generate the translation *non toxique pour les cellules* and the translation *noncytotoxique*.

Finally, let us point out that concatenation regenerates the full form of the source term (i.e. the non-split one). Once more, this enables us to increase the translation possibilities for the term, by going through a cognate and/or a morphological variant. If we know that *noncytotoxic* belongs to the same morphological family as *noncytotoxicity* and we know that *noncytotoxicity* is translated by *noncytotoxicité*, then we can establish a direct translation link from *noncytotoxic* to *noncytotoxicité* which remains an acceptable translation. This is a useful fallback strategy when the term cannot be split into morphemes or the translation of one of the morphemes has failed.

6.2.2. *Translation*

The translation function provides a translation for each split generated by $\mathcal{D}$. As we rely on the compositionality principle, we consider that the translation of the whole can be computed from the translation of the parts: $\mathcal{T}(a,b) = \mathcal{T}(a) \times \mathcal{T}(b)$. For a decomposition $\{c_1, ...c_n\}$ with n components, there are thus $\prod_{i=1}^{n} |\mathcal{T}(c_i)|$ possible translations.

$$\begin{aligned}&\mathcal{T}(\{\text{cyto, toxic}\}, \{\text{cytotoxic}\})\\&= \mathcal{T}(\text{cyto}) \times \mathcal{T}(\text{toxic}), \mathcal{T}(\text{cytotoxic})\\&= \{\text{cyto, toxique}\}, \{\text{cellule, toxique}\}, \{\text{cytotoxicité}\}\end{aligned}$$

The translations are obtained from the $Trans$ and Var resources. If the component is identified as a bound morpheme (prefix, combining form and suffix), its translations will be those given by the morpheme translation table. If the component is a noun, then we will use the general language dictionary and the dictionary of cognates. In the cases in which the component is made of a single letter or corresponds to an acronym, we will also add this component as its own translation. This enables us to find translations of terms which contain names of genes, logos or abbreviations directly borrowed from English, e.g.: *p-value* → *valeur de p*, *er-negative* → *negativ er*.[1] The two bilingual resources can be combined with the monolingual resources (morphological families and synonyms) in order to deal with morphological variation and lexical divergence.

1 ER is the abbreviation of *Estrogen Receptor*.

To summarize, the translation of a word can be:

– a direct translation, obtained by looking at bilingual resources:

- $\mathcal{T}(c) = Trans(c)$, e.g. *toxic* → *toxique*;

– an indirect translation obtained by:

- translating the word then looking for a translation variant:

- $\mathcal{T}(c) = Var^{tgt}(Trans(c))$, e.g. *toxic* → *toxique* → *toxicité* for a morphological variant or *toxic* → *toxique* → *vénéneux* ('poisonous') for a synonym;

– looking for a variant of the source word and translating this variant into the target language:

- $\mathcal{T}(c) = Trans(Var^{src}(c))$, e.g. *toxic* → *toxicity* → *toxicité* for a morphological variant or *toxic* → *poisonous* → *vénéneux* for a synonym.

For a given set of components ($\{c_1, ..., c_i\}$), if one of the components cannot be translated, the translation of the whole fails.

6.2.3. *Recomposition*

The recomposition function $\mathcal{R}$ takes the translations generated by $\mathcal{T}$ as input and recomposes them as a sequence of lexical units. The recomposition is carried out in three stages: permutation of the translated components (PERMUTATE), concatenation into words (CONCATENATE) and filtering (FILTER):

$\mathcal{R}$({cyto,toxique},{cellule,toxique},{cytotoxicité})
=FILTER(CONCATENATE(PERMUTATE({cyto,toxique},{cellule,toxique}, {cytotoxicité})))

6.2.3.1. *Permutation of translated elements (*PERMUTATE*)*

For a translation of n elements, this stage generates the $n!$ permutations of these elements. For example, the translation of {A,B,C} generates six permutations: {A,B,C}, {A,C,B}, {B,A,C}, {B,C,A}, {C,A,B} and {C,B,A}. This phase takes into account the distortion phenomenon: the order of the translated units can be different from one language to the next. It is costly to use these complexity functions $O(n!)$ but in our case we manipulate small sets (a maximum of four components).

FILTER(CONCATENATE(PERMUTATE({cyto,toxique},{cellule,toxique}, {cytotoxicité})))
=FILTER(CONCATENATE({cyto,toxique}, {toxique,cyto}, {cellule, toxique},
{toxique, cellule}, {cytotoxicité}))

6.2.3.2. *Concatenation into words (*CONCATENATE*)*

Once the components have been permuted, we generate for each permutation all the possible concatenations of its components (as we have done after the morphological split). This stage is meant to create the target words from the components that were translated.

FILTER(CONCATENATE({cyto,toxique}, {toxique,cyto}, {cellule, toxique}, {toxique, cellule}, {cytotoxicité}))
=FILTER({cyto, toxique}, {cytotoxique}, {toxique, cyto},{toxiquecyto}, {cellule, toxique}, {celluletoxique}, {toxique, cellule},{toxiquecellule},{cytotoxicité})

6.2.3.3. *Filtering (*FILTER*)*

This stage filters the outputs of CONCATENATE with heuristic rules. For example, a sequence of lexical units in the target language $L = \{l_1, ..., l_n\}$ will be eliminated if one of the lexical units corresponds to a bound morpheme or if the sequence ends with stop words. For example, the recomposition {cytotoxique} will be accepted but not the recomposition {-cyto-, toxique} since *-cyto-* is a bound morpheme which cannot be used as an autonomous lexical unit (word). A sequence such as {traitement, après} is eliminated in French since it ends with the preposition *après* and a target term ending with a stop word is considered to be ill-formed, hence the reason it has been eliminated).

FILTER({cyto, toxique}, {cytotoxique}, {toxique, cyto},{toxiquecyto}, {cellule, toxique}, {celluletoxique}, {toxique, cellule},{toxiquecellule},{cytotoxicité})
= {cytotoxique}, {toxiquecyto}, {cellule, toxique}, {celluletoxique}, {toxique, cellule}, {toxiquecellule}, {cytotoxicité}

These sequences of concatenated components correspond to the lexical units which will be matched with the target corpus by the selection function. For example, the sequence {toxique_A, cellule_B} corresponds to the lexical unit *toxique* followed by *cellule*. The {cytotoxique_{AB}} sequence corresponds to a single lexical unit: *cytotoxique*.

6.2.4. *Selection*

The selection function $\mathcal{S}$ attempts to match the lexical unit sequences generated by $\mathcal{R}$ with the lemma of the target corpus words. We call $L = \{l_1, ...l_n\}$ a sequence of lexical units generated by $\mathcal{R}$. We call $W = \{w_1, ...w_m\}$ a sequence of words in the target corpus, $l(w_k)$ is the lemma of the word w_k and $p(w_k)$ the part-of-speech of the word w_k. L matches W if there is a strictly increasing sequence of indexes $I = \{i_1, ...i_n\}$ such as $l(w_{i_j}) = l_j$ and $\forall j, 1 \leq j \leq n$ and $\forall i, 1 \leq |i_{j-1} - i_j| \leq \mathcal{L}3$ and $\forall w_k | \ k \notin I, \ l(w_k) \in Stop^{tgt}$; $\mathcal{L}3$ having been set empirically to 3.

$\mathcal{S}$({cytotoxique}, {toxiquecyto}, {cellule, toxique}, {celluletoxique}, {toxique, cellule}, {toxiquecellule}, {cytotoxicité})
= {"toxique/A pour/PREP le/DET cellule/N", "cytotoxicité/N"}

In other words, L is a sub-sequence of W lemmas, and we authorize a maximum of $\mathcal{L}3$ stop words between two words which match the lexical units of L. Thus, {toxique, cellule} matches "*toxique pour les cellules*" but not "*toxique étendu aux cellules*" (presence of a lexical word between *toxique* and *cellule*) nor "*toxique pour aucune de ces cellules*" (more than three stop words between *toxique* and *cellule*).

6.2.4.1. *Definition of a candidate translation*

For each sequence of lexical units L, we gather in the target corpus all the word sequences $W_1, W_2, ...W_p$ which match L according to the definition given above. We consider that two sequences $W1$ and $W2$ correspond to the same candidate translation if $|W1| = |W2|$ and $\forall(w1_i, w2_j)$ such as $w1 \in W1, w2 \in W2, i = j$ then $l(w1_i) = l(w2_j)$ and $p(w1_i) = p(w2_j)$, i.e. if two sequences of words correspond to the same sequence of pairs "(lemma, part-of-speech)", then these two sequences are one and the same candidate translation. This allows us to ignore the differences of inflection, for example "*toxique pour la cellule*" and "*toxique pour les cellules*" correspond to the same candidate translation: "toxique/A pour/PREP le/ DET cellule/N". However, "*toxique pour les cellules*" and "*toxique envers les cellules*" are two different candidate translations.

This first section allowed us to present the whole translation generation algorithm. The following sections concern the evaluation of the algorithm. We first evaluated the morphological splitting algorithm (section 6.3), then the translation algorithm in its entirety (section 6.4).

6.3. Morphological splitting evaluation

To evaluate the morphological splitting function SPLIT, we observed:

– the number of words that could not be split;

– among the words that could be split:

  - the number of words with at least one correct split;

  - among those that were incorrectly split:[2]

    – how many were oversplit, e.g. {ligation, de, pendent} instead of {ligation, dependent};

    – how many were undersplit, e.g. {cyclophosphamide, based} instead of {cyclo, phosphamide, based}.

2 We also had cases in which the number of morphemes was correct, but the split was wrong, e.g. {grandpa and rent} instead of {grand and parent} but in those cases, the correct split had also been generated.

These results are shown in Table 6.2. The list S^{FR} (1839 words), respectively S^{DE} (1824 words) corresponds to the list of source terms to be translated into French, respectively into German, presented in section 5.3. Results are equivalent no matter the source language.

We observe that between 3.15 and 3.23% of the terms are not split. As for the terms that were split, 93% of them were given at least one correct split. There is little over-generation: only two terms were given different splits, and among these splits, at least one was correct:

– *grandparent* was split into "grand+parent and into "grandpa+rent

– *lymphoedema* was split into "-lymph-+oedema and into "-lympho-+edema

As for the terms that were incorrectly split, between 76.85% and 77.27% of them were oversplit. For example, *ligation-dependent* was split into "ligation+de-+pendent. The oversplit is not an issue since by using concatenation, we can find the correct split again. However, between 12.12 and 12.37% of the cases were undersplit. For example, *cyclophosphamide-based* was split into "cyclophosphamide+based.

	S^{FR}	S^{DE}
Not split	3.15%	3.23%
Split	96.85%	96.77%
↪ Number of splits/term	1.001	1.001
↪At least 1 correct split	93.82 %	93.88 %
↪No correct split	6.18 %	6.12 %
↪ Over-splitting	77.27 %	76.85 %
↪ Under-splitting	22.73 %	23.15 %

Table 6.2. *Results obtained by the morphological splitting function* SPLIT

6.4. Translation generation evaluation

In this section, we present the evaluation of the translations generated with Algorithm 4. We start by presenting the measures and references used for the evaluation (section 6.4.1) then we present the results of several experiments aiming to highlight the usefulness of resources and generation strategies (sections 6.4.2 to 6.4.6). We end with a qualitative analysis of the generated translations (section 6.4.7).

6.4.1. *Reference data and evaluation measures*

To evaluate the translations generated, we use the two references presented in Chapter 5, section 5.4: *a posteriori* reference and *a priori* reference.

6.4.1.1. A posteriori *reference*

This reference is created from the outputs of the system which are manually annotated (see section 5.4.2). The source terms correspond to the lists S^{FR} and S^{DE} described in section 5.3.

For the *a posteriori* reference evaluation, we use the following measures.

6.4.1.1.1. Coverage (C)

The coverage corresponds to the fraction of the source terms for which the system was able to generate a translation, no matter how exact it is:

$$C = \frac{|ST|}{|S|} \qquad [6.1]$$

$$ST = \{s : |\mathcal{T}(s)| > 1\}$$

in which S is the set of source terms and $\mathcal{T}(s)$ is a set of translations generated by the system for the source term s.

6.4.1.1.2. Precision (P)

The precision indicates the fraction of terms in ST for which the system generated at least one correct translation, i.e. annotated as exact or accurate by the judges:

$$P = \frac{|SC|}{|ST|} \qquad [6.2]$$

$$SC = \{s : s \in ST, \mathcal{A}(s) \cap \{\text{exact, accurate}\} \neq \emptyset\}$$

in which $\mathcal{A}(s)$ is the set of manual annotations allocated to the translations of s. We will subsequently draw the line between a precision only based on exact translations (P_E) and a precision based on exact or accurate translations (P_{EA}).

6.4.1.1.3. Usability (U)

By usability, we mean the fraction of source terms for which the system was able to translate at least one exact translation. Usability is given by the multiplication of coverage by precision:

$$U = \frac{|SC|}{|S|} = C \times P \qquad [6.3]$$

From now on, we will also draw the line between U_E (only exact translations) and U_{EA} (exact or acceptable translations).

6.4.1.1.4. Results obtained

The results obtained are given in Table 6.3. Let us note that the generation is not as good for English–German: both in terms of coverage (40 vs. 36%) and in terms of precision (48 vs. 59%). It is hard to compare this to other works on the machine translation of monolexical units since the approaches and the data used are so different (focalization on a specific morphological structure and use of translation examples). For example, [CAR 05] obtains 94% precision, and all the terms have at least one translation. However, [CAR 05] only focuses on the translation of prefixed words. [HAR 12] also obtain a very high precision (between 96 and 98%) for a smaller coverage (30–37%) but they only focus on the translation of neoclassical compounds. For compound nouns, [GAR 08] obtain an average of 19% precision and 13% coverage over nine language pairs. We suggest, in section 6.4.2, comparing our method to approaches which target a single type of morphological structure.

	C	P_E	U_E	P_{EA}	U_{EA}
EN-FR	.40	.59	.24	.69	.28
EN-DE	.36	.48	.17	.56.	.20

Table 6.3. A posteriori *evaluation of translation generation*

6.4.1.2. A priori *reference*

This reference is a bilingual lexicon obtained by matching the entries of medical meta-thesaurus UMLS with the texts in our corpus (see section 5.4.1). We note SR the set of source terms belonging to this lexicon. The evaluation measures are the standard precision, recall and F1-measure measures.

6.4.1.2.1. Precision (P)

Precision indicates the fraction of terms ST for which the system could generate at least one translation which matches the one given by the UMLS.

$$P = \frac{|SR|}{|ST|} \qquad [6.4]$$

$$SR = \{s : s \in ST, \mathcal{T}(s) \cap \mathcal{R}(s) \neq \emptyset\}$$

in which $\mathcal{T}(s)$ is the set of translations of s and $\mathcal{R}(s)$ is the set of translations of s given by the UMLS.

As we mentioned in section 4.4, if we only use the UMLS translations, we lose out on the cases in which the system has generated a correct translation. For example, for the term *mastectomy*, our system generated the translations *mastektomie*, *entfernung des brust*, *abschnitt ein brust*, *ablation der brust* which are all correct translations.

Yet, the translation given by UMLS is *brustamputation*, which was not generated by our system.

Therefore, we also suggest calculating the precisions P_E and P_{EA}. P_E takes into account the translations given by UMLS and the translations annotated as exact. P_{EA} takes into account the translations given by UMLS and the translations annotated exact and accurate by the judges. Table 6.4 gives examples of translations annotated exact or accurate by the judges but not found in the UMLS.

SOURCE TERM	UMLS TRANSLATION	GENERATED TRANSLATION	ANNOTATION
heterozigozity	heterozygot (DE)	heterozygozity	exact
radiography	roentgen (DE)	radiograpisch	accurate
lumpectomy	ablation d'une tumeur (FR)	lumpectomie	exact
co-repressors	co-répresseur (FR)	corépression	accurate

Table 6.4. *Differences between the* a priori *and* a posteriori *references*

6.4.1.2.2. Recall (R)

Recall indicates the fraction of source terms for which the system was able to generate at least one translation which matches the one given by the UMLS:

$$R = \frac{|SR|}{|S|} \quad [6.5]$$

We also calculate R_E and R_{EA} from the translations annotated exact and/or accurate.

6.4.1.2.3. F1-measure (F1)

Finally, the F1-measure accounts for the compromise between precision and recall:

$$F1 = 2 \times \frac{P \times R}{P + R} \quad [6.6]$$

We also calculate $F1_E$ and $F1_{EA}$ from P_E, R_E and P_{EA}, R_{EA}.

6.4.1.2.4. Results obtained

The results obtained with the *a priori* evaluation are given in Table 6.5. We found very good levels of precision (between 0.8 and 0.7 when using only the UMLS translations), whereas in the case of the *a posteriori* evaluation, precision was between 0.59 and 0.48. The difference between precision P and precisions P_E and P_{EA}, which take into account the exact and accurate translations, shows how only using the UMLS translations eliminates part of the correct translations generated by the system. For example, in the case of P_E, precision levels go from 0.8 to 0.94 in

French and from 0.7 to 0.88 in German. Once more, we can see that the results are not as good in German as they are in French, even though this is not as strong for the *a posteriori* evaluation.

The *a priori* reference enables us to compare our approach to data-driven approaches which also evaluate their algorithms against the UMLS. One of the advantages of these approaches is that just like in our method, they do not target a specific type of morphological construction. However, they require many translation examples. [CLA 09] obtains better results: 88% precision and 88% recall on very close languages (Portuguese → Spanish) and 58% precision and 58% recall on languages further apart (English → Russian). [LAN 09]'s results are not as good: 57% precision and 19% recall for the translation from French into English; 63% precision and 23% recall from the translation from Spanish into English. [CLA 11], who translate from French into Japanese, obtain 63% precision and 45% recall if they only count the translations found in the UMLS. They obtain 89% precision and 64% recall if they take into account all the correct translations generated by their algorithm (their results are then similar to ours).

	P	R	F1	P_E	R_E	$F1_E$	P_{EA}	R_{EA}	$F1_{EA}$
EN-FR	.80	.52	.63	.94	.62	.75	.95	.63	.76
EN-DE	.70	.51	.59	.88	.64	.74	.89	.66	.76

Table 6.5. A priori *evaluation of translation generation*

We have carried out several experiments meant to highlight the usefulness of the generation strategies and the different linguistic resources. For each experiment, we present the results of the *a posteriori* and *a priori* evaluation. The experiments focus on:

– the usefulness of the model's genericity (section 6.4.2);

– the usefulness of the linguistic resources (section 6.4.3);

– the usefulness of the fallback strategy (section 6.4.4);

– the usefulness of fertile translations (section 6.4.5);

– the usefulness of the popular science corpus (section 6.4.6).

Finally, we conclude with a qualitative analysis of the system's silences and errors (section 6.4.7).

6.4.2. *Model genericity influence*

In this experiment, we compare our system to approaches which only try to translate a specific type of morphological construction or which are only based on the identification of cognates. We chose the following four bases for comparison.

Prefixing – This approach only translates prefixed words. The source term is split (when possible) into prefix + lexical base, the prefix is translated using the morpheme translation table (we only retain translations which are themselves prefixes), and the lexical base is translated with the general language dictionary. Lexical base and prefix are concatenated into a single word. This approximatively corresponds to [CAR 09b]'s approach.

The source words made of a prefix and free lexical stem represent 31% of the French *a posteriori* reference (32% of the German one) and 25% of the French *a priori* reference (34% of the German one).

Neoclassical compound – This approach only translates words built by neoclassical compounding. The source term is split (when possible) into a set of combining forms or of combining forms and words, the combining forms are translated with the morpheme translation table (we only retain translations which are themselves combining forms), and the words are translated with the general language dictionary. All the translated morphemes are concatenated into a single word. The order of the elements is not preserved. This approximately corresponds to [HAR 12]'s approach, except they draw the line between initial elements and final elements and the order of the elements is preserved.

The source words made of at least one combining form and of free lexical bases or other combining forms represent 18% of the French and German *a posteriori* reference and 56% of the French *a priori* reference (52% for the German one).

Word compound – This approach only translates words created by word compounding. The source term is split (when possible) into a set of simple words, and the words are translated with the general language dictionary. The translations can be concatenated into a single word or into several words. The order of the words is not preserved. This is an approximate match to [WEL 11]'s approach, if only that they base themselves on predefined translation templates.

The source words made of several lexical stems represent 48% of the French *a posteriori* reference (49% of the German one) and 25% of the French *a priori* reference (21% of the German one).

Cognate – This approach translates any word by assigning as translation its cognate when it exists. The cognates are identified with the method described in section 5.6.6.

We have compared these four "basic" methods with our system which take into account several morphological structures and are also based on resources which manage variation. Results are given in Tables 6.6, 6.7 (*a posteriori* reference) and 6.8, 6.9 (*a priori* reference).

6.4.2.1. A posteriori *evaluation*

For the *a posteriori* reference, we see that most of the other methods are more precise than ours. However, these methods generate very few translations, which in the end means that our method generates the lexicon which is most usable (in the sense given by our usability measure U), no matter the language pair.

	C	P_E	U_E	P_{EA}	U_{EA}
Neoclassical compound	.03	**.95**	.03	**1**	.03
Cognate	.13	.66	.08	.81	.10
Noun compound	.05	.63	.03	.65	.03
Prefixing	.02	.90	.02	.97	.02
Our method	**.40**	.59	**.24**	.69	**.28**

Table 6.6. *Comparing with other generation methods,* a posteriori *evaluation, English–French*

	C	P_E	U_E	P_{EA}	U_{EA}
Neoclassical compound	.03	**.96**	.02	**.98**	.02
Cognate	.10	.58	.06	.66	.07
Noun compound	.04	.55	.02	.62	.03
Prefixing	.03	.86	.02	.92	.03
Our method	**.36**	.48	**.17**	.56	**.20**

Table 6.7. *Comparing with other generation methods,* a posteriori *evaluation, English–German*

If we compare the four basic methods to each other, we observe that neoclassical compounds are the most precise, closely followed by prefixing. These two methods, however, have very low coverage, which can be explained by the fact that our list of source terms contains mostly word compounds. The most useful method of all four appears to be the cognate method. It is the one with the best usability scores (U). Compounds and cognates have a relatively low level of precision. The results are better for cognates when accurate translations are taken into account; indeed, many identified cognates are morphological variants (*aromatherapist* → *aromathérapie*, *comprehensively* → *comprehensive*). Error cases typically involve prefixed words such as *pretreatment* → *treatment* or combinations with another very short word: *fulvestrant-er* → *fulvestrant*.

For word compounds, errors are mainly caused by fertile translations often combined with a different word order than the source term's order, for example:

– *low-risk* is translated by *bas car cela risquer* ('low because at risk') which appears within the context "...*sauf si le nombre de plaquettes est trop* ***bas car cela risquerait*** *de* ..." ('unless the number of platelets is too low because it risks');

– *strong-smelling* is translated by *fort pour bien sentir* ('strong to feel well') which appears in the context "*Presser assez* ***fort pour bien sentir*** *le tissu mammaire*" ('Press strongly so that you can feel the breast tissue').

Nonetheless, certain translations have a rather close meaning to the source terms' meaning: *milk-producing* is translated by *lait produire* ('milk produce') (context: "*canal évacuant le* ***lait produit*** *par la glande mammaire.*", 'duct that evacuates the milk produced by the mammary gland').

6.4.2.2. A priori *evaluation*

The results obtained with the *a priori* reference are similar to those with the *a posteriori* evaluation: the other methods are more precise, but in the end we obtain the best F1-measure. We also consistently obtain the best recall. The precision of cognates is always much higher when we take into account the exact or accurate translations. Prefixing and compounding have high levels of precision, but the cognates remain the best method (of the four basic methods) giving the best F1-measure.

The difference with the *a posteriori* method is that in this case, word compounds obtain very good results. In French, the translations given by the UMLS are immediately found for the four word compounds: *workload* → *charge de travail, lifestyle* → *style de vie, viewpoint* → *point de vue, half-life* → *demivie*. For German, it is hard to draw conclusions: a single word compound found a translation and while the generated translation is exact, it is not the one suggested by the UMLS: *child-birth* is translated by *geburt ein kind* ("birth of a child", translation annotated as exact), whereas the UMLS suggests *geburt* ("birth").[3]

	P	R	F1	P_E	R_E	$F1_E$	P_{EA}	R_{EA}	$F1_{EA}$
Neoclassical compound	.83	.20	.32	.97	.23	.37	**1**	.24	.38
Cognate	.76	.37	.50	.89	.44	.59	.92	.45	.61
Noun compound	**1**	.03	.06	**1**	.03	.06	**1**	.03	.06
Prefixing	.56	.04	.07	.89	.06	.12	**1**	.07	.13
Our method	.80	**.52**	**.63**	.94	**.62**	**.75**	.95	**.63**	**.76**

Table 6.8. *Comparing with other generation methods,* a priori *evaluation, English–French*

6.4.2.3. *Synthesis*

We can conclude that it is useful to try and translate several types of morphological structures while relying on resources which can manage the variation rather than focus on a single type of construction: even if the translations are not as precise, in the end, the number of source terms which returned at least one correct translations is higher. The cognates appear to be a useful method to complete a bilingual lexicon.

Let us note that our system is not equivalent to the union of the four methods to which it has been compared. The wide coverage of our system can be explained by the

3 "*Die* ***Geburt eines Kindes*** *läutet umfassende Veränderungen in der weiblichen Brust ein.*", "The birth of a child announces major changes for women's breasts".

various translation strategies that we use and which are not used by the four methods to which we compared our system:

– None of the four methods uses resources meant to manage variation. For example, the translation method based on prefixing would not be able to draw a parallel between *bioavailable* and *biodisponibilité*.

– Apart from the method based on cognates, the dictionary of cognates is not used by any other method. For example, the translation method based on word compounds would not be able to translate *taxane-treated* as *traitement par taxane* since the translation of *taxane* only exists in the dictionary of cognates.

– Only the translation method based on word compounds generates fertile translations. The other methods do not generate such translations. For example, the method based on the neoclassical compounds would not find any equivalence between *tumorectomy* and *ablation de la tumeur*, and the method based on prefixing would not find any equivalence between *pre-chemotherapy* and *avant la chimiothérapie*.

– None of the methods to which we have compared our own suggests a fallback strategy. The equivalence *uniformly* → *uniforme* can only be found by our method.

– Finally, our method also proposes to translate suffixed terms. This enables us to find translations such as *retrospectively* → *façon retrospective*.

	P	R	F1	P_E	R_E	$F1_E$	P_{EA}	R_{EA}	$F1_{EA}$
Neoclassical compound	**.80**	.18	.29	.95	.21	.35	.95	.21	.35
Cognate	.62	.26	.36	.86	.36	.50	.89	.37	.52
Noun compound	0.0	0.0	0.0	**1**	.01	.02	**1**	.01	.02
Prefixing	.75	.07	.12	**1**	.09	.16	**1**	.09	.16
Our method	.70	**.51**	**.59**	.88	**.64**	**.74**	.89	**.66**	**.76**

Table 6.9. *Comparing with other generation methods,* a priori *evaluation, English–German*

6.4.3. *Linguistic resources influence*

In this experiment, we wanted to evaluate the usefulness of resources which help manage variation (thesaurus and morphological families) and of the dictionary of cognates which can increase the size of the bilingual lexicon.

We carried out four tests whose results are in Tables 6.10 to 6.13:

Basic – The translation was carried out only with the general language dictionary and the morpheme translation table.

Basic + dictionary of cognates – General language dictionary, morpheme translation table and dictionary of cognates.

Basic + morphological families – General language dictionary, morpheme translation table and morphological families.

Basic + thesaurus – General language dictionary, morpheme translation table and thesaurus.

All the resources – General language dictionary, morpheme translation table, dictionary of cognates, morphological family and thesaurus.

6.4.3.1. A posteriori *evaluation*

The results observed are almost identical no matter the language pair. The basic method is the most precise (except in the case in which the accurate translations are taken into account in French: in that case, the combination basic + cognates is as precise as the basic resources on their own, since the cognates identify a good number of morphologically derived words, e.g. *aromatherapist* → *aromatherapy*). As resources are added, coverage increases and precision decreases, but in the end, the usability is higher, except for the combination basic + thesaurus: the latter does not generate a lexicon which is more usable than the basic resources themselves. The dictionary of cognates and morphological families are very useful resources and provide many translations which are judged to be accurate.

	C	P_E	U_E	P_{EA}	U_{EA}
Basic	.16	**.73**	.12	**.77**	.12
Basic + dictionary of cognates	.28	.71	.19	**.77**	.21
Basic + morphological families	.27	.56	.15	.66	.18
Basic + thesaurus	.17	.69	.12	.72	.13
All the resources	**.40**	.59	**.24**	.69	**.28**

Table 6.10. *Linguistic resource usefulness,* a posteriori *evaluation, English → French*

	C	P_E	U_E	P_{EA}	U_{EA}
Basic	.15	**.60**	.09	**.63**	.10
Basic + dictionary of cognates	.27	.56	.15	.61	.16
Basic + morphological families	.24	.48	.12	.57	.14
Basic + thesaurus	.17	.55	.09	.60	.10
All the resources	**.36**	.48	**.17**	.56	**.20**

Table 6.11. *Linguistic resource usefulness,* a posteriori *evaluation, English → German*

6.4.3.2. A priori *evaluation*

If we only count the generated translations which correspond to the ones found in the UMLS, we have the same results for the two language pairs. Overall, the best F1-measure is always obtained by combining all the resources. However, combining basic + cognates can lead to a better precision than just the basic one. If we compare the F1-measures, we observe that morphological families and thesaurus have little impact compared to the basic one on its own. The combination basic + cognates and the combination of all the resources obtain similar F1-measures (especially in English–German).

	P	R	F1	P_E	R_E	$F1_E$	P_{EA}	R_{EA}	$F1_{EA}$
Basic	.78	.29	.42	.93	.34	.50	**.98**	.36	.52
Basic + dictionary of cognates	**.81**	.51	.62	**.94**	.59	.72	.95	.60	.73
Basic + morphological families	.76	.29	.42	**.94**	.37	.53	**.98**	.38	.55
Basic + thesaurus	.77	.29	.42	**.94**	.35	.51	**.98**	.37	.53
All the resources	.80	**.52**	**.63**	**.94**	**.62**	**.75**	.95	**.63**	**.76**

Table 6.12. *Linguistic resource usefulness,* a priori *evaluation, English → French*

	P	R	F1	P_E	R_E	$F1_E$	P_{EA}	R_{EA}	$F1_{EA}$
Basic	.71	.27	.39	**.94**	.36	.52	.94	.36	.52
Basic + dictionary of cognates	**.75**	.49	**.59**	.93	.61	**.74**	**.95**	**.62**	.75
Basic + morphological families	.67	.29	.40	.87	.38	.53	.90	.39	.54
Basic + thesaurus	.63	.27	.38	.87	.37	.52	.87	.37	.52
All the resources	.70	**.51**	**.59**	.88	**.64**	**.74**	.89	.66	**.76**

Table 6.13. *Linguistic resource usefulness,* a priori *evaluation, English → German*

6.4.3.3. *Synthesis*

Overall, we see that adding new resources helps translate more terms but lowers precision. The thesaurus is not very useful. As for the other resources, we note a difference between the results of the *a posteriori* evaluation and the *a priori* evaluation. In the *a posteriori* evaluation, cognates and morphologically derived words have a positive impact, but the best results are obtained by combining all the resources. In the *a priori* evaluation, the morphologically derived words have a small impact (especially in German), only the cognates are genuinely useful. We believe that this difference is due to the nature of the source terms to be translated. In the *a priori* reference, most of the terms to be translated have a spelling which is close to their translations (e.g. *translocation* → *translokation, cytogenetic* → *cytogénétique*), which works well with the identification of translation through cognates. In the *a posteriori* reference, we find many more word compounds and words whose spelling is not close to their translation (*tumor-margin* → *tumorrand*). For example, compounds work well with the generation of fertile translations; moreover, fertility often involves a morphological variation, e.g. *cytoprotection* → *protéger la cellule*.

6.4.4. *Fallback strategy influence*

In this section, we evaluate the usefulness of the fallback strategy described in section 6.2.1.2. When a term could not be decomposed or one of the components is not translated, this strategy enables us to try and find a translation directly either by using the dictionary of cognates or by combining with a variation resource (synonyms and morphological family) and a bilingual resource (general language dictionary and cognates). For example, *exactly* was translated into *exakt* by going from *exactly* to *exact* using English morphological families, and then from *exact* to *exakt* by using English–German cognates. Results are given in Tables 6.14 to 6.17.

6.4.4.1. A posteriori *evaluation*

Overall, the fallback strategy enables us to increase the coverage with a slight decrease in precision which does not have any impact on the final usability of the lexicon. The strategy is rather efficient with cognates for a translation from French to English, but its usefulness is not obvious for German. There is no clear improvement for the synonyms and morphological families. However, there is a clear impact when all the resources are combined: the usability increases by 3 points for German and 4 points for French (exact and accurate translations). The combination of all the resources leads to translations by using the morphologically derived words as well as the cognate, as in the example above (exactly → exakt).

	C	P_E	U_E	P_{EA}	U_{EA}
Basic + Cognate dictionary − fallback	.24	**.72**	.17	**.79**	.19
Basic + Cognate dictionary + fallback	**.28**	.71	**.19**	.77	**.21**
Basic + morphological families − fallback	.26	**.57**	.15	.66	.17
Basic + morphological families + fallback	**.27**	.56	.15	.66	**.18**
Basic + thesaurus − fallback	.17	**.70**	.12	**.73**	.12
Basic + thesaurus + fallback	.17	.69	.12	.72	**.13**
All the resources − fallback	.35	**.60**	.21	.69	.24
All the resources + fallback	**.40**	.59	**.24**	.69	**.28**

Table 6.14. *Fallback strategy usefulness,*
a posteriori *evaluation, English → French*

	C	P_E	U_E	P_{EA}	U_{EA}
Basic + dictionary of cognates − fallback	.24	**.58**	.14	**.62**	.15
Basic + dictionary of cognates + fallback	**.27**	.56	**.15**	.61	**.16**
Basic + morphological families − fallback	.22	**.49**	.11	.56	.12
Basic + morphological families + fallback	**.24**	.48	**.12**	**.57**	**.14**
Basic + thesaurus − fallback	.17	**.56**	.09	**.61**	.10
Basic + thesaurus + fallback	.17	.55	.09	.60	.10
All the resources − fallback	.31	**.50**	.15	.56	.17
All the resources + fallback	**.36**	.48	**.17**	.56	**.20**

Table 6.15. *Fallback strategy usefulness,* a posteriori *evaluation, English → German*

6.4.4.2. A priori *evaluation*

We observe the same phenomenon overall if we base ourselves on the UMLS: a visible impact with the cognates (especially in German), a small impact with the morphological families and the thesaurus, a stronger impact obtained when combining all the resources. However, in this case, the impact is much clearer for English–German than for French-German: when we take into account the exact and accurate translations, the $F1_{EA}$ measure increases by 5 points for German and 1 point for French.

	P	R	F1	P_E	R_E	$F1_E$	P_{EA}	R_{EA}	$F1_{EA}$
Base + dictionary of cognates − fallback	**.82**	.48	.61	**.96**	.56	.71	**.97**	.57	.72
Base + dictionary of cognates + fallback	.81	**.51**	**.62**	.94	**.59**	**.72**	.95	**.60**	**.73**
Base + morphological families − fallback	.75	.29	.41	.94	.36	.52	.98	.37	.54
Base + morphological families + fallback	**.76**	**.29**	**.42**	.94	**.37**	**.53**	.98	**.38**	**.55**
Base + thesaurus − fallback	.77	.29	.42	.94	.35	.51	.98	.37	.53
Base + thesaurus + fallback	.77	.29	.42	.94	.35	.51	.98	.37	.53
All the resources − fallback	.78	.48	.60	**.95**	.59	.73	**.97**	.60	.75
All the resources + fallback	**.80**	**.52**	**.63**	.94	**.62**	**.75**	.95	**.63**	**.76**

Table 6.16. *Fallback strategy usefulness,* a priori *evaluation, English → French*

6.4.4.3. *Synthesis*

Cognates and their combination with morphological families appear to be really useful. The usefulness of this fallback strategy is especially strong when translating into German.

6.4.5. *Fertile translations influence*

In this section, we carry out two comparisons:

Non-fertile vs. fertile translations – We compare here the quality of each type of translation: are the fertile translations more exact than the non-fertile translations? Do they generate more translations?

Non-fertile translations vs. all translations – We observe here the effect of adding fertile translations to a lexicon which would only be made of non-fertile translations: do fertile translations improve the final quality of the lexicon?

	P	R	F1	P_E	R_E	$F1_E$	P_{EA}	R_{EA}	$F1_{EA}$
Basic + dictionary of cognates − fallback	**.76**	.46	.57	.93	.56	.69	.93	.56	.69
Basic + dictionary of cognates + fallback	.75	**.49**	**.59**	.93	**.61**	**.74**	**.95**	**.62**	**.75**
Basic + morphological families − fallback	.67	.29	.40	.87	.38	.53	.90	.39	.54
Basic + morphological families + fallback	.67	.29	.40	.87	.38	.53	.90	.39	.54
Basic + thesaurus − fallback	**.67**	.27	.38	**.89**	.36	.51	**.89**	.36	.51
Basic + thesaurus + fallback	.63	.27	.38	.87	**.37**	**.52**	.87	**.37**	**.52**
All the resources − fallback	**.72**	.48	.57	.87	.58	.69	.88	**.59**	.71
All the resources + fallback	.70	**.51**	**.59**	**.88**	**.64**	**.74**	**.89**	.66	**.76**

Table 6.17. *Fallback strategy usefulness,* a priori *evaluation, English → German*

6.4.5.1. A posteriori *evaluation*

No matter the language (Tables 6.18 and 6.19), fertile translations are of clearly lesser quality than non-fertile translations (precision loses between 6 and 20 points in English–French; between 32 and 39 points for English–German). Moreover, fertile translations do not lead to the generation of a greater number of translations than non-fertile translations.

However, this type of translation is useful when combined with non-fertile translations since fertile translations provide a good complement: they help improve coverage, and although they lower precision, in the end the extracted lexicon is much more usable. We see that fertile translations are more useful in English–French than in English–German: increasing the coverage by 16 points and lowering the precision by 1 point (exact translations) in French; increasing the coverage by 12 points and lowering the precision by 10 points (exact translations) in German.

	C	P_E	U_E	P_{EA}	U_{EA}
Non-fertile translations	.24	**.58**	**.14**	**.75**	**.18**
Fertile translations	.24	.52	.12	.55	.13
Non-fertile translations	.24	.58	.14	**.75**	.18
All translations	**.40**	**.59**	**. 24**	.69	**.28**

Table 6.18. *Fertile translation usefulness,* a posteriori *evaluations, English–French*

	C	P_E	U_E	P_{EA}	U_{EA}
Non-fertile translations	**.24**	**.58**	**.14**	**.69**	**.16**
Fertile translations	.20	.26	.05	.30	.06
Non-fertile translations	.24	**.58**	.14	**.69**	.16
All translations	**.36**	.48	**.17**	.56	**.20**

Table 6.19. *Fertile translation usefulness,* a posteriori *evaluation, English–German*

Tables 6.20 and 6.21 detail the impact of fertile translations when they are combined with non-fertile translations. For the translation of French into English, most of the fertile translations that are found for source tems which have no non-fertile translation are correct. This is not the case, however, for German, where in three-quarters of the cases, fertile translations are wrong. When fertile translations are found for non-fertile translations, the lexicon can only profit from it:

– If there is no non-fertile translations and if:

- the fertile translations lead to at least one correct translations, precision increases;

- none of the fertile translations are correct, precision stays the same.

– If there is at least one correct non-fertile translation and if:

- there is a correct fertile translation: precision remains stable, but a variant has been found;

- no correct fertile translation has been found: precision also remains stable.

433 source terms with fertile translations(s)
↪ **289 (67%) had no translation**
↪ 160 (55%) cases in which fertile translations returned a correct translation★
↪ 129 (45%) cases in which fertile translations returned noise
↪ **144 (33%) already had a (non-fertile) translation**
↪ 16 (11%) cases in which the fertile translations create a correction♦
↪ 60 (42%) cases in which fertile translations add a variant†
↪ 68 (47%) cases in which fertile translations have no effect∗

Table 6.20. *Detailed impact of fertile translations,* a posteriori *evaluation, English–French*

371 source terms with fertile translation(s)
↪ **219 (30%) had no translation**
↪ 57 (26%) cases in which the fertile translations returned on correct translation★
↪ 162 (74%) cases in which the fertile translations returned noise
↪ **152 (70%) already had a (non-fertile) translation**
↪ 11 (7%) cases in which the fertile translations create a correction♦
↪ 162 (28%) cases in which fertile translations add a variant†
↪ 99 (65%) cases in which fertile translations have no effect*

★exact or accurate

♦the fertile translations contain one correct translation when all the non-fertile translations were false

†there is a correct fertile translation and a correct non-fertile translation

*all the fertile translations are false and either all the non-fertile translations are false or one of the non-fertile translations is correct

Table 6.21. *Detailed impact of fertile translations,* a posteriori *evaluation, English–German*

6.4.5.2. A priori *evaluation*

Tables 6.22 and 6.23 show that fertile translations are only a very useful complement for French (from 4 to 3 points higher with the F1-measure depending on whether one is only using the UMLS translations, the exact translations or the exact and accurate translations). Here is the detail of the fertile translations obtained in French (we add an asterisk for the fertile translations which correspond to the UMLS translation):

	P	R	F1	P_E	R_E	$F1_E$	P_{EA}	R_{EA}	$F1_{EA}$
Non-fertile translations	**.77**	**.48**	**.60**	**.92**	**.58**	**.71**	**.95**	**.60**	**.73**
Fertile translations	.38	.05	.08	.75	.10	.17	.75	.10	.17
Non-fertile translations	.77	.48	.60	.92	.58	.71	.95	.60	.73
All translations	**.80**	**.52**	**.63**	**.94**	**.62**	**.75**	.95	**.63**	**.76**

Table 6.22. *Fertile translation usefulness,* a priori *evaluation, English–French*

	P	R	F1	P_E	R_E	$F1_E$	P_{EA}	R_{EA}	$F1_{EA}$
Non-fertile translations	**.74**	**.51**	**.61**	**.90**	**.62**	**.74**	**.92**	**.63**	**.75**
Fertile translations	0.0	0.0	0.0	.31	.06	.09	.38	.07	.11
Non-fertile translations	**.74**	.51	**.61**	**.90**	.62	.74	**.92**	.63	.75
All translations	.70	.51	.59	.88	**.64**	.74	.89	**.66**	**.76**

Table 6.23. *Fertile translation usefulness,* a priori *evaluation, English–German*

At least one correct fertile translation[4] *– no non-fertile*:

– *g-protein* → *protéine g**;

– *lifestyle* → *style de vie** ('style of life').

At least one correct fertile translation and one correct non-fertile translation:

– *cardiotoxicity* → *toxicité cardiaque** ('cardiac toxicity'), *cardiotoxicité* ('cardiotixicity);

– *cytogenetic* → *génétique de cellule*[5] ('genetic of the cell'), *cytogénétique.*

Incorrect fertile translations and at least one correct non-fertile translation:

– *mammaplasty* → *plastique de sein* ('plastic of breast'), *mammoplastie*;

– *overweight* → *supérieur avec et sans charge* ('superior with and without charge), *surcharge* ('overweight').

Incorrect fertile translations and incorrect non-fertile translations:

– *in-patient* → *pas malade, non malade, inverse chez le patient, [...] impatience* ("not ill, opposite in the patient, impatience").

As for the translation into German (Table 6.23), the usefulness of fertile translation is unclear: the F1-measure varies from -2 to +1 when the fertile translations are added to the lexicon. Here are detailed the fertile translations obtained in German:

At least one correct fertile translation – no correct non-fertile translation:

– *childbirth* → *geburt ein kind* "birth of a child";

– *hypercalcaemia* → *zu viel calcium in das blut* "too much calcium in the blood".

At least one correct fertile translation and one correct non-fertile translation:

– *chemo-radiotherapy* → *strahlen und chemotherapie "radiation and chemotherapy", radiochemotherapy, chemoradiotherapy*;

– *self-examination* → *selbst untersuchen* ('self-examine'), *selbstuntersuchung* ('self-examination').

Incorrect fertile translations and at least one correct non-fertile translation:

– *childhood* → *zustand der kind "state of the child", kindheit*;

4 exact or accurate.

5 **cytogenetic** abnormalities / instability → anomalie / instabilité **génétique des cellules**.

– *gynaecomastia → frau brust "woman breast", frau mit brust "woman with breast", [...] gynäkomastie.*

Incorrect fertile translations – no non-fertile translation:

– *breathless → ohne atmen* "without breathing";

– *ultrasound → über die fest* "on the solid".

Incorrect fertile and translations and incorrect non-fertile translations:

– *workplace→ stellen sich noch die aufgabe "to make the task again", aufgabestellung "task".*

6.4.5.3. *Synthesis*

No matter the type of evaluation, fertile translations are less interesting in German. A partial explanation could be that the English–German corpus is less comparable than the English–French corpus (0.45 vs. 0.74): the English–German translations are in general of a lower quality than the English–French translations.

Another explanation involves the morphological type of the languages involved. Indeed, as a Latin language, French has a higher tendency to use phrases made of several words (typically NOUN$_1$ PREPOSITION NOUN$_2$ or NOUN ADJECTIVE structures), whereas English and German are German languages, and will tend toward word compounds (NOUN$_2$+NOUN$_1$ or ADJECTIVE +NOUN structures). For example, compounds, such as *anthracycline-containing* (English) or *Anthracyclin-enthaltende* (German), are common in these languages, whereas in French, there is no non-fertile translations for these compounds: a correct translation would be *contenant de l'anthracycline*, and non-fertile equivalents, such as **anthracycline-contenant* or **contenant-anthracycline*, go against French word formation rules.

6.4.6. *Popular science corpus influence*

In this section, we wish to evaluate the usefulness of integrating popular science texts to a specialized corpus. The terms to be translated are usually terms that tend to belong to the academic discourse, or at least this is what we had observed in our data (see Table 6.24).

Yet, when we use comparable corpora, it is mainly because there is a lack of parallel data in the languages that we wish to deal with. However, sometimes, even comparable data are hard to find in large enough quantities. As we saw when gathering the German corpus, it was hard to gather specialized texts that were representative of the *academic* discourse. Is it a good choice to increase the size of the corpus by adding specialized texts which could belong to the *popular science* discourse? Is there a risk of lowering the quality of the extracted lexicon?

source terms only found in academic texts	69%
source terms only found in popular science texts	20%
source terms found in academic and popular science texts	11%

Table 6.24. *Presence of the source terms in the corpora*

We compared the following situations:

Academic corpus – Takes into account only the translations found in the academic corpus.

Popular science corpus – Takes into account only the translations found in the popular science corpus.

Whole corpus – Takes into account the translations found in the entire corpus.

Tables 6.25 to 6.28 indicate the results obtained. Overall, when we compare an academic corpus to a popular science corpus, the results are always better in the academic corpus, both in terms of coverage/precision (*a posteriori* evaluation) and in terms of precision/recall (*a priori* evaluation). It is difficult to come to a conclusion with the English–French corpus since the academic corpus is larger than the popular science corpus:[6] there are more chances of finding translations in it. On the contrary, for the English–German pair, the sizes are comparable, and it is clear that the academic texts are more interesting than the popular science ones.

When we compare the academic corpus with the whole corpus, the results show that it is useful to use popular science texts to increase an academic corpus. In the case of German, adding the popular science text leads to a slight decrease in precision but in the end, the quality of the lexicon is higher with the whole corpus (usability for the *a posteriori* reference, F1-measure for the *a priori* reference).

6.4.6.1. *Fertility and discourse type*

We also wanted to know if we could establish a link between the discourse type and the fertility of the translations. For example, we can suppose that the popular science texts have more fertile translations. To verify this theory, we have compared the number of times in which fertile and non-fertile translations were found in the

6 The French academic corpus has 1.45 times more words than the English popular science corpus (see section 5.2).

academic corpus and in the popular science corpus. Since the academic and popular corpora's sizes were different, we normalized this count with the number of distinct words in each corpus:

$$freq(f,c) = \frac{|t \in f \cap c|}{|words(c)|} \qquad [6.7]$$

in which f is the type of translation (i.e. fertile or non-fertile), c is a corpus (i.e. academic or popular science corpus), $|t \in f \cap c|$ is the number of exact or accurate translations of type f found in corpus c and $|words(c)|$ is the number of distinct words in corpus c.

	C	P_E	U_E	P_{EA}	U_{EA}
Popular science corpus	.25	.54	.14	.64	.16
Academic corpus	.35	.58	.20	.68	.24
Whole corpus	**.40**	**.59**	**.24**	**.69**	**.28**

Table 6.25. *Popular science corpus usefulness,* a posteriori *evaluation, English → French*

	C	P_E	U_E	P_{EA}	U_{EA}
Popular science corpus	.26	.44	.11	.53	.14
Academic corpus	.29	**.49**	.14	**.57**	.16
Whole corpus	**.36**	.48	**.17**	.56	**.20**

Table 6.26. *Popular science corpus usefulness,* a posteriori *evaluation, English → German*

	P	R	F1	P_E	R_E	$F1_E$	P_{EA}	R_{EA}	$F1_{EA}$
Popular science corpus	.76	.31	.44	**.96**	.39	.55	**.96**	.39	.55
Academic corpus	.77	.44	.56	.94	.53	.68	**.96**	.54	.69
Whole corpus	**.80**	**.52**	**.63**	.94	**.62**	**.75**	.95	**.63**	**.76**

Table 6.27. *Popular science corpus usefulness,* a priori *evaluation, English → French*

Figures 6.1 and 6.2 indicate the distribution of each type of translation in each discourse type. No matter the language, the popular science corpus contains more fertile translations than the academic corpus.

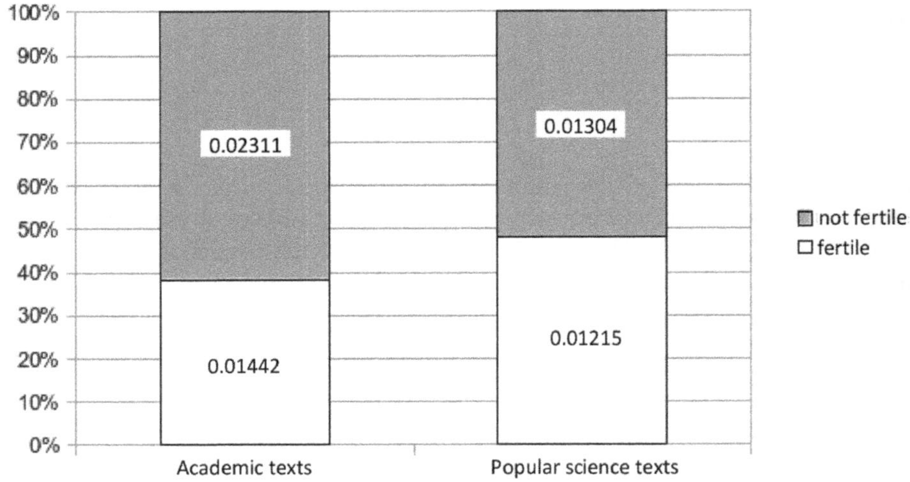

Figure 6.1. *Distribution of fertile and non-fertile translations in academic and popular science texts, English → French*

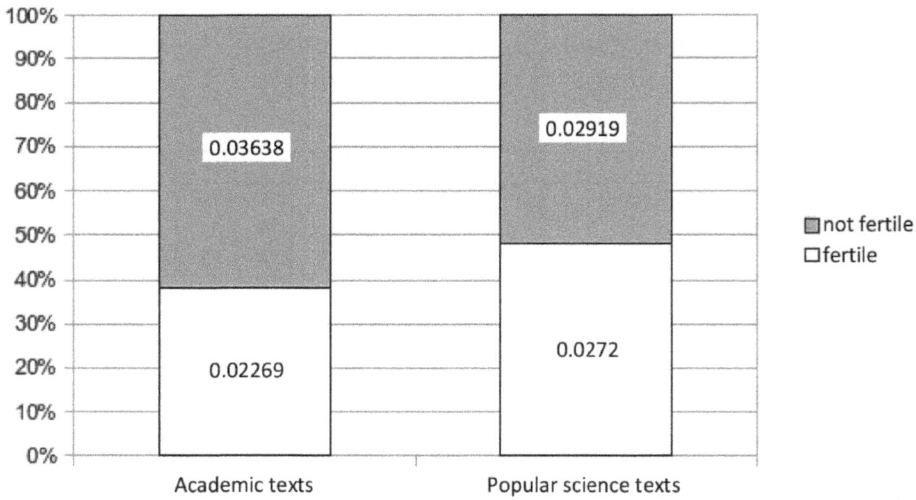

Figure 6.2. *Distribution of fertile and non-fertile translations in academic and popular science texts, English → German*

	P	R	F1	P_E	R_E	$F1_E$	P_{EA}	R_{EA}	$F1_{EA}$
Popular science corpus	.64	.36	.46	.86	.48	.61	.86	.48	.61
Academic corpus	.69	.47	.56	**.89**	.60	.72	**.90**	.61	.73
Whole corpus	**.70**	**.51**	**.59**	.88	**.64**	**.74**	.89	**.66**	**.76**

Table 6.28. *Popular science corpus usefulness,* a priori *evaluation, English → German*

6.4.7. *Qualitative analysis*

Our last analysis presents cases of silence (non-translated source terms) and noise (incorrect translations). For each language pair, the analyzed data consists of:

– 50 cases of silences randomly extracted from the UMLS translations which were not found by our system;

– 50 cases of mis-translations randomly extracted from the translations generated by our system and annotated as "false" or "close" by the judges.

6.4.7.1. *Silence analysis*

The results of the analysis are found in Table 6.29.

	EN-FR	EN-DE
Non-compositionality	20 (40%)	25 (50%)
↪ Same meaning, different morphological split	10	13
↪ No semantic correspondence	10	11
↪ Acronym	0	1
Translation absent from the resources	15 (30%)	18 (36%)
Semi-compositionality	12 (24%)	2 (4%)
↪ Close meaning	8	2
↪ Far meaning	4	0
Recomposition and selection	3 (6%)	5 (10%)
Total	50	50

Table 6.29. *Analysis of silence cases*

Most of the silence cases (from 40% to 48%) are due to cases which cannot be solved through compositional methods:

– Either the meaning of the source term or the target term is identical but the morphological split is different:

- *collarbone* → *klavikula*: two morphemes in English, a single one in German;

- *newborn* → *nourrisson*: two morphemes in English, a single one in French.

– Or the semantic split between the two languages is different, one of the terms has one or more elements of additional meaning:

- *ultrasonography* → *ultrashall*: additional morpheme *-graphy-* in the source language;

- *underam* → *achselhöle*: *achsel* approximately corresponds to *underarm* and *höle* does not have a match in the source term;

- *anti-emetic* → *médicaments antiémétiques*: *médicaments* has no match in the source term.

– Or the source term is translated by an acronym:

- *electrocardiogram* → *ekg*.

The second cause of silence is due to the coverage of our resources. Between 30% and 36% of the translations failed either because the term could not be split or one of the elements could not be translated and the fallback strategy failed:

– *mastectomy* → *brustamputation*: no correspondence between *-ectomy* and *amputation*;

– *pre-eclampsia* → *präeklampsie*: no correspondence between *pre-* and *prä-* or between *eclampsia* and *eklampsie*;

– *pharmacokinetics* → *pharmacocinétique*: no correspondence between *kinetics* and *cinétique*;

– *headache* → *maux de tête*: no correspondence between *ache* and *mal* (the dictionary only offers the phrase *faire mal*, "to hurt").

The third type of silence corresponds to cases of semi-compositionality: the number of morphemes is the same, and there is a translation correspondence between only some of the morphemes. For the other part of the morphemes, the semantic distance can be more or less pronounced:

– Close meaning (case of lexical divergence):

- *bloodstream* → *circulation sanguine*: *stream* means "courant" more than "circulation" ('traffic');

- *intra-abdominal* → *bauchhöhle*: *-intra-* means "inside", which is rather far from *höhle* ("cavity").

– Far meaning:

- *brachytherapie* → *curiethérapie*:*-brachy-* means "short, which does not last long" and *curie* come from the proper name *Curie* referring to Marie Curie;

- *abnormality* → *malformation*: *formation* is not the translation of *normality*, which would be *normalité*.

These cases mainly concern the English → French translation (24% vs. 4% for English → German).

The last cases of silence concern several recomposition and selection issues. For example, in German, we have not generated any intermediary *-s-* between the words of a compound, so we have been unable to find the translation of *workplace* (*arbeitsplatz*). And to this, we can add the issues liked with the pre-processing of texts: characters may have been badly encoded, the standardization of certain terms is poor, which prevents them from being matched, etc.

6.4.7.2. *Noise analysis*

The results of the analysis are provided in Table 6.30.

	EN-FR	EN-DE
Wrong translation of one of the components	41 (82%)	41 (82%)
↪ Meaning does not match the context	23	20
↪ Variant is too far	16	18
↪ Incorrect cognate	2	3
Insertion of stop words	8 (16%)	3 (6%)
↪ Wrong stop words	7	2
↪ Useless stop words	1	1
Element order	1 (2%)	6 (12%)
Total	50	50

Table 6.30. *Noise analysis*

The major part of the errors (82%) comes from wrongly translated components:

– The wrong translation can come from the general language dictionary or the morpheme translation table. It would then be a case of polysemy or of translations which are not valid within the context in which they have been found:

- *patient-related* → *patient et leur famille*: *related* means "*en rapport avec, relié*" ('linked to') but also "*proche, membre de la famille*" ('relatives');

- *gynecomastia* → *brust der frau*: *brust der frau* does indeed mean "woman's breast" and gynecomastia is indeed an overdevelopment of breasts in a man, but it is not the meaning taken on by this expression in the context: "*...Die **Brust der Frau** ist außerdem ein sekundäres Geschlechtsmerkmal...*" ("The woman's breast is also a secondary sexual characteristic").

– The wrong translation can come from variants (morphologically derived or synonyms) which often generate a translation whose meaning is too far from the source morpheme:

- *inactivate* → *inactivité*: although they are morphologically close, *inactivité* ('inactivity') cannot be considered as a correct translation of *inactivate* which would be "*désactiver*" in French;

- *incorrect* → *nicht zu ein verbesserung*: *verbesserung* means "correction" rather than *correct*. In the texts from the corpus, *nicht zu ein verbesserung* means "*not an improvement*": "*die Bestrahlung nach brusterhaltender Therapie* ***nicht zu einer Verbesserung*** *des Gesamtüberlebens* ("*radiation after a breast conservation treatment does not improve overall survival*").

– Finally, in some cases, the translation was found in the dictionary of cognates and it is false:

- *infrequently* → *manière plus fréquent*: the dictionary of cognates gave the translation *infrequent* → *fréquent* ('frequent');

- *in-patient* → *patient*: *patient* was directly obtained by the dictionary of cognates.

Other incorrect translations are due to the stop words allowed between two words when looking for the target term in the corpus:

– Either the stop words are not the right ones:

- *prosurvival* → *favorable de survie* in "*un facteur* ***favorable de survie***" ('a favorable survival factor'). The correct translation should have been "*favorable à la survie*" ('favorable to survival');

- *hormone-sensitive* → *hormon oder empfindlich* in "*...abhängig von bestimmten* ***Hormonen oder empfindlich*** *gegenüber bestimmten Substanzen...*" (sensitive to certain hormones or to certain substances). The correct translation would have been " *empfindlich auf Hormone*".

– Or they are useless, and no stop word should have been allowed:

- *non-mutation* → *non à un mutation* ('not to mutation') "*tumeurs du sein héréditaires liées ou* ***non à des mutations***" ('hereditary breast tumors which are related to mutations or not);

- *hand-foot* → *hand oder fuss* "*...neurotoxische Schädigungen der Nerven an* ***Händen oder Füßen***..." (neurotoxic damage for the nerves in the hands or the feet)". The compound noun *hand-foot* is part of the expression *hand-foot syndrome*[7] which

7 A redness and swelling of hand and feet following chemotherapy.

is translated in German by *Hand-Fuß-Syndrom*. The correct translation should have been *handfuss*.

The last type of errors comes from the order of elements. In the cases observed, this type of error only appears with fertile translations:

– *pre-pregnancy* → *schwangerschaft vor* instead of *vorschwangerschaft* "before the pregnancy"

– *first-year* → *an lors de leur premier* ('year at the time of their first'): in this case, the expected order was rather "*premier an* "

6.5. Discussion

This section discusses our translation generation method: we first present the findings of our experiments then outline the improvement perspectives for this method.

6.5.1. *Findings*

6.5.1.1. A priori *versus* a posteriori *reference*

We have evaluated our generation method from several angles (resource usefulness, techniques used...) and especially using two references: *a priori* reference and *a posteriori* reference. These two references are made from different source terms. With the *a priori* reference, the source terms are effectively the terms of the domain since they are present in the UMLS meta-thesaurus. Not only does it help evaluate cases of silence, this reference also helps evaluate our method from the angle of bilingual terminology extractions and comparing us to other methods. The *a posteriori* reference contains any source term as long as it has no entry in the general language bilingual dictionary or that its translation does not exist in the target corpus. The evaluation angle is more that of helping human translation and enriching general language resources. Depending on the reference used, we have obtained nuances in the results, especially in terms of translation method comparison (word compounds vs. neoclassical compounds vs. cognates, etc.), the usefulness of linguistic resources and the usefulness of the fallback strategy. Word compounds, for example, return more noise with the *a posteriori* reference. The morphological family and cognate combinations are interesting for the *a posteriori* reference but not for the *a priori*, for which only the cognates have an interesting impact.

6.5.1.1.1. Comparing language pairs

As for languages, we have systematically observed better results for the English → French pair than the English → German pair. There may be two reasons for this:

the lesser comparability of the English → German corpus and the language morphological types (for English → German, the search for fertile translations is less relevant). Moreover, our system does not deal as well with German in general. For example, we do not manage the case of the interfix "-s-" which can be found between two nouns in word compounds. We have seen that the morphological families had more impact for French. And we must note that in German, they are much less exhaustive (7348 families for German, made of 2.15 words on average, against 7049 in French, made of 2.45 words on average).

6.5.1.1.2. Fertile translations

The generation of fertile translations, while it is of lesser quality than the generation of classic translations, is an improvement factor for the English → French lexicon but does not bring anything obvious in German. We assume that this is due to the morphological type of the languages, but this has yet to be proven by carrying out experiments on other languages. Overall, the fertile translations provide original translation proposals which are an ideal complement to classical non-fertile translation by suggesting a popular variant, often close to a paraphrase. These translations attest to the linguistic uses that the translator can employ at will in his work. Extracts 6.1 and 6.2 present examples of fertile translations found by the system along with occurrence contexts for each language pair.

Extract 6.1. Examples of fertile translations found in English → French

– *loco-régional → local et régional*:

- "***Loco-regional*** *treatments are potentially curative when disease is confined to the breast and lymph nodes.*",

- "*A la fin des traitements* ***locaux et régionaux*** *(chirurgie, radiothérapie) et après une chimiothérapie si elle a été administrée.*" ('After local and regional treatment (surgery and radiotherapy) and after a chemotherapy if it was administered');

– *post-conception → après fécondation*:

- "*The first stage of foetal development is implantation, which occurs within 2 weeks* ***post-conception***.",

- "***Après fécondation*** *in vitro (FIV), les embryons obtenus sont congelés et seront réimplantés ultérieurement dans l'utérus de la patiente, à distance de la fin des traitements.* " ('After in vitro fertilization, the embryos are frozen and will be relocated later in the uterus of the patient, some time after the end of the treatments.');

– blue-dye → colorer en bleu, colorant bleu:

- "*Motion 4-axillary sampling* ***(blue-dye*** *guided) (For: Mr. Douglas Macmillan.* ",

- "*Une palpation était également pratiquée et était prélevé tout ganglion suspect même s'il n'était ni radioactif ni* ***coloré en bleu***." ('A palpation was also practiced and any suspicious node was removed even if it was not radioactive or was not colored in blue.'),

- "*Un traceur radioactif ou un* ***colorant bleu*** *est injecté dans la zone de la tumeur.* " ('A radioactive tracer or a blue dye is injected into the area of the tumor.');

– *randomly → manière randomisée*:

- "*In this study 52 women were* ***randomly*** *assigned to oestradiol 0.05 mg/day (n = 26) or placebo dermal patches (n = 26) for 12 weeks.* ",

- "*Chez les femmes traitées pour cancer du sein, la voie percutanée (0.1 mg/j) a été la première testée de* ***manière randomisée*** *en double aveugle contre placebo avec crossover chez 110 patientes [27].*" ('In the case of women who had been treated for breast cancer, percutaneous implantation (0.1 mg/day) was first tested in a double-blind placebo-controlled randomized study with crossover in 110 patients [27].').

Extract 6.2. Examples of fertile translations found in English → German

– *hypercalcaemia → zu viel calcium in das blut*:

- "***Hypercalcaemia*** *(excessive calcium in the blood)* ",

- "*Kann auch* ***zu viel Calcium ins Blut*** *kommen im Sinne einer Überdosierung durch tägliche Calcium-Tabletten Einnahme als Vorsorge?" It is possible that there is excessive calcium in the blood at that the overdose is due to the preventive daily intake of calcium tablets?*;

– *tumour-free → frei von tumor*:

- "*Nava emphasizes that oncoplastic procedures often involve wide resections which increase the chance of* ***tumour-free*** *margins.*",

- "*Resektionsrand ist* ***frei von Tumor****gewebe" The edges of the resection margin does not show any sign of tumor*,

- *non-invasive → nicht invasiv*,

- "*Because the cancer cells have not developed the ability to spread, you may hear DCIS described as a pre-cancerous, intraductal or non-invasive cancer.*",

- "*Bei fast allen Tumortypen liegt auch eine nicht invasive (duktale oder lobuläre) Tumorkomponente vor, aus der sie hervorgegangen sind und die für die Größe der Operation mitentscheidend ist." For almost all kinds of tumors, there is also a (ductal or lobular) non-invasive component from which the tumor has appeared and which will determine the seriousness of the surgery to be carried out*;

– *post-mastectomy → nach der entfernung der brust*:

- *"Disease relapse (local or distant recurrences) occurred in 29 women, in whom 25 were **post-mastectomy**. "*,

- *"**Nach der Entfernung** der Brust gibt es unterschiedliche Techniken diese wiederherzustellen." After removing the breasts, there are several techniques for breast reconstruction.*

6.5.2. *Research perspectives*

Finally, the qualitative analysis enabled us to find the limits of our approach as well as future research perspectives, which concern the improvement of linguistic resources and the fine-tuning of the fertile translation generation method.

6.5.2.1. *Improving linguistic resources*

Synonyms dictionary – The various experiments have shown that the thesaurus was not very useful. Yet, we noticed that certain cases of silence are due to semi-compositionality, in which one of the components is translated by a component with a close meaning even if it is not its exact translation. This is a case of lexical divergence which cannot be dealt with with synonyms as such. A research axis would be to use a thesaurus to include semantically close words with the variants. Another axis would be to acquire this list of close words in the target and source corpora, considering two words to be semantically close when they appear in similar contexts or trying to translate a word with the N first candidates given by the distributional method.

Morphological families – As for the morphological families, we must concede that the stemming algorithm [POR 80] is a rather brutal method to extract such a resource. In certain cases, even if two words are morphologically related, their meaning can be too far for this pair to be useful to manage morphological variation in translation. One solution might be to use specific variation templates such as [MOR 10]. We believe, however, that the morphological families obtained by stemming should not be eliminated since it might lower the method's coverage: it would just be a question of giving more weight to the morphological variants obtained from the templates.

Coverage of bilingual resources – We have also noted that a third of the silences were due to the absence of translation in our bilingual resources. One solution to enrich the bilingual dictionary would be to extract the translations of terms of parallel data from other domains. Once these translation examples were extracted, we could use data-driven methods to learn the alignments between morphemes or strings of characters [CLA 09, CLA 11]. The translation equivalences between morphemes could also be learned from cognate pairs extracted from comparable corpora.

6.5.2.2. *Fertile translations*

Candidate translation definition – A first issue concerns the definition of a candidate translation. We believe that there should be a post-processing module for clustering some of the translations. We currently consider that two translations are identical if they match the same sequences of *(lemma, part-of-speech)* pair. While this makes sense when the translations include stop words such as prepositions (*time period of progression* is very different from *time period without progression*), in the same way, it should be possible to neutralize the variation at the level of the articles if necessary: *nach der operation* (after the operation) and *nach ein operation* (after an operation) should be brought back to the same neutral form *nach Article operation.* The question of the intensity adverbs is harder to answer for they involve a chage in meaning. For example, we translate *prematurely* by *manière plus précoce* and *manière très précoce*. Should they be regrouped in a neutral form such as *manière Adverb précoce*? The question remains unanswered.

Inserting stop words – A second type of issue concerning the management of stop words is that they are allowed between each of the translated components, i.e. when we translate *breast-cancer* into two words *cancer* and *sein* then during the selection phase, we consider as candidate translation any word sequence starting with *cancer* and followed by up to three stop words and ending with *sein*. If including the stop words enables us the return correct translations (*cancer du sein*), it also creates false translations and even misinterpretations (*cancer en dehors du sein*).

Component order – The order of the components can create mistakes in the case of non-fertile translation, but it is mostly with fertile translations that it is an issue. For example, for *breast-cancer*, the system will suggest translations such as *sein et cancer, sein mais sans cancer, sein aprés un cancer* ('breast and cancer', 'breast without cancer', 'breast after cancer'). The current generation method uses a brute-force approach: we generate all the permutations to be sure that the right component order is generated, and only the attestation of one of the permutations in the target text enables us to consider it as a potential translation. This approach could be improved. A first solution would be to train a language model and associate a probability with each generated translation. We could also specify translation patterns (e.g. $\text{NOUN}_1\text{+NOUN}_2 \rightarrow \text{NOUN}_2\ \text{PREPOSITION ARTICLE}^?\ \text{NOUN}_1$). As for morphological families, these templates would not replace the current generation method but would have more weight, and the translations generated from these patterns would be pushed forward.

Several improved perspectives have been suggested in this chapter, and we can see that there appears the idea of pushing forward certain translations over others because, for example, they were generated by a more reliable resource (e.g. template rather than brute-force generation) or because we might have information on the probability of finding the target term in the target language (language model). We also know, thanks to the experiments presented in 2, that translators do not like having too many candidate translations. It is thus necessary to be able to rank the candidate translations in order to have the best translation show up in first position. This issue is the focus of the next chapter.

7

Formalization and Evaluation of Candidate Translation Ranking

7.1. Introduction

This chapter describes the exploratory work meant to experiment on several ranking methods for the candidate translations. We will start by detailing the chosen ranking criteria in section 7.2 and then indicate the way in which we combine them in section 7.3. The results are given in section 7.4. The limits of our work as well as the research prospects are discussed in section 7.5

7.2. Ranking criteria

We have tested four ranking criteria:

1) The similarity between source term contexts and target term contexts (section 7.2.1).

2) The target term frequency (section 7.2.2).

3) The parts-of-speech translation probability (section 7.2.3).

4) The reliability of component translations (section 7.2.4).

7.2.1. *Context similarity*

This ranking criteria, which we will refer to as C, corresponds to the similarity score obtained with the direct distributional method (section 1.3.1) and is thus based on the same assumption: the more often two terms tend to appear in similar contexts, the more likely it is that they have a similar meaning and are translations of one another.

The implementation of this method is identical to the method described in section 1.4.1: the size of the contexts is of five words to the right and five words to the left of the vector's head and the standardization of the number of co-occurrences is carried out according to the likelihood ratio (see Appendix A1.1.). The vector translation is carried out using the bilingual general language dictionary (see section 5.6.1). A fertile translation is a polylexical unit: its context vector corresponds to an average vector calculated from the vectors of each of the lexical words that compose it.

The similarity between source term vector s and candidate translation vector t is calculated with a weighted Jaccard index:

$$C(s,t) = \frac{\Sigma_{m \in s \cap t} min(TV(s,m_i), TV(t,m_i))}{\Sigma_{m_i \in s \cup t} max(TV(s,m_i), TV(t,m_i))} \quad [7.1]$$

in which $TV(x, m_i)$ is the standardized number of co-occurrences (likelihood ratio) between term x and context word m_i.

7.2.2. *Candidate translation frequency*

This criterion (given as F) enables us to emit the hypothesis that as the frequency of the target term increases, so does the likelihood that it belongs to the corpus topic and thus that it is a good translation.

The target term frequency t is given by:

$$F(t) = \frac{nbocc(t)}{N} \quad [7.2]$$

in which $nbocc(t)$ is the number of occurrences of t in the target corpus and N the total number of words in the target corpus.

7.2.3. *Parts-of-speech translation probability*

Here we want to capture the fact that it is more probable that a noun is translated by a noun, for example, or by a sequence of NOUN PREPOSITION NOUN than by an adverb (at least in the case of English to French translation). These translation probabilities between parts-of-speech, given as P, were acquired from the EMEA parallel corpus [TIE 09]. This corpus is created from parallel text belonging to the European Medicines Agency. These texts belong to the medical domain. They are aligned at the sentence level and available online in the TMX format.[1] The phrase

1 http://opus.lingfil.uu.se/EMEA.php.

alignments were carried out with the alignment software belonging to LINGUA ET MACHINA, which corresponds to the implementation of the algorithm ANYMALIGN [LAR 10a].

We tokenized, lemmatized and POS-tagged the texts with the XELDA analyzer, and then extracted the aligned phrases. We obtained an alignment table A in which each alignment $a \in A = \{lem_s, pos_s, lem_t, pos_t, p(s|t), p(t|s)\}$, for which lem_s, respectively lem_t, are the lemmas of the source, respectively target, phrase. pos_s, respectively pos_t, are the part(s)-of-speech of the source, respectively target, phrase. $p(s|t)$, respectively $p(t|s)$, is the probability that the target phrase is the translation of the source phrase and vice versa.

The probability that a candidate translation with the part(s)-of-speech y is the translation of a source term with the part-of-speech x corresponds to:

$$P(y|x) = \frac{\sum_{a \in A | pos_s = x, pos_t = y} p(t|s)}{\sum_{a \in A | pos_s = x} p(t|s)} \qquad [7.3]$$

To calculate translation probabilities, we only retained the alignments in which a source lexical unit was aligned with one or more target lexical units. For the two language pairs, we found target lexical units of at least five words (stop words and lexical words).[2]

From an English–German corpus of 363,982 aligned sentences, we acquired translation probabilities for 108,612 pairs of parts-of-speech sequences. For the English–French, we acquired approximately 191,854 pairs of parts-of-speech sequences. The starting corpus had 373,127 aligned sentences. A final lexicon extract is available in Appendix A2.3.6.

7.2.4. *Components translation mode*

Since certain translation modes are more reliable than others, we defined a reliability criteria, given as M, which takes into account the way in which each component of the source term was translated. For example, we can suppose that a component translated by the general language dictionary will have a more correct translation than a component translated with the dictionary of cognates.

2 The candidate translations generated in French are also composed of at least five words. As for the candidate translations in German, four of them have more than five words, which represents 0.16% of the totality of the translations generated in German.

We distinguish ten modes of translation.

– The component corresponds to a word:

- the word is directly translated:

– using the general language dictionary (mode DICO),

– using the dictionary of cognates (mode COGN);

- the word is indirectly translated:

– using the general language dictionary and the morphological families (mode MORPHO);

– using the general language dictionary and the thesaurus (mode SYNO),

– using the dictionary of cognates and the morphological families (mode MORPHOCOGN);

- using the dictionary of cognates and the thesaurus (mode SYNOCOGN),

– The component corresponds to a bound morpheme, it is translated using the morpheme translation table:

- prefix translated as a prefix (mode PREF);

- combining form translated as a combining form (mode CONF);

- suffix translated as a suffix (mode SUFF);

- prefix, combining form or suffix translated by a word (mode FERT).

	Decomposition	Translation	Recomposition
1	{*ab, normal, ly*}	{*a:PREF, normal:DICO, façon:FERT*}	{*façon, anormal*}
2	{*ab, normal, ly*}	{*a:PREF, normal:COGN, façon:FERT*}	{*façon, anormal*}
3	{*abnormal, ly*}	{*anormal:DICO, façon:FERT*}	{*façon, anormal*}
4	{*abnormal, ly*}	{*anormal:COGN, façon:FERT*}	{*façon, anormal*}

Table 7.1. *Example of candidate translation as fruit of multiple generations*

The translation of a source term may have been generated in several manners. For example, the translation of "*façon anormal*" was generated in four different manners, as indicated in Table 7.1:

– Generation 1 separated "*abnormally*" into *ab-*, *normal* and *-ly*. The prefix *ab-* was translated by the prefix *a-*, the noun *normal* was translated using the general language dictionary by *normal* and the suffix *-ly* was translated by the noun *façon*.

– Generation 2 followed the same process only the translation of *normal* was obtained using the dictionary of cognates.

– In generation 3, the source term was separated into *abnormal* and *-ly*, *abnormal* was translated using the general language dictionary and *-ly* was translated by *façon*.

– In the fourth generation, *abnormal* was translated by the dictionary of cognates.

The recomposition stage provides the same target term template: *façon* followed by *anormal*. This template is looked for in the target corpus and the translation *façon/noun anormal/adjective* is obtained ("*...des gènes protecteurs contre le développement de tumeurs sont réduits au silence de* ***façon anormale***.").

No matter the number of generations which helped to reach the target term "*façon anormal*", in the end, only a single translation is taken into account: "*abnormally* $\rightarrow$ *façon anormal*". This multiple generation phenomenon is much stronger in French (4.27 different generations per translation) than in German (2.43).

When we calculate the Mcriterion for a target term t, we take into account all the translation modes used by all the generations, which produced the target term:

$$M(t) = \frac{\sum_{g \in G(t)} \sum_{c \in g} reliability(m(c))}{\sum_{g \in G(t)} |c \in g|} \qquad [7.4]$$

in which $G(t)$ is the set of generations which produced t, each $c \in g$ is a component of the generation g and $reliability(m(c))$ is the reliability of the translation mode m of c.

In our example, if $PREF = 0.6$; $DICO = 0.5$; $COGN = 0.6$ and $FERT = 0.4$, then the reliability score of "*façon anormal*" is of 0.5:

$$M(\text{façon anormal}) = \frac{2 \times 0.6 + 2 \times 0.5 + 2 \times 0.6 + 4 \times 0.4}{10} \qquad [7.5]$$

The reliability of each translation mode was calculated on our training data set T described in section 5.5. For a translation mode m, its reliability is given by:

$$reliability(m) = \frac{|\{g : m \in g, \mathcal{A}(t(g)) \in \{\text{exact}\}\}|}{|\{g : m \in g\}|} \qquad [7.6]$$

in which $\{g : m \in g\}$ are all the generations, which used the construction mode m and $\mathcal{A}(t(g))$ is the annotation of the target term t given by the generation g.

The values obtained are given in Table 7.2.

Table 7.2 shows that the components translated with the general language dictionary are less reliable than those translated with the dictionary of cognates, no matter what the language is. This confirms once again the usefulness of enriching the bilingual dictionary with cognates identified in a comparable corpus.

The components indirectly translated (bilingual resource + variation resource) are among the least reliable. The cognate and morphological variants combination is the most secure, followed by the general language dictionary and thesaurus combination, then the general language dictionary and morphological variants combination. The combination cognates and thesaurus is the translation mode that is the least reliable of the ten translation modes, especially in German.

The most reliable translation modes are the non-fertile translations of combining forms and suffixes. Prefixes are also highly reliable in German but not as much in French. The low reliability of prefixes in French is surprising, especially since the experiments described in section 6.4.2 indicated a high level of precision for the translation of prefixed words. By analyzing the system's outputs, we observed that in French, the lexical base(s) contained in the prefixed words are mainly (71%) translated using variation resources, which can lower the quality of the translation. This phenomenon is not as strong in German (66%).

The fertile translation is the second least reliable translation mode, especially in German.

	EN-FR	EN-DE
DICO	0.49	0.38
COGN	0.57	0.48
MORPHO	0.34	0.29
SYNO	0.43	0.32
MORPHOCOGN	0.41	0.37
SYNOCOGN	0.21	0.05
PREF	0.61	0.79
CONF	0.79	0.67
SUFF	0.63	0.92
FERT	0.37	0.19

Table 7.2. *Reliability of translation modes*

7.3. Criteria combination

7.3.1. *Value standardization*

Our ranking criteria all have a value between 0 and 1, but they present very different value scales. For example, the frequency criterion's values are very low (< 0.005) whereas the translation mode reliability values vary between 0.19 and 0.92.

And if we combine the raw values, the criteria with very low values will be completely hidden by the criteria with the higher values.

We have standardized our values according to the method described in [GEN 77, p. 48-50]: the values observed are replaced by their percentile then the percentile is transformed into a z-score using the normal law table. The details of the standardization are given in Appendix A1.4.

7.3.2. *Linear combination*

Our first experiments consisted of combining each criterion:

$$score(t) = \alpha C + \beta F + \gamma P + \delta M \quad [7.7]$$

in which α, β, γ and δ are weighting coefficients ($0 \leq \alpha, \beta, \gamma, \delta \leq 1$ and $\alpha + \beta + \gamma + \delta = 1$).

We carried out two experiments. In the first experiment, all the weighting coefficients are equal: we consider that the criteria are as informative as one another. In the second experiment, we gave each different criterion a different weight: in this case, we consider that certain types of criteria are more useful than others, and so they have a bigger weight. The weights were automatically learned on the training data set T (see section 5.5) by using Algorithm 6, we simply tested several possible weight sets and retained the one that gave the best precision on Top1.

The weights obtained are given in Table 7.3. Frequency of the target term and part-of-speech have matching weights. The criterion with the highest weight is that of translation modes.

Context similarity is the criterion with the lowest weight. This criterion is less useful, because the source terms and target terms are not usually frequent: between 73% and 81% have five or less occurrences in the corpus (see Tables 7.11 and 7.12). This shows how useful it is to have used compositional translation rather than the distributional approach for complex terms.

As the mean difference calculated for each coefficient will show,[3] the coefficient values are stable no matter the language couple. This seems to indicate that the importance given to each ranking criteria is independent of the languages used in the

3 Average of the differences between the values and the mean of the population: $\frac{1}{n}\sum_{i=1}^{n}|x_i - \bar{x}|$.

translation. It would be interesting to verify this theory with other language pairs. If the theory was true, it would then be possible to use parallel data in languages which are rich in them to train weight coefficients and apply them to a language with fewer resources. It would also be interesting to see if the coefficients are stable for the same language pair but in different domains of speciality.

Criterion	EN-FR	EN-DE	mean difference
Context C (coeff. α)	0.12	0.15	0.015
Frequency F (coeff. β)	0.24	0.22	0.010
Part-of-speech P (coeff. γ)	0.25	0.26	0.005
Translation mode M (coeff. δ)	0.39	0.37	0.010

Table 7.3. *Weight ranking criteria*

7.3.3. *Learning-to-rank model*

Secondly, we experimented with learning-to-rank algorithms. To this end, we based ourselves on the RankLib[4] library, which provides the implementation of several learning-to-rank algorithms. Among the implemented algorithms, we selected those that belonged to the list-wise algorithm family: ADARANK [LI 07], COORDINATE ASCENT [MET 00] and LAMBDA MART [WU 10].

ADARANK and LAMBDA MART are based on the boosting technique. Boosting consists of combining the results provided by several models, which are usually simpler and less efficient (taken separately) than a general model. These models are learned one by one, the weight of each example of the data set is re-evaluated depending on the previously learnt model errors (examples which have not been correctly classified see their weight increase; examples which have been correctly classified see their weight decrease). As for COORDINATE ASCENT, it learns a linear model. Its name is due to the technique used to optimize the choice of parameters.

The variables provided to the algorithms are the four criteria: C, F, P and M. The values were first standardized according to the method described in section 7.3.1. The parameters proposed by the RankLib library offer the chance to specify a measure to be optimized for list-wise algorithms. We have decided to optimize precision on Top1. All the other parameters were left with their default value. The model training was done on the data set T.

4 http://people.cs.umass.edu/ vdang/ranklib.html.

Algorithm 6 Finding the best weights

```
Require: training_data
  step ← 0.01
  best_precision ← 0
  best_weight_set ← ∅
  for α = 0 ; α <= 1; α = α + step do
      for β = 0 ; β <= 1; β = β + step do
          for γ = 0 ; γ <= 1; γ = γ + step do
              for δ = 0 ; δ <= 1; δ = δ + step do
                  if not α + β + γ + δ == 1 then
                      continue
                  end if
                  exact ← 0
                  total ← 0
                  for all source_term, translations in training_data do
                      ranked_translations ← rank(translations, {α, β, γ, δ})
                      if ranked_translations[0] is exact then
                          exact+ = 1
                      end if
                      total+ = 1
                  end for
                  precision = exact/total
                  if precision > best_precision then
                      best_precision ← precision
                      best_weight_set ← {α, β, γ, δ}
                  end if
              end for
          end for
      end for
  end for
  return best_weight_set
```

7.4. Evaluation

7.4.1. *Reference data and evaluation measures*

The ranking methods were evaluated on the data set E (described in section 5.5), which corresponds to the source terms of the *a priori* reference for which the system generated a translation. The training data (used to learn reliability scores, linear combination weights and ranking models) correspond to the data set T, i.e. the source terms, which do not belong to the *a priori* reference and for which the system generated a translation. The data sets E and T do not overlap.

The evaluation measure is the precision at the $TopN$, i.e. the fraction of source terms, which have at least one correct translation among the N first candidate translations:

$$TopN = \frac{1}{|S|}\sum_{j=1}^{|S|} \alpha(T_{j^N}, R_j) \qquad [7.8]$$

$$\alpha(T_{j^N}, R_j) = \begin{cases} 1 & \text{if } T_{j^N} \cap R_j \neq \emptyset \\ 0 & \text{if not} \end{cases}$$

in which:

– S is the set of source terms;

– T_{j^N} is the Top N candidate translations for the source term j;

– R_j is the set of correct translations for the source term j.

The definition of a "correct" translation can vary: either they are only the translations provided by the UMLS (in this case, the precision is given as P); or they are the UMLS translations as well as the translations annotated as exact by the translators (precision written as P_E); or they are the UMLS translations as well as the exact or accurate annotated translations (precision written as P_{EA}).

7.4.2. *Bases of comparison*

We have used six bases of comparison. The lower comparison basis (RANDOM) corresponds to the precision obtained when the translations are randomly ranked (precision indicated is an average over 100 random rankings). The higher comparison basis (BEST PRECISION POSSIBLE) corresponds to the precision that would be obtained if the best translation was also placed in rank 1. The four other comparison bases C, F, P and M each correspond to the four criteria used separately. To understand how difficult the task was, we mention in Figure 7.1 the number of translations per source term for each language couple.

For the English $\rightarrow$ French translations, we observe that almost two-thirds (64%) of the source terms have a single-candidate translation. Only 13% of them have two candidate translations and 23% of them have more than two candidate translations. The maximum number of candidate translations is 13.

For the English $\rightarrow$ German translations, the task is a bit harder: only less than half (46%) of the source terms have one candidate translation, a quarter of them (24%) have two candidate translations and 29% have more than two candidate translations. The maximum number of candidate translations is 28.

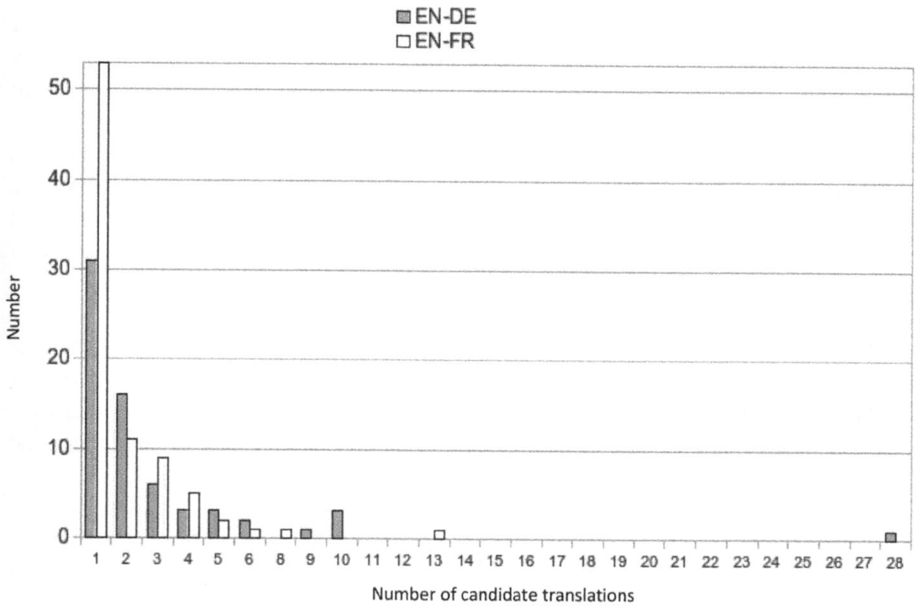

Figure 7.1. *Number of translations per source term*

7.4.3. *Results*

For each language pair, we provide the precision obtained from Top1 to Top5. We also mention the "Maximum precision rank", i.e. the rank from which the best precision was obtained.

7.4.3.1. *Ranking English → French translations*

Results are listed in Tables 7.4 (P), 7.5 (P_E) and 7.6 (P_{EA}). The methods are ranked in a decreasing manner by their precision on the Top1, then the Top2 and then the Top3.

We observe that no matter the definition chosen for a correct translation (UMLS, exact, accurate, etc.), the methods that stand out are the NON-WEIGHTED COMBINATION method and WEIGHTED COMBINATION method followed by the COORDINATE ASCENT method, LAMBDA MART method and M criteria. We also observe that all the tested methods systematically perform better than the random ranking. This is especially visible with the translations of the UMLS only: the worse method (isolated C criterion) is 9 points higher than the random on Top1 and the best method obtains up to 10.5 points more than the random (still on the Top1). Obviously, as we go down in the Top, the gap with random ranking narrows. This is also the case for the flexibility given to the definition of a correct translation: the more flexible a definition is, the less interesting the ranking is.

Ranking seems to be mostly relevant when trying to find a UMLS translation or an exact translation on Top1 or Top2. Since the candidate translation lists are usually shorts (only 23% have more than two candidate translations from English to French; 29% from English to German), the best precision possible is quickly obtained. For the translations of only the UMLS (P), the best precision possible is obtained at Top3. This is all the more visible when one takes into account the exact or accurate translations. For the UMLS translations and exact (P_E), the best precision possible is obtained at Top2. For the UMLS, exact and accurate translations (P_{EA}), the best precision possible is obtained at Top1.

It does not seem interesting to learn weight when using linear combination: the results are almost equivalent (+1.2 to -1.2 point). Among the learning-to-rank methods, ADARANK is different because it did not perform as well as the other two. In general, the methods that rely on training data do not stand out as better than the simple non-weighted combination of the four criteria.

If we compare each of the criteria used separately, the M criterion (reliability of the translation modes) is the one that offers the best results (it was given the biggest weight during the training: 0.39). The context similarity (criterion C) is clearly the worst criterion, and has been given the smallest weight (0.12). Nonetheless, it is still better than random ranking: it enables us to obtain the best precision at rank 4 instead of rank 13 for the random ranking. Finally, the frequency criterion (F) appears to be a bit more interesting than that of the parts-of-speech translation probability (P).

	Precision (UMLS)					Rank precision maximum
	Top1	Top2	Top3	Top4	Top5	
BEST PRECISION POSSIBLE	.795	.795	.795	.795	.795	1
WEIGHTED COMBINATION	**.759**	**.783**	**.795**	**.795**	**.795**	**3**
NON-WEIGHTED COMBINATION	.747	**.783**	**.795**	**.795**	**.795**	**3**
COORDINATE ASCENT	.747	**.783**	**.795**	**.795**	**.795**	**3**
LAMBDA MART	.747	**.783**	**.795**	**.795**	**.795**	**3**
M	.747	.771	**.795**	**.795**	**.795**	**3**
F	.723	.783	**.795**	**.795**	**.795**	**3**
ADARANK	.687	.759	.783	**.795**	**.795**	4
P	.687	.759	.783	**.795**	**.795**	4
C	.663	.747	.783	**.795**	**.795**	4
RANDOM	.654	.733	.772	.783	.787	13

Table 7.4. *English → French (P) ranking results*

7.4.3.2. *Ranking English → German translations*

The results are given in Tables 7.7 (P), 7.8 (P_E) and 7.9 (P_{EA}). The methods were also ranked according to their precision on Top1, then Top2, then Top3.

	Precision (UMLS or exact)					Rank precision maximum
	Top1	Top2	Top3	Top4	Top5	
BEST PRECISION POSSIBLE	.94	.94	.94	.94	.94	1
NON-WEIGHTED COMBINATION	**.928**	**.94**	**.94**	**.94**	**.94**	**2**
WEIGHTED COMBINATION	**.928**	**.94**	**.94**	**.94**	**.94**	**2**
COORDINATE ASCENT	**.928**	**.94**	**.94**	**.94**	**.94**	**2**
LAMBDA MART	**.928**	**.94**	**.94**	**.94**	**.94**	**2**
M	**.928**	**.94**	**.94**	**.94**	**.94**	**2**
F	.916	.928	**.94**	**.94**	**.94**	3
ADARANK	.892	.904	.928	**.94**	**.94**	4
P	.892	.904	.928	**.94**	**.94**	4
C	.88	.904	.928	**.94**	**.94**	4
RANDOM	.836	.898	.928	.931	.932	13

Table 7.5. *English → French (P_E) ranking results*

For German, there is a strong margin of progression since there are many more candidate translations per source term. All the methods tried behave better than random ranking. The worse method obtains between 5 and 1.2 points more than random ranking at Top1 depending on whether the UMLS, exact or accurate translations are taken into account.

In this case, the weighted combination systematically performs better than non-weighted combination (4.5 to 1.5 points higher on Top1 depending on the type of "correct" translation chosen). As for the English → French ranking, COORDINATE ASCENT, LAMBDA MART and NON-WEIGHTED COMBINATION are some of the more interesting methods. Nonetheless, with the UMLS translations, COORDINATE ASCENT, LAMBDA MART and NON-WEIGHTED COMBINATION are only really interesting from Top2 (P = 0.682). At Top1, they are distanced by methods, which are generally less efficient elsewhere (P and ADARANK criteria). The M criterion based on translation modes also obtains good results from the Top1 (P) and the Top2 (P_E and P_{EA}).

Finally, the P and C criteria obtain the worst results. Even if P has a good precision at Top1 (especially with UMLS translations), we have to wait for rank 17 to reach maximum precision. With the C criteria, which is the worst of them all, we have to wait for rank 28.

7.5. Discussion

We conclude this chapter with a general discussion of the results obtained. First we present the findings of our experiments and then suggest several research prospects.

	Precision (UMLS or exact or accurate)					Rank precision maximum
	Top1	Top2	Top3	Top4	Top5	
BEST PRECISION POSSIBLE	.952	.952	.952	.952	.952	1
NON-WEIGHTED COMBINATION	**.952**	**.952**	**.952**	**.952**	**.952**	**1**
COORDINATE ASCENT	**.952**	**.952**	**.952**	**.952**	**.952**	**1**
WEIGHTED COMBINATION	.94	**.952**	**.952**	**.952**	**.952**	2
LAMBDA MART	.94	**.952**	**.952**	**.952**	**.952**	2
M	.94	**.952**	**.952**	**.952**	**.952**	2
ADARANK	.94	.94	**.952**	**.952**	**.952**	3
F	.94	.94	**.952**	**.952**	**.952**	3
P	.94	.94	**.952**	**.952**	**.952**	3
C	.928	.94	**.952**	**.952**	**.952**	3
RANDOM	.917	.942	.949	.95	.951	8

Table 7.6. *English → French (P_{EA}) ranking results*

	Precision (UMLS)					Rank precision maximum
	Top1	Top2	Top3	Top4	Top5	
BEST PRECISION POSSIBLE	.697	.697	.697	.697	.697	1
WEIGHTED COMBINATION	**.621**	.667	**.697**	**.697**	**.697**	**3**
M	**.621**	.652	**.697**	**.697**	**.697**	**3**
ADARANK	**.621**	.652	.652	.667	.667	17
P	**.621**	.652	.652	.667	.667	17
LAMBDA MART	.606	**.682**	**.697**	**.697**	**.697**	**3**
C	.606	.667	.667	.682	.682	28
F	.591	.667	**.697**	**.697**	**.697**	**3**
NON-WEIGHTED COMBINATION	.576	**.682**	**.697**	**.697**	**.697**	**3**
COORDINATE ASCENT	.576	**.682**	**.697**	**.697**	**.697**	**3**
RANDOM	.526	.627	.654	.665	.672	28

Table 7.7. *English → German (P) ranking results*

7.5.1. *Findings*

7.5.1.1. *Usefulness of criteria combination*

Overall, we observe that four ranking methods rise above the rest, no matter what the language pairs: NON-WEIGHTED COMBINATION, WEIGHTED COMBINATION, COORDINATE ASCENT and LAMBDA MART. These four methods are closely followed by the M score, which actually obtained the highest weight during the training (0.39 for English → French and 0.37 for English → German).

	Precision (UMLS or exact)					Rank precision
	Top1	Top2	Top3	Top4	Top5	maximum
BEST PRECISION POSSIBLE	.879	.879	.879	.879	.879	1
WEIGHTED COMBINATION	**.848**	**.879**	**.879**	**.879**	**.879**	**2**
LAMBDA MART	**.848**	.864	.864	.864	**.879**	**5**
NON-WEIGHTED COMBINATION	.833	.864	**.879**	**.879**	**.879**	**3**
COORDINATE ASCENT	.833	.864	**.879**	**.879**	**.879**	**3**
F	.833	.848	**.879**	**.879**	**.879**	**3**
ADARANK	.833	.848	.848	.848	.848	17
P	.833	.848	.848	.848	.848	17
M	.818	.864	**.879**	**.879**	**.879**	**3**
C	.803	.864	.864	.864	.864	28
RANDOM	.77	.832	.846	.853	.857	28

Table 7.8. *English → German (P_E)ranking results*

	Precision (UMLS or exact or accurate)					Rank precision
	Top1	Top2	Top3	Top4	Top5	maximum
BEST PRECISION POSSIBLE	.894	.894	.894	.894	.894	1
WEIGHTED COMBINATION	**.879**	**.894**	**.894**	**.894**	**.894**	**2**
LAMBDA MART	**.879**	.879	.879	.879	**.894**	5
NON-WEIGHTED COMBINATION	.864	**.894**	**.894**	**.894**	**.894**	**2**
COORDINATE ASCENT	.864	**.894**	**.894**	**.894**	**.894**	**2**
M	.864	.879	**.894**	**.894**	**.894**	3
ADARANK	.864	.879	.879	.879	.879	17
P	.864	.879	.879	.879	.879	17
F	.848	.864	**.894**	**.894**	**.894**	3
C	.818	.879	.879	.879	.879	28
RANDOM	.806	.859	.872	.877	.88	28

Table 7.9. *English → German (P_{EA}) ranking results*

We also notice that the techniques based on training do not clearly perform better than the combination of the four criteria. We mostly observe a difference in German between WEIGHTED COMBINATION and LAMBDA MART which obtain between 4.5 and 1.5 points more than simple (non-weighted) combination.

However, experiments have clearly shown the usefulness of combining several criteria, even in a simple manner: no matter the reference used or the language pair, the combination of criteria offers better or at least as good results as the best criterion on its own. One exception is the case of the M criterion, which is better on the Top1 for English → German (UMLS translations), but when reaching Top2, the non-weighted combination becomes better. Overall, the M criterion is the best of all the criteria taken separately.

7.5.1.2. *Inconclusive results of the methods based on training*

We believe that the lesser input of the methods based on training can be explained by the fact that our training data and evaluation data are rather different. Table 7.10 summarizes the number of candidate translations per source term, depending on the language pairs and the data set: training (T) and evaluation (E). The training data set has more candidate translations per source term than the evaluation data set (3.04 versus 1.92 for English $\rightarrow$ French; 3.11 versus 2.83 for English $\rightarrow$ German).

	EN-FR		EN-DE	
	T	E	T	E
Source terms with one candidate	39%	64%	44%	46%
Source terms with two candidate translations	23%	13%	21%	24%
Source terms with three candidate translations	14%	11%	11%	9%
Source terms with four candidate translations	7%	6%	8%	4%
Source terms with five and more candidate translations	18%	6%	17%	16%
number of translations/source terms	3.04	1.92	3.11	2.83

Table 7.10. *Number of candidate translations per source term*

This is also the case for the frequency of the source terms and candidate translations (Tables 7.11 and 7.12). Many more source terms/translations appear in the lower frequencies in the training data set. Let us note that as a general rule, source terms and candidate translations are infrequent. For English $\rightarrow$ French, between 63% and 81% of the terms have a number of occurrences lower than or equal to 5. For English $\rightarrow$ German, between 56% and 80% of the source terms appear five times or fewer in the corpus. This high number of terms associated with a small number of occurrences explains the low performances of the C criterion (the distributional approach requires that the terms to be translated are frequent). German has the most terms with low frequencies and is also the language in which the C criterion had the worst results.

Finally, training data and evaluation data are also different in terms of annotation allocation (Table 7.13). As a general rule, training data has many more translations annotated false or close than in the evaluation data. As a corollary, there are fewer examples of translations annotated exact in the training set. The proportion of accurate translations remains the same.

All these reasons partly explain that the methods based on training did not obtain results that were clearly better than those coming from methods that appeared simpler at first. We initially chose to use the *a priori* reference as evaluation data so as to conform ourselves to the uses of the domain: the UMLS is considered to be the reference resource for medical term translation.

	Source terms		Candidate translations	
	T	E	T	E
# Minimum occ.	1	1	1	1
# Average occ.	5.33	11.42	14.22	10.72
# Median occ.	2	3	2	3
# Maximum occ.	116	260	2,196	230
% Terms with # occ. = 1	47%	24%	45%	34%
% Terms with # occ. <= 5	81%	66%	73%	63%
% Terms with # occ. <= 10	88%	80%	81%	80%

Table 7.11. *Number of source term and candidate translation occurrences (English → French)*

	Source terms		Candidate translations	
	T	E	T	E
# Minimum occ.	1	1	1	1
# Average occ.	5.25	19.36	14.22	6.74
# Median occ.	2	4	1	2
# Maximum occ.	83	260	1,248	196
% Terms with # occ. = 1	47%	21%	51%	47%
% Terms with # occ. <= 5	77%	56%	80%	80%
% Terms with # occ. <= 10	88%	68%	88%	88%

Table 7.12. *Number of occurrences of the source terms and candidate translations (English → German)*

	EN-FR		EN-DE	
	T	E	T	E
Exact	30%	67%	24%	61%
Accurate	10%	16%	7%	6%
Close	18%	6%	14%	6%
False	41%	11%	55%	27%

Table 7.13. *Annotations allocated to the candidate translations*

In conclusion, the overall findings are inconclusive. On the one hand, we have shown the usefulness of combining several ranking criteria. On the other hand, we expected the ranking models based on training to provide better results.

7.5.2. *Research perspectives*

7.5.2.1. *Language and domain independent models*

A first research perspective would be to use all the annotated translations to evaluate the training input: we would then use cross-validation to create several training/evaluation sets from the *a priori* reference. However, we consider that it is not a very realistic endeavor to train on translations coming from a comparable corpus and manually annotated. In real conditions, when we use comparable corpora, it is because we lack parallel data for the language pair and/or the domain of speciality in question.

A first research axis would be to study how parallel data coming from other domains or even other languages could be used as training data. For example, to learn the parts-of-speech, we used a corpus in the medical domain but it would be interesting to see if these translation probabilities can be learnt on a corpus from a different domain without having much impact on precision. In the same way, the stability of the weighting coefficients leads us to believe that each criterion is independent of the languages (section 7.3.2).

7.5.2.2. *Better suited evaluation methods*

The evaluation method used can also be questioned. We have used precision at the TopN, since it is the most frequent evaluation measure found to evaluate comparable corpora lexicon extraction. However, other measures could be considered, especially to evaluate the *ranking* algorithms. Indeed, the TopN does not take into account the ability to rank the translations from the most useful to the less useful for the translator. For example, even if the algorithm places a correct translation in the first spot, it is always useful to find other correct translations below rather than at the rank 10.

In Chapter 1, we presented several measures that could provide a different viewpoint on the ranking results. The mean reciprocal rank (MRR) indicates the mean rank at which the first correct translation can be found. The mean average precision (MAP) indicates the mean precision obtained when all the correct translations are selected. We could also use Kendall's Tau [KEN 83] to evaluate the correlation between the rank allocated by the system to each candidate translation and the rank allocated to them by the judges.

7.5.2.3. *Identification of correct translations*

Until now, we only tried to rank the candidate translations to select the best translation(s). Yet, this approach is useless if all the generated translations are incorrect. Another way to proceed would be to use the quality criteria to directly rank a translation as exact, accurate and close or false.

7.5.2.4. *Combining different methods*

We believe that the criteria combination models could be used to rank translations obtained from different methods: distributional, compositional, data-driven or cognates. We could thus combine methods to find the best advantage of each of them: we would then increase the size of the extracted lexicon without hurting its precision.

In the translation industry context, it is common to be confronted with the need to combine lexicons from several originals. The learning-to-rank techniques could be used to aggregate several lexica. When the lexicons suggest different translations for a single source term, these translations could be ranked depending on the origin of the translation. For example, more weight would be given to translations coming from manually created lexica. Translations coming from parallel corpora would have more weight than those coming from comparable corpora.

7.5.2.5. *Looking for new ranking features*

To conclude this discussion, while value-added machine learning still needs to be proven for candidate translation ranking, the combination of criteria showed encouraging results (for English $\rightarrow$ French, the weighted combination obtained 75.9% precision on the Top1 versus 74.7% for the best criterion taken separately; for English $\rightarrow$ German, the non-weighted combination obtained 68.2% precision on Top2 versus a 65.2% for the best criterion taken separately). Thus, the possibilities of exploring new features for estimating translation quality are opened up: source term frequency, source term and target term frequency rating, number of generations leading to the target term, source term part-of-speech, target term part-of-speech and number of occurrences in academic texts, in popular texts, etc.

In this chapter, we looked at exploratory work aiming to improve the ranking of translations generated by our system. This chapter corresponded to the last axes of our plan to improve compositional translation, which was mentioned at the end of Chapter 3.

The last pages of this book are devoted to a general conclusion on our work as well as to putting our work into perspective within an applicative context.

Conclusion and Perspectives

C1.1. Results review

The aim of this book was to explore the ways of using comparable corpora in Computer-Assisted Translations (CAT). We had two objectives: first, we wished to observe the extracted lexicons in an applicative perspective and analyze how they were approached by translators to discern useful research axes for CAT; second, we wished to implement these research axes and further the progression of current comparable corpora lexicons extraction techniques.

C1.1.1. *Applicative perspective*

To find an answer to our first objective, we started by implementing the reference method for comparable corpora lexicon extraction. This method is based on the distributional theory and consists of aligning terms that tend to appear in similar contexts. The terms were first identified in the source and target corpora by using a term extractor. Based on the needs mentioned in several translation study works, we enriched the bilingual lexicon with peripheral information extracted from the corpora and from the Internet (collocations, frequency, links to the Wikipedia page, etc.) and then developed an interface to find the term alignments, their concordances as well as their terminology records.

This tool enabled us to implement an applicative evaluation of bilingual lexica. Our evaluation protocol consisted of comparing the quality of human translations generated with and without lexicons extracted from comparable corpora: we decided that the quality difference observed reflected the usefulness of the lexica. The evaluation was done with two corpora: one of the corpora dealt with BREAST CANCER (medical domain) and the other dealt with WATER SCIENCE (environmental domain). The results of the evaluation were inconclusive. In the case of the WATER

SCIENCE topic, the extracted lexicons had little vocabulary in common with the lexicons to be translated (14% for the source part), which did not enable us to reach a conclusion. However, this highlighted the fact that we had to use topics with a fine granularity to expect any benefits from comparable corpora. The breast cancer corpora had better coverage (67% for the target part and 94% for the source part) and we observed that the comparable corpus extracted lexicon had a visible improvement effect on the quality of the translations compared to a situation in which the translator only had general language resources available. However, in such a well-resourced domain as the medical domain, comparable corpora are not very useful compared to a situation in which the translator had access to resources available on the internet.

This experiment enabled us to collect the translators' impressions when faced with this new type of lexicon which they were not used to manipulating. We learned that the ambiguity of the lexicons (i.e. the fact that a source term is associated with several candidate translations) is a hindrance and that translators prefer a very short list of candidate translations, even if this means that fewer source terms are translated.

On the basis of this conclusion, we decided to focus on translation generation techniques that had been recently successfully applied to comparable corpora lexicon extraction [MOR 10]. These techniques do not consist of the alignment of terms previously extracted from the corpora but consist of the generation of source term translations, which are then filtered by using comparable corpora. We also considered "data-driven" generation methods, i.e. methods based on translation relation training based on bilingual terminology examples. However, these methods were set aside since they required a previously existing minimum of bilingual specialized resources. We then focused on translation generation methods based on the compositionality principle.

C1.1.2. *Contributions to compositional translation*

Our contributions to compositional translation focused on the translation of morphologically complex monolexical units. The state of the art of these methods enabled us to find three research axes:

– The first axis focused on the generation of fertile translations, i.e. translation pairs in which the target term has more lexical words than the source term. These translations, which are often closed to paraphrasing variants of the "canonical" target term, fit nicely within the remit of our research: they helped us to identify the translational equivalences whose structure was far from the source term's structure and thus leverage the specificity of comparable corpora which contain natural formulations that have not been influenced by the source language. For example, "*cytogenetic*" can be translated as "*génétique des cellules*".[1] Fertile translation also provides popular variants of the canonical term which is useful when the translator is working on popular science texts. For example, "*oophorectomy*" can be translated to "*ovariectomie*" or "*ablation des ovaires*".

– The purpose of our second research axis was to generate a translation system which would be relatively independent of the morphological structure of the terms to be translated. Indeed, the existing methods are each suited for one or two morphological construct types and do not offer any generic solution. The system we implemented can translate prefixed terms, word compounds and neoclassical compounds as well as some cases of suffixation. For example, the term "*abnormally*" is decomposed into *ab-+normal+-ly* and translated as "*(de) façon anormale*"; the term "*over-represented*" is separated into *over+re-+presented* and translated as "*sur-représentation*"; the term "*phyto-estrogens*" is separated into *-phyto-+-estro-+-gen-* and translated as "*Pflanzenöstrogen*".

– Our third and last research axis focused on the issue of ranking the generated translations: we explored several ranking criteria as well as combination methods for these criteria. We introduced the use of algorithms taken from Information Research which directly model the issue of ranking (listwise in learning-to-rank approaches).

We evaluated our translation method over a medical corpus corresponding to the topic of breast cancer. We studied two language pairs: English → French and English → German. The evaluations showed us that the generation of fertile translations increase the quality of the lexicon only for translations from English to French. We presented the theory that in the case of translations from English to German, fertile translations were less interesting due to the morphological type of the German language which, as a Germanic language, tends to create words by agglutinating morphemes rather than creating locutions or phrases.

As for the independence of the source term's morphological structure, experiments have also shown that it was better for the algorithm to take input in several cases of morphological constructs rather than focus on a certain type of structure. This genericness increased the lexicon's coverage and we did not observe any significant loss in precision.

Finally, as for the candidate translation ranking, we showed that the combination of several criteria provided us with results superior to those obtained with random ranking or by only using a single criterion, and this was true even without the use of trained models from translation examples.

1 English context: "A molecular **cytogenetic** approach to studying platinum resistance"; French context: "*Parmi les anomalies moléculaires ou **génétiques des cellules** tumorales.*"

C1.2. Work limitations and perspectives

C1.2.1. *Choice of knowledge field*

In our opinion, the main limit to our work is the knowledge field to which the corpora on which we have worked belong. Indeed, the medical domain has a great number of parallel resources. Thus, it is not very relevant to carry out research meant for the acquisition of linguistic resources in domains that lack such resources on such a rich environment. However, working in the medical domain provided us with reference resources (from the UMLS, on-line medical dictionaries or reference translations for the applicative evaluation). These references enabled us to quickly and easily evaluate our methods. In a less rich environment, we would have had to use an expert to evaluate the relevance of the translations generated.

The medical domain is also an ideal domain to test a method based on the analysis of neoclassical compounds (among others). Even if combining forms can be found in many technical domains, we know that they are particularly frequent in the medical domain [NAM 07]. Thus, our first perspective will be to test our methods on a domain with few resources, for example on a topic linked to environmental studies.

C1.2.2. *Languages and morphological structures*

A second limit in our work concerns the small number and morphological variety of the language pairs we tested. We saw that the translation from English to French was open to the generation of fertile translations. It would be interesting to test the influence of the translation direction and the morphological type of languages used in the generation of such a type of translations. We are specifically thinking of testing our method by agglutinating source languages such as Turkish or Finnish.

We have tried to improve the genericness of the current compositional translation techniques. However, we remained focused on four morphological construction processes frequently found in Western European languages. Moreover, we considered the issue of fertility only from the angle of monolexical unit translation into polylexical units. Thus, the genericness of the system can still be increased by managing infixes and circumfixes, translating polylexical units into monolexical units, etc.

C1.2.3. *Applicative evaluation*

We have evaluated our translation generation method by comparing it to a reference. We would like to carry out an applicative evaluation of this method, especially by comparing the quality of the translations obtained with a lexicon which is only created from the distributional method versus a lexicon containing translations created from the distributional as well as the compositional method.

Linked to the issue of the knowledge field, we would like to renew our applicative evaluation experiment in better conditions. First of all, we would choose texts belonging to a domain which has very few bilingual resources. Moreover, we would check that the source corpus provides good coverage of the vocabulary of the texts to be translated so that the source and target corpora are sufficiently comparable.

C1.2.4. *Contextualization and tooling*

As a conclusion to this book, we wish to go over the four research axes highlighted at the end of Chapter 2, which are: (1) the automatic gathering of comparable corpora; (2) the search for translational equivalences; (3) the contextualization of terms and (4) the development of CAT tools created for comparable corpora.

From the viewpoint of the industry, we believe that the first two research topics have been sufficiently explored and that today there are reasonably mature techniques that could be transferred into the translation industry. However, as has been highlighted by our experiments, comparable corpora lexicons cannot be used in the same way as a lexicon extracted from parallel corpora. Indeed, lexicons extracted from comparable corpora will always be small and ambiguous. We believe that the role of comparable corpora belongs not during the translation phase itself but prior to the translation, during the documentation research phase described by [DUR 10]: they must allow the translator to become familiar with a new domain, to understand its notions and observe its uses. They can also be of great help to terminologists since they enable them to identify and observe the terms in contexts which have not been influenced by the source language.

To use all the potential of comparable corpora, it would thus be helpful to investigate in more detail the research aiming to contextualize terms, and develop suitable exploration tools. We should, for example, be able to select the most informative contexts of a term for the translator, whether it is on a semantic level (definition context) or a linguistic level (collocation and subcategorization). It would also be interesting to be able to "align" the contexts, i.e. compare as parallel corpora concordancers do, a source context and a target context which share a large part of their vocabulary. Finally, the comparable corpora cruelly lack tools to explore them.

It would be useful to integrate advanced functionalities such as research engines managing complex queries to CAT tools[2] or the possibilities for visualizing the semantic proximity between terms.

2 For example, the NETSPEAK engine [RIE 12] has an advanced query language: the query "*{ a b c }*" is matched with all the permutations of *a*, *b* and *c* and provides their frequency on the Internet – http://www.netspeak.cc.

PART 3

Appendices

Appendix 1

Measures

A1.1. Vectors normalization

In the following formulas, M is the head of the vector, m is one of its co-occurrents, $nbOcc(M, m)$ is the number of times when M and m co-occur, $nbOcc(M)$ is the number of co-occurrences of M, $nbOcc(m)$ is the number of occurrences of m.

A1.1.1. *Likelihood ratio [MOR 04]*

The likelihood ratio is calculated based on the following contingency table:

	m	$\neg m$	TOTAL
M	a	b	e
$\neg M$	c	d	h
TOTAL	f	g	N

Table A1.1. *Contingency table for the co-occurrence of words observed in the corpus*

in which a is the number of times when M and m co-occur ($nbOcc(M, m)$), b is the number of times when M co-occurs with another word than m, etc. N is the total number of co-occurrences calculated in the corpus.

The likelihood ratio TV between M and m can be obtained with:

$$TV(M,m) = a\log(a) + b\log(b) + c\log(c) + N\log(N) - e\log(e) - f\log(f) - g\log(g) - h\log(h) \qquad [A1.1]$$

A1.1.2. *Discounted log-ods [LAR 10b]*

Calculation of the *discounted log-ods* is also done based on Table A1.1:

$$odds\_ratio = log\frac{(a+\frac{1}{2})(d+\frac{1}{2})}{(b+\frac{1}{2})(c+\frac{1}{2})} \quad [A1.2]$$

A1.1.3. *Mutual Information [MOR 04, p. 106]*

$$IM(M,m) = \log\frac{nbOcc(M,m)}{nbOcc(M)\cdot nbOcc(m)} \quad [A1.3]$$

A1.1.4. *TFIDF [FUN 98, p. 8-11]*

$$TFIDF(M,m) = TF\cdot IDF \quad [A1.4]$$

$$TF = nbOcc(M,m) \quad [A1.5]$$

$$IDF(m) = \log\frac{nbMax}{nbOcc(m)} + 1 \quad [A1.6]$$

in which $nbMax$ is the highest frequency found on the corpus.

A1.2. Vectors similarity

In the following formulas, V_S is the source vector with the head M_S, V_C is the target vector with the head M_C, n is the number of bilingual lexicon entries, m_i is an entry in the bilingual lexicon, $P(M_S, m_i)$ is the number of standardized co-occurrences between m_i and the head of the source vector M_S, and $P(M_C, m_i)$ is the number of standardized co-occurrences between m_i and the head of the target vector M_C.

A1.2.1. *Cosine similarity [FUN 98, p. 12]*

$$Cosine(V_S, V_C) = \frac{\sum_{i=1}^{n} P(M_S,m_i)\cdot P(M_C,m_i)}{\sqrt{\sum_{i=1}^{n} P(M_S,m_i)^2 \cdot \sum_{i=1}^{n} P(M_C,m_i)^2}} \quad [A1.7]$$

A1.2.2. *Weighted Jaccard [PRO 10, p. 62]*

$$J(V_S, V_C) = \frac{\sum_{i=1}^{n} min(P(M_S,m_i), P(M_C,m_i))}{\sum_{i=1}^{n} max(P(M_S,m_i), P(M_C,m_i))} \quad [A1.8]$$

A1.2.3. *Euclidean distance [FUN 97, p. 196]*

$$DE(V_S, V_C) = \sum_{i=1}^{n} |P(M_S, m_i) - P(M_C, m_i)| \qquad [A1.9]$$

A1.2.4. *Normalized Euclidean distance [HAZ 12, p. 128]*

$$DEN(V_S, V_C) = \sqrt{\sum_{i=1}^{n} (\frac{P(M_S, m_i)}{||V_S||} - \frac{P(M_C, m_i)}{||V_C||})} \qquad [A1.10]$$

A1.3. Corpus comparability [LI 10, p. 645–646]

$$M(C_e, C_f) = \frac{\sum_{w \in C_e^v \cap D_e^v} \sigma(w, C_f^v) + \sum_{w \in C_f^v \cap D_f^v} \sigma(w, C_e^v)}{|C_e^v \cap D_e^v| + |C_f^v \cap D_f^v|} \qquad [A1.11]$$

$$\sigma(w, C^v) = \begin{cases} 1 & \text{if } T_w \cap C^v \neq \emptyset \\ 0 & \text{ifnot} \end{cases}$$

in which:

– C_e, C_f are the source and target corpora, respectively.

– C_e^v and C_f^v are the vocabulary of the source and target corpus, respectively (only lexical words).

– D_e^v, D_f^v are, respectively, the source and target entries of a bilingual dictionary.

– $\sigma(w, C^v)$ is a function returning 1 if at least one translation of the word w is found in the vocabulary of the corpus C.

A1.4. Values standardization [GEN 77, p. 48–50]

A1.4.1. *Value percentile*

The percentile of a value v is obtained by the formula:

$$percentile(v) = \frac{lower(v) + 0.5\, eff(v)}{N} \qquad [A1.12]$$

where $lower(s)$ is the number of individuals with a value lower than v, $eff(v)$ is the number of individuals with the value v and N is the total number of values.

A1.4.2. *Z-score*

The z-score is obtained with the standard normal table (Table A1.2). In the standard normal table T, the cell T_{ij} corresponds to the percentile matching to the z-score $i+j$. For example, the percentile 0.5438 matches the z-score 0.11 (line 0.1; column 0.01).

For percentiles lower than 0.5, we obtain the z-score as follows:

$$zscore(percentile) = -T(1 - percentile) \qquad [A1.13]$$

For example, the percentile 0.4562 matches the z-score -0.11.

A1.5. Evaluation measures

A1.5.1. *Coverage [LAN 08]*

$$C = \frac{|ST|}{|S|} \qquad [A1.14]$$

$$ST = \{s : |\mathcal{T}(s)| > 1\}$$

where:

– S is the set of source terms.

– $\mathcal{T}(s)$ is the set of translations generated by the system for the source term s.

A1.5.2. *TopN/precision at rank N [LAN 08]*

$$P_N = \frac{|SR_N|}{|ST|} \qquad [A1.15]$$

$$SR_N = \{s : \mathcal{T}_N(s) \cap \mathcal{R}(s) \neq \emptyset\}$$

$$ST = \{s : |\mathcal{T}(s)| > 1\}$$

where:

– $\mathcal{T}(s)$ is the set of translations generated by the system for the source term s.

– $\mathcal{T}_N(s)$ is the set Top N translations of s.

– $\mathcal{R}(s)$ is the set of reference translations of s.

z	0.00	0.01	0.02	0.03	0.04	0.05	0.06	0.07	0.08	0.09
0.0	0.5000	0.5040	0.5080	0.5120	0.5160	0.5199	0.5239	0.5279	0.5319	0.5359
0.1	0.5398	0.5438	0.5478	0.5517	0.5557	0.5596	0.5636	0.5675	0.5714	0.5753
0.2	0.5793	0.5832	0.5871	0.5910	0.5948	0.5987	0.6026	0.6064	0.6103	0.6141
0.3	0.6179	0.6217	0.6255	0.6293	0.6331	0.6368	0.6406	0.6443	0.6480	0.6517
0.4	0.6554	0.6591	0.6628	0.6664	0.6700	0.6736	0.6772	0.6808	0.6844	0.6879
0.5	0.6915	0.6950	0.6985	0.7019	0.7054	0.7088	0.7123	0.7157	0.7190	0.7224
0.6	0.7257	0.7291	0.7324	0.7357	0.7389	0.7422	0.7454	0.7486	0.7517	0.7549
0.7	0.7580	0.7611	0.7642	0.7673	0.7704	0.7734	0.7764	0.7794	0.7823	0.7852
0.8	0.7881	0.7910	0.7939	0.7967	0.7995	0.8023	0.8051	0.8078	0.8106	0.8133
0.9	0.8159	0.8186	0.8212	0.8238	0.8264	0.8289	0.8315	0.8340	0.8365	0.8389
1.0	0.8413	0.8438	0.8461	0.8485	0.8508	0.8531	0.8554	0.8577	0.8599	0.8621
1.1	0.8643	0.8665	0.8686	0.8708	0.8729	0.8749	0.8770	0.8790	0.8810	0.8830
1.2	0.8849	0.8869	0.8888	0.8907	0.8925	0.8944	0.8962	0.8980	0.8997	0.9015
1.3	0.9032	0.9049	0.9066	0.9082	0.9099	0.9115	0.9131	0.9147	0.9162	0.9177
1.4	0.9192	0.9207	0.9222	0.9236	0.9251	0.9265	0.9279	0.9292	0.9306	0.9319
1.5	0.9332	0.9345	0.9357	0.9370	0.9382	0.9394	0.9406	0.9418	0.9429	0.9441
1.6	0.9452	0.9463	0.9474	0.9484	0.9495	0.9505	0.9515	0.9525	0.9535	0.9545
1.7	0.9554	0.9564	0.9573	0.9582	0.9591	0.9599	0.9608	0.9616	0.9625	0.9633
1.8	0.9641	0.9649	0.9656	0.9664	0.9671	0.9678	0.9686	0.9693	0.9699	0.9706
1.9	0.9713	0.9719	0.9726	0.9732	0.9738	0.9744	0.9750	0.9756	0.9761	0.9767
2.0	0.9772	0.9778	0.9783	0.9788	0.9793	0.9798	0.9803	0.9808	0.9812	0.9817
2.1	0.9821	0.9826	0.9830	0.9834	0.9838	0.9842	0.9846	0.9850	0.9854	0.9857
2.2	0.9861	0.9864	0.9868	0.9871	0.9875	0.9878	0.9881	0.9884	0.9887	0.9890
2.3	0.9893	0.9896	0.9898	0.9901	0.9904	0.9906	0.9909	0.9911	0.9913	0.9916
2.4	0.9918	0.9920	0.9922	0.9925	0.9927	0.9929	0.9931	0.9932	0.9934	0.9936
2.5	0.9938	0.9940	0.9941	0.9943	0.9945	0.9946	0.9948	0.9949	0.9951	0.9952
2.6	0.9953	0.9955	0.9956	0.9957	0.9959	0.9960	0.9961	0.9962	0.9963	0.9964
2.7	0.9965	0.9966	0.9967	0.9968	0.9969	0.9970	0.9971	0.9972	0.9973	0.9974
2.8	0.9974	0.9975	0.9976	0.9977	0.9977	0.9978	0.9979	0.9979	0.9980	0.9981
2.9	0.9981	0.9982	0.9982	0.9983	0.9984	0.9984	0.9985	0.9985	0.9986	0.9986
3.0	0.9987	0.9987	0.9987	0.9988	0.9988	0.9989	0.9989	0.9989	0.9990	0.9990

Source: http://en.wikipedia.org/wiki/Standard_normal_table#Cumulative_table

Table A1.2. *Normal standard table*

A1.5.3. *Recall at rank N [LAN 08]*

$$R_N = C \times P_N = \frac{|SR_N|}{|S|} \qquad [A1.16]$$

$$SR_N = \{s : \mathcal{T}_N(s) \cap \mathcal{R}(s) \neq \emptyset\}$$

where:

– S is the set of source terms.

– $\mathcal{T}_N(s)$ is the set of Top N translations of s.

– $\mathcal{R}(s)$ is the set of reference translations of s.

A1.5.4. *F1-measure at rank N*

$$F1_N = 2 \times \frac{P_N \times R_N}{P_N + R_N} \quad [A1.17]$$

where:

– P_N is the precision at rank N.

– R_N is the recall at rank N.

A1.5.5. *MRR: mean reciprocal rank [YU 09]*

$$MRR = \frac{1}{|S|} \sum_{i=1}^{|S|} \frac{1}{rank_i} \quad [A1.18]$$

where S is the set of source terms with at least one candidate translation and $rank_i$ is the rank of the first correct candidate translation of the source term i.

A1.5.6. *MAP: mean average precision [MAN 08]*

$$MAP(Q) = \frac{1}{Q} \sum_{j=1}^{|Q|} \frac{1}{m_j} \sum_{k=1}^{m_j} Precision(R_{j^k}) \quad [A1.19]$$

where:

– Q is the set of queries.

– m_j is the number of documents to be retrieved for the queryQ_j.

– R_{jk} is the set of documents retrieved by the system for the query Q_j before the document k.

A1.5.7. *NDCG: normalized discounted cumulative gain [MAN 08]*

NDCG is based on discounted cumulative gain (DCG). DCG is calculated for a given rank (k):

$$DCG@k = rel_1 + \sum_{i=2}^{k} \frac{rel_i}{log_2(i)} \quad [A1.20]$$

where rel_i is the document relevance score i.

NDCG is:

$$NDCG@k = \frac{DCG@k}{IDCG@k} \quad [A1.21]$$

where $IDCG@k$ is the maximum DCG that can be reached, obtained by calculating DCG over the list of correctly ranked documents.

Finally, the average NDCG for all the queries Q is:

$$NDCG(Q,k) = \frac{1}{Q} \sum_{j=1}^{|Q|} \frac{DCG@k}{IDCG@k} \quad [A1.22]$$

A1.6. Annotators agreement

A1.6.1. $Kappa$ measure [CAR 96]

The $Kappa$ score is calculated from $P(a)$, the agreement observed among annotators, and $P(e)$, the probability of a random agreement ($1/N$ for which N is the number of categories used in the annotation):

$$Kappa = \frac{P(a) - P(e)}{1 - P(e)} \quad [A1.23]$$

A1.6.2. *Kappa* ***interpretation***

The *Kappa* score can thus be interpreted [LAN 77]:

Kappa	interpretation
< 0	no agreement
0.0 – 0.20	slight agreement
0.21 – 0.40	fair agreement
0.41 – 0.60	moderate agreement
0.61 – 0.80	substantial agreement
0.81 – 1.00	almost perfect agreement

Table A1.3. *Kappa scores*

Appendix 2

Data

A2.1. Comparable corpora

A2.1.1. *Water science*

The Water science corpus was created from academic abstracts from the English language journal *Water Science Technology*[1] and from academic papers from the French language journal *Sciences de l'eau*.[2] Its comparability rate is of 0.77.

	EN	FR
Number of words	2,202,523	2,382,033
Number of documents	11,914	500

Table A2.1. *Size of the Water science corpus (number of words and number of documents)*

A2.1.1.1. *English*

Extract A2.1. Paragraph from the English Water science corpus

```
The pseudo first-order rate constant (k obs)  for PCE
    dechlorination by 0.06 wt % Cu/Si was 0.028 h -1,
    which was 2.8 times higher than that by Si(0) alone.
```

1 http://www.iwaponline.com/wst/

2 http://www.rse.inrs.ca/

```
However, the k obs for PCE dechlorination decreased to
    0.0016 h -1 when the loading of Cu(II) increased to 3
    wt %. The EPMA results showed that the distribution of
    loading of 0.06 wt % Cu on the Si(0) surface constant
    was observed before the total coverage of the active
    sites on the reductive metal by the catalytic metal
    layer. The surface coverage of Cu to Si(0) can
    theoretically calculate by estimation of the lowest
    energy fcc(111) crystallographic orientation.
```

source: http://www.ncbi.nlm.nih.gov/pubmed/20595750

A2.1.1.2. *French*

Extract A2.2. Paragraph from the French Water science corpus

```
L'Interprétation des résultats de près de 150 essais de
    pompage fournit les valeurs suivantes (DASSARGUES é
    tal., 1987) 1.10-9 $<$ K $<$ 2.10-7 m/sec - pour les
    limons -pour le conglomérat résiduel 1.10-5 $<$ K $<$
    8.10-3 m/sec - pour les craies supérieures (fracturées)
    2.1 $<$H$<$ K $<$ 5.10-3 m/sec - pour les craies
    inférieures (compactes) 1.10-5 $<$ K $<$ 5.10-4 m/sec
    La porosité efficace (CASTANY, 1982) ou de drainage (DE
    MARSILY, 1981), déterminée par les essais de pompage et
    par observation des fluctuations de la surface
    piézométrique en fonction de l'infiltration efficace,
    serait de l'ordre de 5 % ; elle dépasserait toutefois
    10 % dans de nombreuses zones où la craie est plus
    fracturée et altérée.
```

http://www.rse.inrs.ca/art/volume4/v4n1_39.pdf

A2.1.2. *Breast cancer*

For the academic part, the Breast cancer corpus was created from academic papers gathered from the *Elsevier* portal[3] and *Google Scholar*.[4] For the popular science part, the corpus was created from articles on popular science websites meant for patients and their kin.

3 http://www.elsevier.com/

4 http://scholar.google.com/

	EN	FR	DE
Academic	198,244	267,180	197,187
Popular science	218,336	184,504	201,760
Total	416,580	451,684	398,947

Table A2.2. *Composition and size of the corpora in terms of number of occurrences*

	EN	FR	DE
Academic	70	78	103
Popular science	272	217	162
Total	342	295	265

Table A2.3. *Composition and size of the corpora in terms of number of documents*

	EN-FR	EN-DE
Academic	0.71	0.42
Popular science	0.69	0.46
All	0.74	0.45

Table A2.4. *Corpora comparability*

A2.1.2.1. *German*

A2.1.2.1.1. Academic discourse

Extract A2.3. Paragraph from the German academic Breast cancer corpus

```
In diesem Jahr werden rund 50000 bis 60000 Frauen an
    Brustkrebs erkranken. Zirka ein Drittel der betroffenen
    Frauen wird daran versterben. Damit ist das
    Mamma-Karzinom die häufigste Krebserkrankung bei Frauen
    in der westlichen Welt - Tendenz steigend. Die deutsche
    Antwort darauf heißt
    Interdisziplinäres-Zertifiziertes-Brustzentrum. Seit
    Einführung der Zertifizierung vor drei Jahren werden
    rund die Hälfte aller Brustkrebspatientinnen dort
    behandelt und die Erfolge geben dieser
    Therapieeinrichtung recht.
```

http://www.uni-frauenklinik-tuebingen.de/bereiche/brustzentrum/aktuelles/pressearchiv.html

A2.1.2.1.2. Popular science

Extract A2.4. Paragraph from the German popular science Breast cancer corpus

```
Wichtig ist, dass die behandelnden Ärzte Bescheid wissen, was der
    Patient selbst einnimmt oder anwendet. Der Gedanke "vielleicht␣
    hilft␣es␣nicht,␣es␣schadet␣aber␣auch␣nicht" sei falsch, sagt
    Kümmel. Schon ein Glas Grapefruitsaft oder Johanniskraut kann
    die Wirkung einer Chemotherapie aushebeln. Mulitvitaminkuren
    sind zum Beispiel bei Bestrahlungen kontraproduktiv.
    Brustkrebspatienten mit hormonempfindlichen Brustkrebs sollten
    keine hochdosierten Pflanzenextrakte einnehmen, die
    Phytoöstrogene enthalten, zum Beispiel Soja oder Ginseng. Die
    Finger lassen sollten Krebspatienten auch von Mitteln, die
    Heilung versprechen. Beispiele sind bittere Aprikosenkerne, in
    denen Amygdalin steckt, oder Galavit, ein Stoff, der im
    Internet als Krebstherapeutikum vermarktet wird. Auch bei
    Noni-, Goji- und Mangostinsäften gibt es bislang keinen
    Nachweis, dass sie gegen Krebs wirken.
Medizinische Datenflut
```

http://www.netdoktor.de/Magazin/Komplementaermedizin-bei-Kreb-11741.html

A2.1.2.2. *English*

A2.1.2.2.1. Academic discourse

Extract A2.5. Paragraph from the English academic Breast cancer corpus

```
Summary scores were calculated according to the EORTC manual.22
    Summary statistics were calculated for baseline scores,
    according to categories of type of surgery (Mx, WLE), time
    since surgery, CT, ET and age. Subscale scores were compared
    between groups of patients defined according to age and the
    set of clinical variables tested using t-tests and analysis of
    variance (ANOVA) as appropriate. In order to investigate the
    effect of confounding on observed associations with QOL
    scores, multiple regression was used, and the significance of
    variables tested using the F-test from an ANOVA that included
    all relevant independent variables (surgery, time since
    surgery, CT, ET and age). Hence the p-values from the F-test
    indicate the significance of each variable after allowing for
    the effects of the other variables listed. Variables which
    remain significant in the multiple regression can be said to
    have independent statistically significant effects on the
    outcome in question.
```

http://www.sciencedirect.com/science/article/pii/S0960977606002165

A2.1.2.2.2. Popular science discourse

Extract A2.6. Paragraph from the English popular science Breast cancer corpus

```
Breast awareness
Most breast cancers are detected by women who report
    unusual changes to their GP. This highlights the
    importance of being breast aware.
Breast awareness means knowing what your breasts look and
    feel like normally, so you can be aware of any changes
    and check them out with your doctor as soon as
    possible. If cancer is diagnosed, prompt treatment
    offers the best chance of a successful outcome.

So the message from Breakthrough Breast Cancer is simple:
Show your breasts some TLC. Touch. Look. Check. Be breast
    aware visit www.touchlookcheck.org.uk
```

http://www.plumslingerie.com/breastawareness-article-from-breakthroughorguk-z-18.html

A2.1.2.3. *French*

A2.1.2.3.1. Academic discourse

Extract A2.7. Paragraph from the French academic Breast cancer corpus

```
L'évaluation histopathologique est importante, puisqu'elle
    peut permettre aux cliniciens de modifier le schéma
    thérapeutique. Ainsi, des patientes en réponse complète
    histologique (RCH) et ayant subi une mammectomie
    pourront ne pas recevoir de radiothérapie. De plus, une
    chimiothérapie adjuvante sera plus volontiers proposée à
     une patiente qui n'est pas en RCH qu'à une patiente
    qui est en RCH.
Classifications histopathologiques de la réponse à la
    chimiothérapie
Plusieurs équipes de pathologistes ont proposé des
    classifications histopathologiques de la réponse à la
    chimiothérapie néoadjuvante. Il faut cependant
    souligner qu'il n'existe pas à l'heure actuelle de
    consensus permettant de privilégier une classification
    plutôt qu'une autre. Cela complique notablement les
    comparaisons des taux de réponses complètes
    histopathologiques (RCH) obtenues dans différentes é
    tudes. Le tableau 1( Tableau 1 ) résume les différentes
    classifications qui ont été décrites dans la
    littérature.
```

http://www.cancerdusein.org/cds/index.php?option=com_content&task=view&id=74&Itemid=169

A2.1.2.3.2. Popular science discourse

Extract A2.8. Paragraph from the French popular science Breast cancer corpus

```
L'adolescente
Quelles sont les précautions à prendre si l'on découvre une
    petite boule chez une adolescente ? Bien évidemment, il
    convient de consulter un médecin. Celui-ci procédera
    tout d'abord à l'interrogation de la patiente,
    c'est-à-dire, à la recherche d'apparition de la boule, à
     ses variations de volume par rapport aux règles, à sa
    sensibilité... puis à la recherche des antécédents
    personnels et familiaux, des facteurs de risques...
    etc. Le médecin procédera ensuite à l'examen clinique
    des seins par leur palpation méthodique zone par zone.
    Lorsque la boule décelée n'excède guère plus de 2 cm et
    que le bilan général de l'interrogatoire et de l'examen
    clinique est normal, le médecin pourra avancer le
    diagnostic de fibroadénome du sein de l'adolescente. Il
    s'agit d'une sorte de petit fibrome, comme pour
    l'utérus.
```

http://www.cancerdusein.org/cds/index.php?option=com_content&task=view&id=74&Itemid=169

A2.2. Texts to be translated and reference translations

A2.2.1. *Water sciences*

The academic texts to be translated and their translations correspond to academic paper abstracts from the *Sciences de l'eau* journal.[5] The popular science texts to be translated and their translations correspond to Web pages from the *Lenntech* company.[6]

	Number of documents	Number of words
Academic texts	3 paper abstracts	499
Popular science texts	1 Web page	425

Table A2.5. *Size of the texts to be translated in the Water science topic*

5 http://www.rse.inrs.ca/

6 http://www.lenntech.com/

A2.2.1.1. *Academic discourse*

A2.2.1.1.1. Text to be translated

Extract A2.9. Paragraph from a text to be translated, Water science topic, academic discourse

```
Health Significance of Bacterial Regrowth in Drinking
    Water: Free Opinion
The presence of heterotrophic bacteria in drinking water
    (tap, point-of use treated or bottled) poses a
    difficult problem because we do not clearly know if
    they are really innocuous.
 Two points of views are presented: they could be totally
     unimportant whatever their number or they can be
     opportunistic pathogens and even frank pathogens if
     they are allowed to multiply in large numbers.
These bacteria are not of faecal origin and are not
    indicators of faecal pollution even if occasionally
    some can be described as coliforms.
```

http://www.erudit.org/revue/rseau/1995/v8/n3/705225ar.html

A2.2.1.1.2. Reference translation

Extract A2.10. Paragraph from a reference translation, Water science topic, academic discourse

```
Effets sur la santé de la recroissance bactérienne dans les
    eaux de consommation / Health significance of bacterial
    regrowth in drinking water
La présence de bactéries hétérotrophes dans les eaux de
    consommation (robinet filtrée sur unités domestiques ou
    embouteillées) constitue un problème difficile à
    résoudre car on connaît très mal leurs effets sur la
    santé humaine.
Deux points de vue s'affrontent: l'une perçoit ces
    bactéries comme des bactéries sans aucune importance
    quel que soit leur nombre, l'autre suppose que
    certaines d'entre elles sont potentiellement pathogènes
    et que l'on ne doit pas leur permettre de se multiplier
    indûment dans l'eau de consommation.
Ces bactéries hétérotrophes sont présentes partout et elles
    trouvent dans l'eau de consommation une niche
    écologique qui permet parfois leur croissance en grand
    nombre (e.g., nodules du réseau, tuyauterie des
    maisons, chauffe-eau, eaux embouteillées, filtre à
    charbon actif, etc.).
```

http://www.erudit.org/revue/rseau/1995/v8/n3/705225ar.html

A2.2.1.2. *Popular discourse*

A2.2.1.2.1. Text to be translated

Extract A2.11. Paragraph from a text to be translated, Water science topic, popular science discourse

```
Examples from active carbon in different processes:

    * Ground water purification
    * The de-chlorination of process water
    * Water purification for swimming pools
    * The polishing of treated effluent

Process description:

Water is pumped in a column which contains active carbon,
    this water leaves the column through a draining system.
    The activity of an active carbon column depends on the
    temperature and the nature of the substances. Water
    goes through the column constantly, which gives an
    accumulation of substances in the filter. For that
    reason the filter needs to be replace periodically. A
    used filter can be regenerated in different ways,
    granular carbon can be regenerated easily by oxidizing
    the organic matter. The efficiency of the active carbon
    decreases by 5 - 10 % 1). A small part of the active
    carbon is destroyed during the regeneration process and
    must be replaced. If you work with different columns in
    series, you can assure that you will not have a total
    exhaustion of your purification system.
```

http://www.lenntech.fr/adsorption.htm

A2.2.1.2.2. Reference translation

Extract A2.12. Paragraph from a reference translation, Water science topic, popular science discourse

```
Exemples d'application :
    * Traitement des eaux souterraines polluées
    * Traitement contre les micropolluants, adsorption des
       traces de certains métaux lourds
    * Rétention de chlore
    * Filtration fine pour piscines
    * Filtration finale pour le rejet d'effluents

Les performances des filtres à charbon actif dépendent de
    la température, ainsi que du composé à adsorber.
```

```
Pour les applications de traitement d'eau dans les procédés
    des industries alimentaires, la filtration au charbon
    actif est souvent accompagnée d'une désinfection UV.

Description du processus

L'eau est pompée dans une colonne qui contient du charbon
    actif, cette eau quitte la colonne à travers un système
    drainant. L'activité de la colonne de charbon actif
    dépend de la température et de la nature des
    substances. L'eau passe à travers la colonne
    continuellement, ce qui entraîne une accumulation des
    substances sur le filtre. Pour cette raison, le filtre
    a besoin d'être remplacé périodiquement. Un filtre
    utilisé peut être régénéré de différentes façons, le
    charbon granulaire peut être régénéré facilement en
    oxydant la matière organique. L'efficacité du charbon
    actif diminue alors de 5 à 10%. Une petite partie du
    charbon actif est détruite pendant le processus de
    régénération et doit être remplacée. Si vous travaillez
    avec différentes colonnes en série, vous pouvez vous
    assurer que vous n'aurez pas un épuisement total de
    votre système de purification.
```

http://www.lenntech.com/library/adsorption/adsorption.htm

A2.2.2. *Breast cancer*

A2.2.2.1. *Academic discourse*

The academic texts to be translated and their translations correspond to academic paper abstracts from the *Elsevier* portal.[7] The popular science texts to be translated and their translations are taken from web pages of the Canadian Breast Cancer Foundation.[8]

	Number of documents	Number of words
Academic texts	3 paper abstracts	508
Popular science texts	1 web page	613

Table A2.6. *Size of the texts to the translated, Water science topic*

7 http://www.elsevier.com/

8 http://www.cbcf.org/

A2.2.2.1.1. Text to be translated

Extract A2.13. Paragraph from a text to be translated, Breast cancer topic, academic discourse

```
Furthermore, these studies have shown that these pathways
    direct and in turn are influenced by the tissue
    structure. Tissue structure is directed by the
    cooperative interactions of the cell-cell and
    cell-ECM pathways and can be modified by stromal
    factors. Not surprisingly then, loss of tissue
    structure and alterations in ECM components are
    associated with the appearance and dissemination of
    breast tumors, and malignancy is associated with
    perturbations in cell adhesion, changes in adhesion
    molecules, and a stromal reaction.
```

http://pmcc.web-t.cisti.nrc.ca/articlerender.cgi?artid=1705474

A2.2.2.1.2. Reference translation

Extract A2.14. Paragraph from a text to be translated, Breast cancer topic, academic discourse

```
De plus, ces études ont montré que ces voies règlent la
    structure tissulaire et qu'en retour, elles sont
    influencées par elle. La structure tissulaire est
    réglée par des interactions coopératives entre les
    voies de signalement entre cellules et entre les
    cellules et la MEC; elle peut également être modifiée
    par des facteurs du stroma. Il n'est donc pas
    surprenant qu'une perte de structure tissulaire et que
    des modifications de constituants de la MEC soient
    associées à l'apparence et la dissémination des
    tumeurs mammaires, et que la malignité soit associée à
    des perturbations de l'adhérence cellulaire, à des
    changements dans les molécules d'adhérence et à une
    réaction du stoma.
```

http://www.nrcresearchpress.com/doi/abs/10.1139/o96-089

A2.2.2.2. *Popular discourse*

A2.2.2.2.1. Text to be translated

Extract A2.15. Paragraph from a text to be translated, Breast cancer topic, popular science discourse

Breast cancer starts in the cells of the breast. The breast tissue covers an area larger than just the breast. It extends up to the collarbone and from the armpit across to the breastbone in the centre of the chest. The breasts sit on the chest muscles that cover the ribs. Each breast is made of glands, ducts (thin tubes) and fatty tissue. Lobules are groups of glands that can produce milk. Milk flows from the lobules through a network of ducts to the nipple. The nipple is in the centre of a darker area of skin called the areola. Fatty tissue fills the spaces between the lobules and ducts and protects them.

A woman's breasts may feel different at different times of her menstrual cycle, sometimes becoming lumpy just before her period. Breast tissue also changes with age. Breast tissue in younger women is mostly made of glands and milk ducts, but older women's breasts are made up mostly of fatty tissue.

A2.2.2.2.2. Reference translation

Extract A2.16. Paragraph from a reference translation, Breast cancer topic, popular science discourse

Le cancer du sein se forme dans les cellules du sein. Le tissu mammaire ne comprend pas seulement le sein, mais aussi la partie du corps comprise entre la clavicule, l'aisselle et la lame du sternum, au milieu de la poitrine. Les seins reposent sur les muscles de la poitrine qui recouvrent les côtes. Chaque sein est constitué de glandes mammaires, de canaux galactophores (petits conduits) et de tissu adipeux. Les glandes mammaires, groupées en lobules, produisent le lait maternel, qui circule depuis les lobules jusqu'au mamelon par un réseau de canaux. Le mamelon se trouve au centre d'une région cutanée plus foncée, appelée aréole. Le tissu adipeux occupe l'espace entre les lobules et les canaux, et les protège.

À différents moments de son cycle menstruel, la femme pourra éprouver des sensations différentes au niveau de ses seins; ceux-ci deviendront parfois grumeleux juste avant les règles. Le tissu mammaire subit également des changements au cours de la vie. Chez les femmes plus jeunes, le tissu mammaire est principalement constitué de glandes et de canaux galactophores alors que chez les femmes plus âgées, le tissu adipeux prédomine.

A2.3. Linguistic resources

A2.3.1. *General-language bilingual dictionary*

The general-language bilingual dictionary is integrated in the linguistic analyzer XELDA (version 2.8.1).[9] It is not directly accessible. The number of entries mentioned is the one provided by the software publishing company.

	EN → FR	EN → DE
General-language bilingual dictionary	37,655 → 59,495	37,655 → 69,285

Table A2.7. *Size of the general-language dictionaries (number of entries)*

A2.3.2. *Thesaurus*

The general-language bilingual dictionary is integrated in the linguistic analyzer XELDA (version 2.8.1).[10] It is not directly accessible. The number of entries mentioned is the one provided by the software publishing company.

	EN	FR	DE
Synonyms	5,064 → 7,596	2,387 → 3,169	4,209 → 4,883

Table A2.8. *Size of the thesauri (number of entries)*

A2.3.3. *Bound morphemes translation table*

The bound morphemes translation table was manually created from online resources,[11] and from an encyclopedic dictionary [DRO 06].

A2.3.3.1. *Caption*

:p: prefix;

:c: combining form;

:s: suffix;

:w: word.

9 http://www.temis.com

10 http://www.temis.com

11 http://medical-dictionary.thefreedictionary.com/; http://georges.dolisi.free.fr/Terminologie/Menu/terminologie__medicale_menu.htm.

EN	DE	FR
ab:p	a:p, ab:p, abs:p, gegenteil:w, nicht:w, umgekehrt:w	a:p, anti:p, contraire:w, inverse:w
anti:p	anti:p, anti:w, gegen:w, gegenteil:w	anti:p, anti:w, contr:p, contraire:w, contre:p, contre:w
auto:p	aut:p, auto:p, eigen:w, persönlich:w, selbst:p, selbst:w, unmittelbar:w	auto:p, propre:w, soimême:w
bi:p	bi:p, doppelheit:w, zwei:w, zweiheit:w	bi:p, deux:w, di:p, double:w
co:p	co:p, com:p, con:p, ko:p, kom:p, kon:p, mit:w, zusammen:w	co:p, ensemble:w, parallèle:w
contra:p	contra:p, gegen:w, gegenteil:w, kontra:p	contr:p, contra:p, contre:p, contre:w, contro:p
counter:p	contra:p, gegen:w, gegenteil:w, kontra:p	contr:p, contra:p, contre:p, contre:w, contro:p
cyto:p	cyto:p, zelle:w, zyto:p	cellule:w, cyto:p
de:p	de:p, entfernen:w, nicht:w, ohne:w, privat:w, stoppen:w	arrêter:w, de:p, dé:p, dés:p, enlever:w, privé:w, sans:w, ôter:w
di:p	bi:p, di:p, doppelheit:w, zwei:w, zweiheit:w	bi:p, deux:w, di:p, double:w
dis:p	dis:p, entfernen:w, in:p, nicht:w, ohne:w, privat:w, stoppen:w, un:p	arrêter:w, de:p, dé:p, dés:p, enlever:w, privé:w, sans:w, ôter:w
dys:p	dys:p, krank:w, schlecht:w, störung:w	dys:p, dé:p, mal:w, mauvais:w
epi:p	auf:w, epi:p, top:w, über:w	dessus:w, supérieur:w, sur:w, épi:p
extra:p	ausserhalb:w, außerhalb:w, extern:w, extra:p, extra:w, mehr:w	dehors:w, externe:w, extra:p, extra:w, extérieur:w, hors:w
fore:p	anterioren:w, vor:p, vor:w, vorherige:w, vorwärts:w	antérieur:w, avant:w, devant:w, pro:p, pré:p
hyper:p	hyper:p, top:w, zu:w, übermässig:w, übermäßig:w	excessif:w, hyper:p, outrance:w, supérieur:w, sur:p, trop:w
hypo:p	boden:w, hypo:p, niedrig:w, unten:w, unter:p, unter:w	dessous:w, endessous:w, hypo:p, inférieur:w, sous:p, sous:w, sub:p

in:p	gegenteil:w, in:w, innen:w, nicht:w, ohne:w, umgekehrt:w, un:p	contraire:w, in:p, inverse:w, ir:p, non:w, pas:w, sans:w
inter:p	dazwischen:w, inter:p, mitten:w, unter:w, zwischen:w	entr:p, entre:p, entre:w, inter:p
intra:p	in:w, innen:w, innerhalb:w, intern:w, intra:p	dans:w, dedans:w, entre:w, interne:w, intra:p, intra:w, intérieur:w
ir:p	gegenteil:w, nicht:w, ohne:w, umgekehrt:w, un:p, un:w	contraire:w, in:p, inverse:w, ir:p, non:w, pas:w, sans:w
meta:p	met:p, meta:p, meta:w, oben:w, top:w, über:w, überlegen:w	audessus:w, dessus:w, meta:p, supérieur:w, sur:w
micro:p	klein:w, micro:p, mikro:p, winzig:w	micro:p, minuscule:w, petit:w
mid:p	dazwischen:w, halb:w, hälfte:w, mid:p, mitt:p, mitte:w, mitter:w, teilweise:w, während:w	durant:w, en_partie:w, mi:p, moitié:w, semi:p
mis:p	falsch:w, krank:w, miss:p, schlecht:w	erroné:w, faux:w, mal:w, mauvais:w, mé:p
mono:p	allein:w, ein:w, einzeln:w, einzig:w, einzigartig:w, mon:p, mono:p	mono:p, seul:w, un:w, uni:p, unique:w
multi:p	mehr:w, mehrere:w, multi:p, verschiedene:w, viel:w, viele:w	multi:p, multiple:w, plusieurs:w, poly:p
neo:p	erneuert:w, jung:w, neo:p, neu:w, neun:w	neuf:w, nouveau:w, néo:p
non:p	anti:w, gegenteil:w, nicht:p, nicht:w, non:w, umgekehrt:w, un:p	contr:p, contre:p, ne_pas:w, non:p, non:w, pas:w
out:p	aus:p, ausgehen:w, ausserhalb:w, außerhalb:w, extern:w, extra:w, hinaus:p, out:w, äussere:w, äußere:w, über:p	dehors:w, externe:w, extra:p, extra:w, extérieur:w, hors:w, sortir:w
over:p	oberhalb:w, zu_viel:w, über:p, über:w, überlegen:w, übermässig:w, übermäßig:w	audessus:w, dessus:w, excessif:w, hyper:p, outrance:w, super:p, super:w, supérieur:w, sur:p, sur:w, trop:w

para:p	durch:w, nahe:w, neben:w, par:p, para:p, via:w	au_moyen_de:w, côté:w, par:p, para:p, à_côté_de:w, à_travers:w
peri:p	herum:w, peri:p	autour:w, péri:p
poly:p	mehr:w, mehrere:w, poly:p, verschiedene:w, viel:w, viele:w	multi:p, multiple:w, plusieurs:w, poly:p
post:p	hinter:w, hintere:w, nach:p, nach:w, post:p	après:w, post:p, post:w, postérieur:w
pre:p	anterioren:w, pre:p, vor:p, vor:w	antérieur:w, avant:w, devant:w, pro:p, pré:p
pro:p	für:w, günstig:w, pro:p, pro:w, vor:w, zugunsten:w	antérieur:w, avant:w, devant:w, en_faveur_de:w, favorable:w, pour:w, pro:p, pré:p
re:p	erneut_starten:w, etwas_wieder:w, neu:w, re:p, red:p, wieder:w	encore:w, r:p, re:p, recommencer:w, refaire:w, ré:p, à_nouveau:w
self:p	auto:p, eigen:w, eigenen:w, persönlich:w, selbst:p, selbst:w	auto:p, propre:w, soimême:w
semi:p	halb:p, halb:w, hälfte:w, in_teil:w, semi:p, teilweise:w	durant:w, en_partie:w, mi:p, moitié:w, semi:p
sub:p	hypo:p, sub:p, unter:p, unter:w, unterlegen:w	dessous:w, endessous:w, hypo:p, inférieur:w, sous:p, sous:w, sub:p
super:p	für:w, hinaus:w, hoch:p, oberhalb:w, super:p, super:w, zu_viel:w, über:p, über:w, überlegen:w, übermässig:w, übermäßig:w	audessus:w, dessus:w, excessif:w, outrance:w, super:p, super:w, supérieur:w, sur:p, sur:w, trop:w
tel:p	abstand:w, entfernt:w, fern:w, tel:p, tele:p	distant:w, tel:p, tél:p, télé:p
tele:p	abstand:w, entfernt:w, fern:w, tel:p, tele:p	distant:w, tel:p, tél:p, télé:p
trans:p	durch:w, hindurch:w, quer_durch:w, trans:p	:w, trans:p, à_travers:w
tri:p	drei:w, tri:p, trio:w	tri:p, trio:w, trois:w, à_trois:w
ultra:p	jenseits:w, ultra:p, über:w, über_hinaus:w, überlegen:w	dessus:w, supérieur:w, sur:w, ultra:p

un:p	gegenteil:w, nicht:w, ohne:w, umgekehrt:w, un:p	contraire:w, in:p, inverse:w, ir:p, non:w, pas:w, sans:w
under:p	hypo:p, unter:p, unter:w, unterlegen:w	dessous:w, endessous:w, inférieur:w, sous:p, sous:w
uni:p	allein:w, ein:p, einheitlich:w, einmal:w, einzig:w, einzigartig:w, uni:p	mono:p, seul:w, un:w, uni:p, unique:w
adeno:c	adeno:c, druse:w, gangliom:c, ganglion:c, geschwulst:w, glandula:c	adéno:c, ganglion:w, glande:w, glandulaire:w
adreno:c	adrenal:c, nebennieren:w	adréno:c, surrénal:w
aemia:c	blut:w, ämie:c	hémie:c, sang:w, émie:c, émique:c
afro:c	afrikan:w, afrikanisch:w, afro:c	africain:w, afro:c
algia:c	algie:c, schmerz:w, schmerzzustand:w	algie:c, algique:c, douleur:w
amino:c	amin:c, amine:w, amino:c	amine:w, amino:c
andr:c	andro:c, mann:w, männlich:w	andr:c, andro:c, homme:w, masculin:w, mâle:w
andro:c	andro:c, mann:w, männlich:w	andr:c, andro:c, homme:w, masculin:w, mâle:w
angi:c	angio:c, blutgefäß:w	angi:c, angio:c, vaisseau:w
angio:c	angio:c, blutgefäß:w, schiff:c	angi:c, angio:c, vaisseau:w
anthra:c	anthra:c, kohle:w	anthra:c
aroma:c	aroma:c, aromat:c, aromat:w	aroma:c, arôme:w
arthr:c	arthr:c, arthri:c, arthro:c, bandscheiben:w, knochen:w	arthr:c, arthro:c, articulation:w
astro:c	astero:c, astro:c, astron:c, stern:w	astr:c, astre:w, astro:c, étoile:w
audio:c	audi:c, audio:c, gehör:w, hörbar:w	audio:c, son:w, écouter:w
bio:c	bio:c, biologie:w, biologisch:w	bio:c, biologie:w, biologique:w
blast:c	blast:c, blasto:c, embryo:w, embryonal:w, keim:w	blast:c, blastique:c, blastique:w, blasto:c, embryon:w, embryonnaire:w, germe:w, immature:w

blastic:c	blastom:c, blastom:w, keim:w	blast:c, blastique:c, blastique:w, blasto:c, blastome:w, embryon:w, embryonnaire:w, germe:w, immature:w
brachy:c	brachy:c, brachys:c, kurz:w	brachy:c, court:w, raccourcissement:w
bromo:c	brom:c, brome:w, bromo:c, duft:w, riechend:w	brom:c, brome:w, bromide:w, bromo:c, odeur:w, puanteur:w
broncho:c	bronch:c, bronchial:w, bronchitis:w, broncho:c, bronchus:w	bronch:c, bronche:w, bronchio:c, broncho:c
calc:c	calcium:c, calcium:w, kalk:c, verkalkung:w	calc:c, calcium:w, calco:c
carbo:c	karb:c, karbo:c, kohl:w, kohlenstoff:w	carb:c, carbo:c, carbone:w, charbon:w
carcino:c	carcinome:w, karzino:c, karzinom:c, karzinom:w, kreb:w, krebs:w, onco:c, tumor:w	cancer:w, cancér:c, cancéro:c, carcin:c, carcino:c, onco:c
cardio:c	herz:w, kard:c, kardi:c, kardio:c	cardi:c, cardiaque:w, cardio:c, coeur:w
centro:c	zentr:c, zentro:c, zentrum:w	centr:c, centre:w, centrie:c, centrique:c, centrisme:c, centro:c
cerebro:c	gehirn:w, kohlenstoff:w, zerebr:c, zerebralen:w, zerebro:c	cerveau:w, cérébr:c, cérébral:w, cérébro:c
charactero:c	charakter:c, charaktero:c, persönlichkeit:w	charactér:c, charactéro:c
chem:c	chem:c, chemi:c, chemikalie:w, chemikalien:w, chemische:w, chemo:c	chimie:w, chimio:c, chimique:w, chémo:c
chemi:c	chem:c, chemi:c, chemikalie:w, chemikalien:w, chemische:w, chemo:c	chimie:w, chimio:c, chimique:w, chémo:c
chemo:c	chem:c, chemi:c, chemikalie:w, chemikalien:w, chemische:w, chemo:c	chimie:w, chimio:c, chimique:w, chémo:c
chloro:c	chlor:c, chlore:w, chloro:c	chlor:c, chlorine:w, chloro:c, vert:w

chondr:c	chondr:c, chondri:c, chondriale:c, chondrio:c, chondrium:c, chondro:c, knorpel:w	cartilage:w, chondr:c, chondrie:c, chondro:c, grain:w, granulaire:w
chondri:c	chondr:c, chondri:c, chondriale:c, chondrio:c, chondrium:c, chondro:c, knorpel:w	cartilage:w, chondr:c, chondrie:c, chondro:c, grain:w, granulaire:w
chondrion:c	chondr:c, chondri:c, chondriale:c, chondrio:c, chondrium:c, chondro:c, knorpel:w	cartilage:w, chondr:c, chondrie:c, chondro:c, grain:w, granulaire:w
chondro:c	chondr:c, chondri:c, chondriale:c, chondrio:c, chondrium:c, chondro:c, knorpel:w	cartilage:w, chondr:c, chondrie:c, chondro:c, grain:w, granulaire:w
choreo:c	choreo:c, tanz:w	choré:c, choréo:c, danse:w
chorio:c	chori:c, chorio:c, chorion:w, choroidal:w, chorr:c, membran:w	chor:c, chori:c, chorio:c, chorion:w, choro:c, choroïde:w
chromato:c	chrom:c, chromato:c, farbe:w	chrom:c, chromat:c, chromato:c, chromo:c, couleur:w
chromo:c	chrom:c, chromato:c, farbe:w	chrom:c, chromat:c, chromato:c, chromo:c, couleur:w
chrono:c	chron:c, chrono:c, zeit:w	chron:c, chrono:c, temps:w
claustro:c	klaustr:c, klaustro:c, käfig:w, raum:w	claustr:c, claustro:c, cloîtrer:w, clôture:w
clinico:c	klinik:c, klinik:w, klinisch:w	clinico:c, clinique:w
colo:c	darm:w, kolo:c	coli:c, colo:c, colon:w, intestin:w
cryo:c	eis:w, frost:w, kry:c, kryo:c, kälte:w	cry:c, cryo:c, froid:w
cyclo:c	rund:w, zykl:c, zyklo:c	cercle:w, cycl:c, cycle:c, cyclique:w, cyclo:c, rond:w, roue:w, récurrent:w
cyte:c	cyto:c, zell:w, zyt:c, zyto:c	cellule:w, cyt:c, cyte:c, cyto:c
cyto:c	cyto:c, zell:w, zyt:c, zyto:c	cellule:w, cyt:c, cyte:c, cyto:c

demo:c	bevölkerung:w, dem:c, demo:c, staat:w, volk:w	démo:c, peuple:w, population:w
densito:c	densit:c, densito:c, dichte:c, dichte:w	dense:w, densit:c, densito:c, densité:w
dermo:c	derm:c, derm:w, derma:c, derme:c, dermo:c, haut:w	dermat:c, dermato:c, dermo:c, peau:w
di:c	di:c, dia:c, doppelt:w, paar:w, zwei:w	bi:c, deux:w, di:c, double:w
dosi:c	dosi:c, dosis:c, dosis:w, messen:w, rationieren:w	dose:w, dosi:c
eco:c	eco:c, umwelt:w, öko:c, ökologie:w	éco:c, écologie:w, écologique:w
ectasia:c	ausdehnung:w, ectasia:c, erweiterung:w	dilatation:w, ectasie:c
ectomy:c	ablation:w, abschnitt:w, ektomie:c, entfernung:w, resektion:w	ablation:w, coupe:w, ectomie:c, section:w
electro:c	electr:c, electro:c, elektr:c, elektrisch:w, elektro:c, strom:w	électr:c, électricité:w, électrique:w, électro:c
embryo:c	embr:c, embryo:c, embryo:w, leibesfrucht:w, ungeborene:w, ur:c, ur:w	embry:c, embryo:c, embryon:w, foetus:w
endocrino:c	absondern:w, endokrin:c, endokrin:w, endokrinen:w, sekret:w, sekretion:w	endocrino:c
epi:c	auf:w, epi:c, über:w	dessus:w, supérieur:w, sur:w, épi:c
epidemio:c	epidem:c, epidemi:c, epidemie:w, epidemio:c	épidémio:c
erythro:c	erythr:c, erythro:c, rot:w	rouge:w, érythro:c
estro:c	estr:c, estro:c, weibliches_geschlechtshormon:w, östr:c, östro:c, östrogen:w	oestro:c, oestrogène:w
fibro:c	faser:w, fiber:w, fibr:c, fibro:c	fibr:c, fibre:w, fibrille:w, fibro:c, fibrosis:w, filament:w, lobe:w
fluoro:c	fluor:c, fluor:w, fluoreszenz:w, fluori:c, fluoro:c	fluor:c, fluorine:w, fluoro:c, flurorescence:w
fluro:c	fluor:c, fluor:w, fluoreszenz:w, fluori:c, fluoro:c	fluro:c

gastro:c	bauch:w, gaster:c, gastr:c, gastro:c, magen:w	estomac:w, gastr:c, gastrique:w, gastro:c, ventre:w
gen:c	ausgangspunkt:w, auslöser:w, gen:c, hervorbringend:w, hervorgebracht:w, verursachend:w, verursacht:w	gène:c
gene:c	ausgangspunkt:w, auslöser:w, gen:c, hervorbringend:w, hervorgebracht:w, verursachend:w, verursacht:w	gène:c, producteur:w, produire:w
geneous:c	ausgangspunkt:w, auslöser:w, gen:c, hervorbringend:w, hervorgebracht:w, verursachend:w, verursacht:w	gène:c, produit:w, résultant:w
genic:c	gen:c, hervorbringend:w, hervorgebracht:w, verursachend:w, verursacht:w	génique:c
genicity:c	genick:c, hals:w, hervorbringend:w, hervorgebracht:w, kopfgelenk:w, verursachend:w, verursacht:w	génicité:c
geno:c	genitalien:w, geschlecht:c, geschlecht:w	gén:c, génit:c, génital:w, génito:c, géno:c
gens:c	ausgangspunkt:w, auslöser:w, gen:c, hervorbringend:w, hervorgebracht:w, verursachend:w, verursacht:w	gènes:c
glyco:c	glyk:c, glyko:c, zucker:w	gluc:c, gluco:c, glucose:w, glyc:c, glyco:c, sucre:w
gonado:c	geschlechtsdrüse:w, gonad:c, gonade:w, gonado:c, keimdrüse:w	gonade:w, gonado:c
grapher:c	aufnehmen:w, graf:c, graph:c, schreiben:w	enregistrer:w, grapheur:c, écrire:w, écriture:w
graphic:c	aufgernommen:w, graphisch:c, schriftlich:w	enregistrer:w, graphique:c, graphique:w, écrire:w, écriture:w
graphy:c	aufnahme:w, graphie:c, schreiben:w	enregistrer:w, graphie:c, écrire:w, écriture:w
gynaeco:c	frau:w, gynäk:c, gynäko:c	femme:w, gyn:c, gyno:c, gynéco:c

gynec:c	frau:w, gynäk:c, gynäko:c	
gyneco:c	frau:w, gynäk:c, gynäko:c	
haemato:c	blut:w, hämat:c, hämato:c	hém:c, hémat:c, hémato:c, hémo:c, sang:w
hemato:c	blut:w, hämat:c, hämato:c	hém:c, hémat:c, hémato:c, hémo:c, sang:w
hepato:c	hepat:c, hepato:c, leber:w	foie:w, hépar:c, héparo:c, hépat:c, hépato:c
hetero:c	hetero:c, unterschiedlich:w	autre:w, hétéro:c
histio:c	gewebe:w, histo:c	hist:c, histi:c, histio:c, histo:c, tissu:w
histo:c	gewebe:w, histo:c	hist:c, histi:c, histio:c, histo:c, tissu:w
homo:c	entsprechend:w, gleich:w, gleichartig:w, homo:c	homo:c, homéo:c, ressemblant:w, semblable:w
hydro:c	hydr:c, hydro:c, wasser:w	eau:w, hyd:c, hydr:c, hydro:c, liquide:w
hypno:c	hypn:c, hypno:c, schlaf:w	hypn:c, hypno:c, hypnose:w, sommeil:w
hypo:c	hyp:c, hypo:c, unter:c, unter:w	bas:w, dessous:w, endessous:w, faible:w, hypo:c, inférieur:w, sous:c, sous:w, sub:c
hyster:c	gebärmutter:w, hyster:c, hysteri:c, hysterio:c	hystér:c, hystéro:c, utérus:w
immuno:c	immun:c, immun:w, immunität:w, immuno:c	dispense:w, exemption:w, immun:c, immunité:w, immuno:c, remise:w
iso:c	gleich:w, iso:c	iso:c, régulier:w, symétrique:w, uniforme:w, égal:w
kinesio:c	bewegung:w, kinesi:c, kinesio:c	kin:c, kinési:c, kinésio:c, mouvement:w
leio:c	glatt:w, leio:c	lio:c, lisse:w, lisso:c, léio:c
loco:c	lokal:w, loko:c	local:w, loco:c
logic:c	logik:w, logiken:w, logisch:c, logish:w	logique:c, logique:w
logist:c	fachmann:w, loge:c, logik:w, logiken:w, logish:w, wissenschaftler:w	logiste:c

logy:c	lehre:w, logie:c, logik:w, logiken:w, logish:w, wissenschaft:w	logie:c
lymph:c	lymph:c, lymph:w, lympho:c	lymph:c, lymphe:w, lympho:c
lympho:c	lymph:c, lymph:w, lympho:c	lymph:c, lymphe:w, lympho:c
macro:c	gross:w, lang:w, makr:c, makro:c	gros:w, incluant:w, long:w, macrie:c, macro:c
mamma:c	brust:w, mamm:c, mamma:c, mammo:c	mamelle:w, mamm:c, mamma:c, mammaire:w, mammo:c, sein:w
mammo:c	brust:w, mamm:c, mamma:c, mammo:c	mamelle:w, mamm:c, mamma:c, mammaire:w, mammo:c, sein:w
mast:c	brust:w, mast:c, mastie:c, masto:c	mamelle:w, mammaire:w, mast:c, masto:c, mastoïd:c, mastoïdo:c, sein:w
mastia:c	brust:w, mast:c, mastie:c, masto:c	mastie:c
medio:c	medio:c, mitte:w	milieu:w, médi:c, média:c, médio:c
meric:c	mer:c, mere:c, segment:w	mère:c, mér:c, mérisme:c, méro:c, partie:w, élément:w
meta:c	absiedelungen:w, meta:c, stamm:w	audessus:w, dessus:w, meta:c, méta:c, supérieur:w, sur:w
methodo:c	method:c, methode:w, weise:w	méthodo:c
metric:c	mass:w, messen:w, metrisch:c	mesure:w, mesurer:w, métrique:c
metry:c	mass:w, messen:w, metrie:c, metrik:c	calcul:w, calculer:w, mesure:w, mesurer:w, métrie:c
micro:c	fein:w, gering:w, klein:w, mikr:c, mikro:c, millionstel:w	micro:c, minuscule:w, petit:w
milli:c	milli:c, tausendstel:w	milli:c, millième:w
mito:c	faden:w, fadenförmige:w, mito:c	filament:w, mito:c, mitose:w
mmastia:c	brust:w, mast:c, mastie:c, masto:c	mastie:c
mono:c	allein:w, einzeln:w, einzig:w, mon:c, mono:c	mono:c, seul:w, un:w, uni:c, unique:w
morpho:c	form:w, morpho:c	forme:w, morph:c, morphie:c, morphique:c, morphisme:c, morpho:c
musculo:c	musculo:c, muskel:c, muskel:w, muskulär:w	muscle:w, muscul:c, musculo:c, myo:c

mycin:c	hyaluronsäure:w, mycin:c	champignon:w, mucéto:c, myc:c, myce:c, mycine:c, myco:c, mycète:c, mycét:c
myco:c	myko:c, pilz:w	
myo:c	muskel:w, my:c, myo:c	muscle:w, my:c, myo:c
neo:c	erneuert:w, jung:w, neo:c, neu:w	jeune:w, nouveau:w, né:c, néo:c
neuro:c	nerven:c, nerven:w, neur:c	nerf:w, neur:c, neural:c, neurie:c, neuro:c
nucleo:c	kern:w, nucleo:c, zellkern:w	noyau:w, nucleus:w, nuclé:c, nucléo:c
oculo:c	augen:w, okular:c, okulär:c	ocul:c, oculo:c, oeil:w, ophtalm:c, ophtalmo:c
oestro:c	estr:c, estro:c, weibliches_geschlechtshormon:w, östr:c, östro:c, östrogen:w	oestr:c, oestro:c
oligo:c	O:w, olig:c, oligo:c, spuren:c	insuffisant:w, olig:c, oligo:c, petit:w, peu:w
onco:c	anschwellung:w, carcinom:w, karcinom:w, karzin:c, karzino:c, krebs:w, onc:c, onco:c	courbure:w, grosseur:w, onc:c, onch:c, oncho:c, onco:c, tumeur:w, volume:w
oophor:c	eierstock:w, oophor:c, oophori:c, ovar:c, ovarek:c, ovari:c, ovariek:c, ovarien:w, ovarium:w	oo:c, oophor:c, oophoro:c, ovaire:w, ovar:c, ovari:c
ophthalmo:c	augen:w, oculär:c, okular:c, ophtalmo:c	ocul:c, oculo:c, oeil:w, ophtalm:c, ophtalmo:c
organo:c	organ:c, organ:w, organisch:w, organo:c	organ:c, organe:w, organo:c, outil:w
ortho:c	aufrecht:w, ortho:c	correct:w, droit:w, normal:w, ortho:c, régulier:w
osteo:c	knochen:w, osteo:c	os:w, ossi:c, osté:c, ostéo:c
ovar:c	eierstock:w, oophor:c, oophori:c, ovar:c, ovarek:c, ovari:c, ovariek:c, ovarien:w, ovarium:w	oo:c, oophor:c, oophoro:c, ov:c, ovaire:w, ovar:c, ovari:c, ovario:c, ovo:c
ovari:c	eierstock:w, oophor:c, oophori:c, ovar:c, ovarek:c, ovari:c, ovariek:c, ovarien:w, ovarium:w	oo:c, oophor:c, oophoro:c, ovaire:w, ovar:c, ovari:c

patho:c	behandlung:w, krankheit:w, leiden:w, path:c, pathie:c, patho:c	maladie:w, path:c, pathie:c, patho:c, souffrance:w
pathy:c	behandlung:w, krankheit:w, leiden:w, path:c, pathie:c, patho:c	maladie:w, path:c, pathie:c, patho:c, souffrance:w
pharmaco:c	arzneimittel:w, pharmaco:c	pharmac:c, pharmaco:c, remède:w
pheno:c	pheno:c, phenol:w, phäno:c	briller:w, phén:c, phénique:c, phéno:c, phénol:c, phénol:w, phényl:c
phospho:c	leuchten:w, licht:w, phosph:c, phosphat:c, phosphato:c, phospho:c, phosphoreszenz:w	lumineux:w, lumière:w, phosph:c, phosphat:c, phosphato:c, phospho:c, phosphore:w
photo:c	foto:c, foto:w, fotografisch:w, licht:w, photo:c	lumière:w, photo:c
physio:c	nature:w, phys:c, physikalisch:w, physio:c	nature:w, physio:c
phyto:c	pflanze:w, pflanzen:w, phyt:c, phyto:c	bourgeon:w, excroissance:w, phyt:c, phyto:c, plante:w, végétal:w
plasia:c	plasie:c, plastisch:c, plastischer:w, umformbarkeit:w, verformung:w	modeler:w, plase:c, plasie:c, plasique:c
plastia:c	plasie:c, plastisch:c, plastischer:w, umformbarkeit:w, verformung:w	
plasty:c	plasie:c, plastisch:c, plastischer:w, umformbarkeit:w, verformung:w	plastie:c, plastique:c, plastique:w, réparation:w
plasy :c	plasie:c, plastisch:c, plastischer:w, umformbarkeit:w, verformung:w	
progesto:c	gesta:c, progest:c, progesto:c, schwangerschaft:w	progesto:c

proto:c	erster:w, prot:c, proto:c, ur:w, vorderster:w, wichtigster:w	premier:w, prot:c, proto:c, protéin:c, protéino:c
pseudo:c	anschein:w, falsch:w, pseudo:c, schein:c	faux:w, mensonger:w, menteur:w, pseud:c, pseudo:c
psycho:c	pscych:c, psych:c, psyche:w, psychische:w, psycho:c, psychologisch:w, seele:w	esprit:w, mental:w, psych:c, psycho:c, psychologie:w, psychologique:w
radio:c	radio:c, strahl:w, strahlen:w, strahlung:w	radi:c, radiation:w, radio:c, radio:w, rayon:w, rayonnement:w
reflexo:c	reaktion:w, reflex:c, reflex:w, reflexo:c, widerstand:w	retourner:w, réflex:c, réflexe:w, réflexo:c
retin:c	netzhaut:w, retin:c, retino:c	rétin:c, rétine:w, rétino:c
retino:c	netzhaut:w, retin:c, retino:c	rétin:c, rétine:w, rétino:c
retro:c	hinten:w, retro:c, rückgang:w, stange:w, stäbchenförmigen:w, zurück:w	arrière:w, avant:w, derrière:w, rétro:c
rhabdo:c	rhabdo:c, rhabdoider:w, rhadb:c, stäbchenförmige:w	baguette:w, rhabd:c, rhabdo:c
ribo:c	rib:c, ribo:c, ribose:w	ribo:c, ribose:w
scope:c	betrachtung:w, skop:c, untersuchung:w	examiner:w, observer:w, regarder:w, scope:c, scopie:c, scopique:c
scopol:c	besonderer_alcaloid:w, scopol:c, skopol:c	scopol:c
socio:c	gesellschaftlich:w, gesellschafts:w, sozial:w, sozialen:w, sozio:c	social:w, socio:c, société:w
some:c	körper:w, leich:w, som:c, some:c, somen:c	corps:w, soma:c, somat:c, somato:c, some:c, somie:c
sono:c	akustik:w, sona:c, sono:c	son:w, sono:c
soya:c	soja:c, soja:w	soya:c
spectro:c	spektr:c, spektro:c, spektrum:w	spectr:c, spectre:w, spectro:c
stat:c	regulierung:w, stabilisierung:w, stat:c	stat:c
stereo:c	fest:w, hart:w, stereo:c	solide:w, stéréo:c
steroido:c	steroid:c, steroid:w, steroido:c	stérol:w, stérone:c, stéroïd:c, stéroïdo:c
strepto:c	geflochten:w, gewunden:w, strept:c, strepto:c	contourné:w, strep:c, strepto:c

tetra:c	tetr:c, tetra:c, vier:w	quadr:c, quadri:c, quatre:w, têtr:c, têtra:c
thelial:c	brustwarze:w, thel:c, thelal:c, thelialen:c	mamelon:w, thelial:c, thélial:c
thelium:c	brustwarze:w, thel:c, thelal:c, thelialen:c	mamelon:w, thelium:c, thélium:c
thermo:c	hitze:w, temperatur:w, thermo:c	chaleur:w, chaud:w, chauffer:w, therm:c, thermo:c
thrombo:c	blutgerinnsel:w, thromb:c, thrombo:c	caillot:w, thromb:c, thrombo:c
tumor:c	carcinom:w, karzinom:w, tumor:c, tumor:w	gonfler:w, tumeur:w, tumor:c, tumoral:w, tumori:c, tumoro:c
tumori:c	carcinom:w, karzinom:w, tumor:c, tumor:w	gonfler:w, tumeur:w, tumor:c, tumoral:w, tumori:c, tumoro:c
tumour:c	carcinom:w, karzinom:w, tumor:c, tumor:w	gonfler:w, tumeur:w, tumor:c, tumoral:w, tumori:c, tumoro:c
tumouri:c	carcinom:w, karzinom:w, tumor:c, tumor:w	gonfler:w, tumeur:w, tumor:c, tumoral:w, tumori:c, tumoro:c
vasculo:c	blutgefäss:w, blutgefäß:w, gefass:w, gefäß:w, vasculo:c, vaskulo:c, vaskulären:w, vaso:c	vaisseau:w, vas:c, vascul:c, vasculo:c, vaso:c
vaso:c	blutgefäss:w, blutgefäß:w, gefass:w, gefäß:w, vasculo:c, vaskulo:c, vaskulären:w, vaso:c	vaisseau:w, vas:c, vascul:c, vasculo:c, vaso:c
xeno:c	fremd:w, fremde:w, fremder:w, gast:w, xen:c, xeno:c	xén:c, xéno:c, étranger:w
zygous:c	paarig:w, verbunden:w, zygo:c, zygos:c, zygote:c	paire:w, zyg:c, zygo:c, zygote:c, zygotique:c
ability:s	barkeit:s, ilität:s, kapazität:w, keit:s	abilité:s, capacité:w, ibilité:s
able:s	abel:s, bare:s, gemacht_werden_kann:w, können:w	able:s, ible:s, pouvoir:w
hood:s	heit:s, schaft:s, sensein:w, tat:s, tat:w, zustand:w	fait:w, état:w
less:s	a:p, ab:p, abs:p, los:s, nicht:w, ohne:w	a:p, ab:p, aucun:w, privé:w, sans:w
like:s	gleich:w, lich:s, wie:w, ähnlich:w	ressembler:w, semblable:w
ly:s	mit:w, mässig:s, mäßig:s, weg:w, weise:w	avec:w, ement:s, façon:w, manière:w, ment:s

wise:s	richtung:w, weise:s, weise:w, während:w	sens:w

Table A2.9. *Bound morphemes translation table*

A2.3.4. *Morphological families*

The morphological families were created by using the [POR 80] algorithm.

	EN	FR	DE
Morphological families	5,835 $\rightarrow$ 14,659	7,049 $\rightarrow$ 17,410	7,348 $\rightarrow$ 15,818

Table A2.10. *Size of the thesauri (number of entries)*

A2.3.4.1. *German*

A2.3.4.1.1. Evaluation

The evaluation covered 116 words clustered into 50 families. We thus obtained 6,670 word pairs classified as belonging to the same morphological family or not belonging to the same morphological family. When we were unable to determine whether a pair belongs to the same family or not, we took it out of the evaluation ("undecided" column).

		Manual annotation		
		Same family	Different family	Undecided
Stemmer	Same family	72	1	16
	Different family	0	4,680	1,901

Table A2.11. *Morphological family evaluation*

Extract A2.17. German morphological families

angstig	ängstigen:ADJECTIVE, ängstigen:PARTICIPLE, ängstigen:VERB
pinkfarb	pinkfarbig:ADJECTIVE, pinkfarben:ADJECTIVE
Mammographiegerat	Mammographiegeräte:NOUN, Mammographiegerät:NOUN
sympath	sympathisch:ADJECTIVE, sympathisch:NOUN
lakon	lakonisch:ADJECTIVE, lakonisch:NOUN
abruck	abrücken:VERB, abrücken:ADJECTIVE, abrücken:PARTICIPLE, abrücken:NOUN
bimmeln	bimmeln:VERB, bimmeln:ADJECTIVE
Zeh	Zehe:NOUN, Zeh:NOUN
Doblin	Döblins:NOUN, Döblin:NOUN
McQuaid	McQuaids:NOUN, McQuaid:NOUN
SEDMitglied	SEDMitglied:NOUN, SEDMitglieder:NOUN
Pattison	Pattisons:NOUN, Pattison:NOUN
Strass	Strasse:LEX, Strass:NOUN, Strasse:NOUN
Danton	Dantons:NOUN, Danton:NOUN
MDax	MDax:LEX, MDax:NOUN
masturbi	masturbieren:PARTICIPLE, masturbieren:VERB
bedank	bedanken:PARTICIPLE, bedanken:VERB
FraktionsFuhr	FraktionsFührung:NOUN, FraktionsFührer:NOUN
leck	lecken:VERB, leck:ADJECTIVE, lecken:PARTICIPLE, lecker:NOUN, lecker:ADJECTIVE, leck:NOUN
verlob	verloben:PARTICIPLE, verloben:VERB, verloben:NOUN, verloben:ADJECTIVE
spielenStatt	spielenStätte:NOUN, spielenStatt:NOUN
Pech	Pech:NOUN, Pech:LEX
Gnadl	Gnadl:NOUN, Gnadls:NOUN
ausraub	ausrauben:PARTICIPLE, ausrauben:VERB, ausrauben:ADJECTIVE
Werfel	Werfels:NOUN, Werfel:NOUN

Table A2.12. *German morphological families*

A2.3.4.2. *English*

A2.3.4.2.1. Evaluation

The evaluation covered 140 words clustered into 50 families. We thus obtained 9,370 word pairs classified as belonging to the same morphological family or not belonging to the same family. When we were unable to determine whether a pair belonged to the same family or not, we took it out of the evaluation ("undecided" column).

		Manual annotation		
		Same family	Different family	Undecided
Stemmer	Same family	127	18	1
	Different family	22	9,286	276

Table A2.13. *Morphological family evaluation*

Extract A2.18. English morphological families

fiduciari	fiduciary:ADJECTIVE, fiduciary:NOUN
careen	careen:VERB, careen:NOUN, careen:PARTICIPLE
carous	carouse:PARTICIPLE, carousal:NOUN
anti-oestrogen	anti-oestrogens:ADJECTIVE, anti-oestrogens:NOUN, anti-oestrogenic:ADJECTIVE, anti-oestrogen:ADJECTIVE, anti-oestrogen:NOUN
reverber	reverberation:NOUN, reverberate:VERB, reverberate:PARTICIPLE
deaf	deafness:NOUN, deaf:NOUN, deaf:ADJECTIVE
p21waf1	p21waf1:PROPER_NOUN, p21waf1:NOUN
contemporari	contemporary:NOUN, contemporary:ADJECTIVE
tend	tended:ADJECTIVE, tend:PARTICIPLE, tend:VERB
seldom	seldom:ADVERB, seldom:ADJECTIVE
earli	early:ADJECTIVE, early:ADVERB
shoulder	shoulder:VERB, shoulder:NOUN
idealist	idealist:NOUN, idealistic:ADJECTIVE
televis	televise:VERB, televised:ADJECTIVE, television:NOUN, televise:PARTICIPLE
Edmund	Edmunds:PROPER_NOUN, Edmund:PROPER_NOUN
play_against	play_against:VERB, play_against:PARTICIPLE
yoke	yoke:VERB, yoke:NOUN
stink	stink:VERB, stink:PARTICIPLE, stinking:ADJECTIVE, stink:NOUN
dupe	dupe:NOUN, dupe:PARTICIPLE
pervas	pervasive:ADJECTIVE, pervasiveness:NOUN
home	home:PARTICIPLE, homely:ADJECTIVE, home:VERB, home:NOUN
fidget	fidget:VERB, fidget:NOUN
mind-boggl	mind-boggling:NOUN, mind-boggling:PARTICIPLE
strappi	strappy:NOUN, strappy:ADJECTIVE
amass	amass:PARTICIPLE, amass:VERB, amass:NOUN

Table A2.14. *English morphological families*

A2.3.4.3. *French*

A2.3.4.3.1. Evaluation

The evaluation covered 126 words clustered into 50 families. We thus obtained 7,875 word pairs classified as belonging to the same family or not belonging to the same family. When we were unable to determine whether a pair belongs to the same family or not, we took it out of the evaluation ("undecided" column).

		Manual annotation		
		Same family	Different family	Undecided
Stemmer	Same family	104	6	0
	Different family	19	7,746	0

Table A2.15. *Morphological family evaluation*

Extract A2.19. French morphological families

Nyon	Nyon:PROPER_NOUN, Nyons:PROPER_NOUN
demeur	demeure:NOUN, demeuré:ADJECTIVE, demeurer:VERB, demeuré:NOUN, demeurer:PARTICIPLE
grommel	grommeler:VERB, grommeler:PARTICIPLE
sadiqu	sadique:NOUN, sadique:ADJECTIVE
Wild	Wilde:PROPER_NOUN, Wild:PROPER_NOUN, Wilder:PROPER_NOUN
compte-tenu	compte-tenu:ADJECTIVE, compte-tenu:NOUN
Bo	Bo:PROPER_NOUN, Boé:PROPER_NOUN, Boer:PROPER_NOUN
reten	retenir:PARTICIPLE, retenir:VERB, retenir:ADJECTIVE
faire_le_diagnostic	faire_le_diagnostic:PARTICIPLE, faire_le_diagnostic:VERB
decoul	découler:PARTICIPLE, découler:VERB
demol	démolir:ADJECTIVE, démolir:VERB, démolir:PARTICIPLE
creol	créole:ADJECTIVE, créole:NOUN
souten	soutenable:ADJECTIVE, soutenir:ADJECTIVE, soutenir:VERB, soutenir:PARTICIPLE
abolition	abolitionniste:ADJECTIVE, abolitionniste:NOUN
coherent	cohérent:ADJECTIVE, cohérence:NOUN
philanthrop	philanthrope:NOUN, philanthropie:NOUN, philanthropique:ADJECTIVE
nevros	névrosé:NOUN, névrosé:ADJECTIVE, névrose:NOUN
barrag	barragiste:NOUN, barrage:NOUN
reaffirm	réaffirmation:NOUN, réaffirmer:PARTICIPLE, réaffirmer:VERB, réaffirmer:ADJECTIVE
artisanal	artisanalement:ADVERB, artisanal:ADJECTIVE
rendre_hommage_	rendre_hommage_à:PARTICIPLE, rendre_hommage_à:VERB
judici	judicieux:ADJECTIVE, judicieusement:ADVERB
Schwarz	Schwarzer:PROPER_NOUN, Schwarz:PROPER_NOUN
Moin	Moins:PROPER_NOUN, Moïn:PROPER_NOUN
sabot	saboter:VERB, sabot:NOUN, saboter:PARTICIPLE

Table A2.16. *French morphological families*

A2.3.5. *Dictionary of cognates*

The dictionaries of cognates were generated according to the [HAU 11] method.

	EN→FR	EN→DE
# Positive examples	21,202	7,399
# Negative examples	21,202	7,399
Error rate (%)	3.49	6.93

Table A2.17. *Cognate identification: training data and error rate*

	EN↔FR	EN↔DE
Cognate pairs	6,708	6,391

Table A2.18. *Size of the specialized dictionaries (number of entries)*

A2.3.5.1. *English ↔ German*

Extract A2.20. English ↔ German dictionary of cognates

light:NOUN	Licht:NOUN
car:NOUN	Carl:NOUN
function:NOUN	Funktion:NOUN
bear:PARTICIPLE	Beat:NOUN
phytoestrogen:NOUN	PhytoÖstrogen:NOUN
home:VERB	hom:ADJECTIVE
actin:PROPER_NOUN	Action:NOUN
department:NOUN	Department:NOUN
strong:ADJECTIVE	streng:ADJECTIVE
express:ADJECTIVE	Expression:NOUN
synthesise:PARTICIPLE	Synthese:NOUN
assay:VERB	Assay:LEX
quantity:NOUN	Quality:NOUN
categorise:VERB	Kategorie:NOUN
randomized:ADJECTIVE	Randomized:NOUN
extreme:NOUN	extrem:ADJECTIVE
News:PROPER_NOUN	new:ADJECTIVE
chi2:ADJECTIVE	Chi:NOUN
droop:VERB	Drop:LEX
Garber:PROPER_NOUN	Gerber:NOUN
GAIC:PROPER_NOUN	GAIN:NOUN
primarily:ADVERB	primary:ADJECTIVE
mastitis:ADJECTIVE	Mastitis:NOUN
treat:ADJECTIVE	treat:ADJECTIVE
senior:ADJECTIVE	Sensor:NOUN

Table A2.19. *English ↔ German dictionary of cognates*

A2.3.5.2. *English ↔ French*

Extract A2.21. English ↔ French dictionary of cognates

car:NOUN	car:NOUN
preferred:ADJECTIVE	préférer:PARTICIPLE
choose:VERB	chose:NOUN
function:NOUN	fonction:NOUN
phytoestrogen:NOUN	phyto-estrogène:NOUN
homogeneity:NOUN	homogénéité:NOUN
MSKCC:PROPER_NOUN	MSKCC:PROPER_NOUN
home:VERB	homme:LEX
actin:PROPER_NOUN	action:NOUN
department:NOUN	département:NOUN
dissociate:VERB	dissocier:PARTICIPLE
express:ADJECTIVE	exprès:ADJECTIVE
synthesise:PARTICIPLE	synthèse:NOUN
cut:ADJECTIVE	cut:LEX
quantity:NOUN	quantité:NOUN
categorise:VERB	catégorie:NOUN
extreme:NOUN	extrême:NOUN
chi2:ADJECTIVE	Chi2:PROPER_NOUN
embolus:NOUN	Emboles:PROPER_NOUN
bombard:VERB	bomber:VERB
inject:VERB	injecté:ADJECTIVE
P=0.009:PROPER_NOUN	p=0.003:NOUN
mastitis:ADJECTIVE	mastite:NOUN
senior:ADJECTIVE	senior:ADJECTIVE
degenerate:VERB	dégénérer:VERB

Table A2.20. *English ↔ French dictionary of cognates*

A2.3.6. *Parts-of-speech translation probability*

The parts-of-speech translation probabilities were acquired from the European Medecine Evaluation Agency (EMEA) corpus [TIE 09].

	EN→FR	EN→DE
# Aligned sentences	373,127	363,982
# Aligned parts-of-speech sequences	191,854	108,612

Table A2.21. *Acquisition of parts-of-speech translation probabilities: size of the data*

A2.3.6.1. *English → German*

Extract A2.22. English → German parts-of-speech translation probabilities

_ADVERB	NOUN	0.2014960293
_ADVERB	_ADVERB	0.1946567909
_ADVERB	ADJECTIVE	0.0841178903
_ADVERB	NOUN NOUN	0.0477002124
_ADVERB	VERB	0.0292847442
_ADVERB	_PREP	0.0180966766
_ADVERB	ADJECTIVE NOUN	0.0164627438
_ADVERB	_ADVERB NOUN	0.0157798611
_ADVERB	PARTICIPLE	0.0150926129
_ADVERB	_NUM	0.0146408467
_ADVERB	_CONJ	0.0109107886
_ADVERB	NOUN NOUN NOUN	0.0104185454
_ADVERB	NOUN PARTICIPLE	0.0102317638
_NUM	_NUM _DET _PREP _PREP _DET	0.000000000315865288145686
_AUX	_PREP _ELIM _CONJ _DET NOUN	0.0000000235290034672843
_AUX	ADJECTIVE NOUN PARTICIPLE	0.00000128821293983382
_PUNCT	_DET _PRO _PREP _PUNCT	0.000000000714239298007896
_PRO	_PRO _PREP _AUX	0.00000244990842009058
_PREP	_DET _DET _ADVERB _DET _DET	0.0000000318176503188138
ADJECTIVE	ADJECTIVE _PREP VERB _PUNCT	0.000000000621283163425878
_PREP	_AUX _PRO _PUNCT _PUNCT _PUNCT	0.0000000204542037763803
_PRO	_ADVERB _CONJ _DET	0.0000000499981310222567
PARTICIPLE	NOUN _NUM VERB	0.00000168907402961649
PROPRE	VERB _DET NOUN _PART	0.0000000654167427917883
_NUM	_NUM _NUM _PREP _DET	0.000000000282022578701506
_DET	_AUX _PREP _DET _PUNCT _PUNCT	0.0000000685651382097666

Table A2.22. *English → German parts-of-speech translation probabilities*

A2.3.6.2. *English → French*

Extract A2.23. English → French parts-of-speech translation probabilities

_NUM	_NUM	0.5869649849
_PUNCT	_PUNCT	0.4934448322
NOUN	NOUN	0.4835526372
PROPRE	PROPRE	0.4696379662
_ELIM	NOUN	0.3716330294
ADJECTIVE	NOUN	0.3414517609
_DET	_DET	0.2581942818
ADVERB	ADVERB	0.2562987002
VERB	VERB	0.2549051439
PARTICIPLE	NOUN	0.2273221307
_PRO	NOUN	0.2237807336
_AUX	VERB	0.2195352295
VERB	NOUN	0.209632155
VERB	_NUM VERB ADJECTIVE NOUN	0.0000143047001026882
_PRO	_PUNCT NOUN _PUNCT	0.00000497600446840555
_DET	_PUNCT _AUX _DET NOUN	0.0000000971339457971694
ADJECTIVE	ADJECTIVE VERB ADJECTIVE NOUN _ADVERB	0.000000135277384277605
VERB	NOUN PARTICIPLE _CONJ VERB	0.000000757334158528157
_AUX	_AUX _PREP _DET _PUNCT	0.00000189408477911639
_PREP	_PUNCT _DET _DET _PUNCT	0.000000789759534699127
NOUN	_PUNCT NOUN _PART _PUNCT	0.00000000296264864581992
_PUNCT	NOUN _PREP _PUNCT _PREP	0.00000000324654226367225
_DET	_NUM NOUN _CONJ NOUN	0.0000000342825691048833
_CONJ	_PREP _PUNCT _PRO NOUN	0.0000000921022892234539

Table A2.23. *English → French parts-of-speech translation probabilities*

A2.4. Source terms

The list of source terms was built in a semi-supervised manner and was manually approved (see section 5.3). The source terms to be translated are the terms for which the bilingual dictionary does not provide any translation which is attested in the target texts.

	FR	*DE*
Morphologically complex source terms	2,025	2,025
Source terms translated with the general language bilingual dictionary	186	201
Source terms to be translated (S)	1,839	1,824

Table A2.24. *Source terms to be translated*

A2.4.1. *Excerpt of the source terms to be translated*

Extract A2.24. Source terms to be translated

	S^{DE}	S^{FR}
soft-tissue:ADJECTIVE	✔	✔
pair-wise:ADJECTIVE	✔	✔
extra-renal:ADJECTIVE	✔	✔
epidermal:ADJECTIVE	✔	✔
watered-down:ADJECTIVE	✔	✔
mammotome:NOUN	✔	✔
overgrowth:NOUN	✔	✔
dedifferentiated:ADJECTIVE	✔	✔
fairly:ADVERB		
overreact:VERB	✔	✔
two-site:ADJECTIVE	✔	✔
uk-specific:ADJECTIVE	✔	✔
fluorometry:NOUN	✔	✔
breast-feeding:PARTICIPE	✔	✔
inconvenient:ADJECTIVE	✔	✔
erythroblastic:ADJECTIVE	✔	✔
bromocriptine:NOUN	✔	✔
medroxyprogesterone:NOUN	✔	✔
time-to-progression:NOUN	✔	✔
anti-p21:ADJECTIVE	✔	✔
cost-effective:ADJECTIVE	✔	✔
cancer-free:ADJECTIVE	✔	✔
in-frame:ADJECTIVE	✔	✔
low-power:ADJECTIVE	✔	✔
high-risk:ADJECTIVE	✔	✔
flu-like:ADJECTIVE	✔	✔

Table A2.25. *Source terms to be translated*

A2.5. Reference data for translation generation evaluation

A2.5.1. *A priori reference*

The *a priori* reference (R) was created from the UMLS [LIN 93].

	FR	DE
$\|R\|$	126 → 163	90 → 104

Table A2.26. *Number of entries and translations in the a posteriori reference*

A2.5.1.1. *English → German extract*

Extract A2.25. English → German *a priori* reference

EN	DE
discomfort:NOUN	unwohlsein, fuehlt sich nicht wohl
meta-analyses:ADJECTIVE	metaanalyse
rapamycin:ADJECTIVE	sirolimus
progestogen:ADJECTIVE	gestagene, progestine
quadrantectomy:ADJECTIVE	quadrantektomie
overweight:ADJECTIVE	übergewicht
neo-adjuvant:ADJECTIVE	neoadjuvante behandlung, neoadjuvante therapie
adriamycin:NOUN	adriamycin
antibody:NOUN	antikörper
immunotherapy:NOUN	immuntherapie
childbirth:NOUN	geburt
x-ray:VERB	röntgenuntersuchung, röntgenaufnahme, röntgenstrahlen, radiografie, roentgen
ultrasonography:ADJECTIVE	ultraschall, sonographie
dosimetry:NOUN	dosimetrie
glycoprotein:NOUN	glykoproteine
intra-abdominal:ADJECTIVE	bauchhöhle
brachytherapy:NOUN	brachytherapie
workflow:ADJECTIVE	workflow, arbeitsfluss, arbeitsablauf
radiosurgery:NOUN	radiochirurgie
childhood:NOUN	kindheit
hysterectomy:NOUN	hysterektomie
polymorphism:NOUN	vielgestaltigkeit
androstenedione:NOUN	androstendion
heterozygous:ADJECTIVE	heterozygot
breastfeed:VERB	stillen

Table A2.27. *English → German a priori reference*

A2.5.1.2. *English → French extract*

Extract A2.26. English → French *a priori* reference

EN	FR
oophorectomy:ADJECTIVE	ablation d'un ovaire, ovariectomie
radiograph:NOUN	radiographie
cytoskeleton:NOUN	cytosquelette
self-esteem:NOUN	estime de soi
ownership:NOUN	propriété, possession
cytoplasm:NOUN	cytoplasme
chromatography:NOUN	chromatographie
overweight:ADJECTIVE	surcharge pondérale, excès de poids
subpopulation:NOUN	groupes de population, groupes
hydrocortisone:NOUN	hydrocortisone
downregulation:NOUN	régulation négative
aftercare:NOUN	suivi
re-operation:NOUN	réintervention, reprise chirurgicale
housework:NOUN	ménage
ataxia-telangiectasia:NOUN	ataxietélangiectasie
inpatient:NOUN	patients hospitalisés
osteoarthritis:NOUN	arthrose
database:NOUN	base de données
cardiotoxicity:NOUN	toxicité cardiaque
workload:NOUN	charge de travail
indomethacin:NOUN	indométacine
decision-making:ADJECTIVE	prise de décision
biomarker:NOUN	biomarqueur
anti-androgen:NOUN	antiandrogène
physiotherapist:NOUN	kinésithérapeute

Table A2.28. *English → French a priori reference*

A2.5.2. *A posteriori reference*

The *a posteriori* reference (P) was created by manually annotating the system's outputs.

	FR	DE
$\|P\|$	730 → 2,129	654 → 2,016

Table A2.29. *Number of entries and translations in the a posteriori reference*

	EN-FR	EN-DE
Kappa	0.71	0.77

Table A2.30. *Annotator agreement on the reference annotation*

A2.5.2.1. *Caption of the extracts*

E: exact translation;

A: accurate translation;

P: close translation;

F: false translation.

A2.5.2.2. *English → German extract*

Extract A2.27. English → German *a posteriori* reference

EN	An.	DE (lemmas + parts-of-speech)	
hands-on:ADJECTIVE	F	auf der hand	_PREP _DET NOUN
discontinuation:NOUN	P	nicht fortsetzen	_ADVERB _ELIM
increasingly:ADVERB	F	sich nicht weiter vermehren	_PRO _ADVERB _ADVERB VERB
greatly:ADVERB	F	grat	NOUN
one-breasted:ADJECTIVE	F	einer oder sogar beide brust	_ELIM _CONJ _ADVERB _DET NOUN
non-selective:ADJECTIVE	E	nichtselektiv	ADJECTIVE
high-risk:ADJECTIVE	E	hochrisiko	LEX
well-fitted:ADJECTIVE	P	gut zu sie passen	ADJECTIVE _PREP _PRO VERB
workflow:ADJECTIVE	E	workflow	NOUN
increasingly:ADVERB	A	zunehmen	ADJECTIVE
ultimately:ADVERB	E	schliesslich	_ADVERB
metaphase:ADJECTIVE	F	metaplasie	_ADVERB
pretreatment:NOUN	F	treatments	ADJECTIVE
three-year:ADJECTIVE	F	jahr drei	NOUN _NUM
self-examination:NOUN	P	untersuchung selbst	NOUN _ADVERB
adjuvant-therapy:NOUN	E	adjuvante therapie	NOUN NOUN
inter-patient:ADJECTIVE	E	zwischen der patient	_PREP _DET LEX
well-differentiated:ADJECTIVE	F	differenzierung der echt	NOUN _DET ADJECTIVE
co-operative:ADJECTIVE	F	mit ein operation	_PREP _DET NOUN
three-year:ADJECTIVE	F	jahr nur drei	NOUN _ADVERB _NUM
helpless:ADJECTIVE	F	nicht jede so hilfsbereit	_ADVERB _PRO _ADVERB ADJECTIVE
privately:ADVERB	F	eigen	ADJECTIVE
retinoblastoma:NOUN	E	retinoblastom	NOUN
in-frame:ADJECTIVE	F	infrage	_ADVERB
increasingly:ADVERB	P	mit ein erhöhen	_PREP _DET ADJECTIVE

Table A2.31. *English → German a posteriori reference*

A2.5.2.3. *English → French extract*

Extract A2.28. English → French extract

EN	An.	FR (lemmas + parts-of-speech)	
fabric-covered:ADJECTIVE	F	tissu le recouvrir	NOUN _PRO VERB
pre-menopausal:ADJECTIVE	E	avant la ménopause	_PREP _DET NOUN
primarily:ADVERB	E	fondamentalement	ADVERB
co-operative:ADJECTIVE	A	coopérateur	ADJECTIVE
angiogenesis:NOUN	A	angiogenèser	VERB
disappearance:NOUN	F	disparité	NOUN
interphase:ADJECTIVE	F	interposer	PARTICIPE
breast-cancer:NOUN	P	cancer in_situ du sein	NOUN _ADVERB _PREP NOUN
post-operative:ADJECTIVE	E	après cette intervention	_PREP _DET NOUN
disorderly:ADJECTIVE	F	avec l'affection	_PREP _DET NOUN
double-blind:ADJECTIVE	E	double aveugle	NOUN ADJECTIVE
cross-talk:ADJECTIVE	E	crosstalk	NOUN
adversely:ADVERB	F	opposé	ADJECTIVE
one-piece:ADJECTIVE	F	un morceau	_DET NOUN
co-repressors:ADJECTIVE	A	corépression	NOUN
disorderly:ADJECTIVE	E	manière désordonné	NOUN ADJECTIVE
colourless:ADJECTIVE	E	sans colorant	_PREP NOUN
part-time:ADJECTIVE	F	taille et le temps	NOUN _CONJ _DET NOUN
last-timed:ADJECTIVE	F	passetemps	NOUN
comparatively:ADVERB	F	relative	NOUN
cancer-trained:ADJECTIVE	F	cancer et son traitement	NOUN _CONJ _PREP _DET NOUN
oophorectomy:ADJECTIVE	E	ovariectomie	NOUN
on-treatment:NOUN	E	sur un traitement	_PREP _DET NOUN
consecutively:ADVERB	A	consécutif	ADJECTIVE
lymphocyte:NOUN	E	lymphocyte	NOUN

Table A2.32. *English → French* `a posteriori reference`

A2.6. Translation ranking training and evaluation data

The training data (T) corresponds to the annotated system's outputs which are not part of the *a priori* reference. The evaluation data (E) corresponds to the annotated system's outputs which are part of the *a priori* reference.

	FR	*DE*
$\vert T\vert$	647 → 1,970	588 → 1,829
$\vert E\vert$	83 → 159	66 → 187

Table A2.33. *Number of entries and translations for training and evaluating the ranking model*

A2.6.1. *Extract of training data*

A2.6.1.1. *Extract caption*

$a > b$ translation a is more relevant than translation b;

a, b translation a is as relevant as translation b.

E: exact translation(s);

A: accurate translation(s);

P: close translation(s);

F: false translation(s).

A2.6.1.2. *English → German extract*

Extract A2.29. English → German learning-to-rank training data

EN	Ranked DE translations (lemmas)
metastasis-free|ADJECTIVE	E: metastasefrei
vasomotor|ADJECTIVE	E: vasomotorisch
stick-on|ADJECTIVE	A: ankleben (VERB), aufkleben, ankleben (NOUN)
prickly|ADJECTIVE	F: stich, trick
non-specific|ADJECTIVE	E: unspezifisch > P: nicht spezifisch > F: nicht oder nur wenig spezifisch
first-line|ADJECTIVE	E: first line, firstline
factor-a|NOUN	F: factor (_ADVERB), factor (ADJECTIVE)
high-risk|ADJECTIVE	E: gross risiko, hoch risiko, high risk, hochrisiko > F: hoch das risiko, hoch oder ein risiko, risiko an das hoch, risiko hoch, hoch thrombose risiko, risiko in etwa so hoch, hoch ihr risiko, risiko gross
tumour-bearing|PARTICIPE	E: tumortragen
workstation|NOUN	E: workstation

Table A2.34. *English → German learning-to-rank training data*

A2.6.1.3. *English → French extract*

Extract A2.30. English → French learning-to-rank training data

<table>
<tr><th>EN</th><th>Ranked FR translations (lemmas)</th></tr>
<tr><td>dinucleotide|NOUN</td><td>P: nucléotide, nucléotider, nucléotidique</td></tr>
<tr><td>non-african|ADJECTIVE</td><td>E: nonafricaines</td></tr>
<tr><td>stick-on|ADJECTIVE</td><td>F: à coller, surmonter, à déterminer</td></tr>
<tr><td>socio-economic|ADJECTIVE</td><td>E: socioéconomique, social ou économique, économique et social, social et économique</td></tr>
<tr><td>whole-genome|ADJECTIVE</td><td>E: ensemble de génome</td></tr>
<tr><td>incomplete|ADJECTIVE</td><td>E: incomplet > A: pas complètement, incomplètement > P: pas totalement > F: pas moins tout_à_fait, non le totalité, non totalement, non un fin</td></tr>
<tr><td>non-randomised|ADJECTIVE</td><td>E: non randomiser (_ADVERB ADJECTIVE), non randomiser (_ADVERB PARTICIPE)</td></tr>
<tr><td>prickly|ADJECTIVE</td><td>P: piquer, piqûre, piquer</td></tr>
<tr><td>non-specific|ADJECTIVE</td><td>E: non spécifique > F: pas déterminer, pas encore déterminer, pas encore bien déterminer, pas toujours de déterminer, pas de déterminer</td></tr>
<tr><td>cardioprotective|ADJECTIVE</td><td>E: protection de coeur, protection cardiaque, cardioprotecteur</td></tr>
</table>

Table A2.35. *English → French learning-to-rank training data*

A2.6.2. *Extract of evaluation data*

$a > b$ translation a is more relevant than translation b;

a, b translation a is as relevant as translation b.

E: exact translation;

A: accurate translation;

P: close translation;

F: false translation.

A2.6.2.1. *English → German extract*

Extract A2.31. English → German learning-to-rank evaluation data

<table>
<tr><th>EN</th><th>ranked DE translations (lemmas)</th></tr>
<tr><td>ultrasound|NOUN</td><td>F: über die fest</td></tr>
<tr><td>headache|NOUN</td><td>E: kopfschmerzen</td></tr>
<tr><td>gynaecomastia|NOUN</td><td>E: gynäkomastie > F: frau durch brust, frau zu die brust, brust der frau, frau nach brust, frau brust, frau nicht an brust, frau bereits an ein brust, frau der brust, frau in der brust, frau an brust, frau gegen brust, brust durch der frau, frau nach ein brust, frau an brust, frau bereits an brust, frau weniger an brust, frau nach ein brust, frau ein brust, frau ohne brust, frau brust, frau mit ein brust, frau mit brust, frau ihr brust, frau mit brust, frau trotz brust, frau die brust, brust bei frau</td></tr>
<tr><td>radiograph|NOUN</td><td>A: radiographisch, radiography, radiographie</td></tr>
<tr><td>wellbeing|ADJECTIVE</td><td>F: wellen (NOUN), wellen (VERB)</td></tr>
<tr><td>fibroblast|NOUN</td><td>E: fibroblasten, fibroblast</td></tr>
<tr><td>mammogram|NOUN</td><td>E: mammogramm, mammogramme</td></tr>
<tr><td>dosimetry|NOUN</td><td>E: dosimetrie</td></tr>
<tr><td>overweight|ADJECTIVE</td><td>A: übergewicht > F: gewicht über</td></tr>
<tr><td>antibody|NOUN</td><td>E: antikörper (NOUN), antikörper (ADJECTIVE), antikörper (_ADVERB) > P: antikörper (LEX)</td></tr>
</table>

Table A2.36. *English → German learning-to-rank evaluation data*

A2.6.2.2. *English → French extract*

Extract A2.32. English → French learning-to-rank evaluation data

EN	ranked FR translations (lemmas)
radiograph|NOUN	E: radiographie > A: radiographier, radiographier, radiographique
overweight|ADJECTIVE	E: surcharge > F: supérieur avec et sans charge
intramuscular|ADJECTIVE	E: dans le muscle, intramusculaire, dans un muscle > A: intramusculaire > F: entre le muscle
orchidectomy|NOUN	E: orchidectomie
cytoplasmic|ADJECTIVE	E: cytoplasme
g-protein|NOUN	E: protéine g
brachytherapy|NOUN	E: brachythérapie
fibroblast|NOUN	E: fibroblaste
radioactivity|NOUN	E: radioactiviter
cardiovascular|ADJECTIVE	E: cardiovasculaire, cardiovasculaire > A: cardiovasculairer

Table A2.37. *English → French learning-to-rank evaluation data*

A2.6.3. *Extract of system output*

The translations represented in the extract were ranked with a non-weighted combination.

A2.6.3.1. *Extracts caption*

$a > b$ translation a was placed before translation b by the algorithm.

A2.6.3.2. *English → German extract*

Extract A2.33. Ranked outputs by the English → German system

EN	ranked DE translations (lemmas)
ultrasound|NOUN	über die fest
headache|NOUN	kopfschmerzen
gynaecomastia|NOUN	gynäkomastie > frau mit brust > frau an brust > frau nicht an brust > frau nach brust > frau die brust > frau brust > frau in der brust > frau ihr brust > frau mit brust > frau weniger an brust > frau ohne brust > frau nach ein brust > frau bereits an ein brust > frau mit ein brust > frau trotz brust > frau zu die brust > frau der brust > frau gegen brust > frau an brust > frau brust > brust durch der frau > brust bei frau > frau ein brust > frau nach ein brust > frau durch brust > frau bereits an brust > brust der frau
radiograph|NOUN	radiography > radiographie > radiographisch
wellbeing|ADJECTIVE	wellen (NOUN) > wellen (VERB)
fibroblast|NOUN	fibroblast > fibroblasten
mammogram|NOUN	mammogramm > mammogramme
dosimetry|NOUN	dosimetrie
overweight|ADJECTIVE	übergewicht > gewicht über
antibody|NOUN	antikörper (NOUN) > antikörper (LEX) > antikörper (_ADVERB) > antikörper (ADJECTIVE)

Table A2.38. *Ranked outputs by the English → German system*

A2.6.3.3. *English → French extract*

Extract A2.34. Ranked outputs by the English → French system

<table>
<tr><th>EN</th><th>Ranked FR translations (lemmas)</th></tr>
<tr><td>radiograph|NOUN</td><td>radiographie > radiographique> radiographier (PARTICIPE) > radiographier (VERB)</td></tr>
<tr><td>overweight|ADJECTIVE</td><td>surcharge > supérieur avec et sans charge</td></tr>
<tr><td>intramuscular|ADJECTIVE</td><td>intramusculaire (ADJECTIVE) > intramusculaire (NOUN) > dans le muscle > dans un muscle > entre le muscle</td></tr>
<tr><td>orchidectomy|NOUN</td><td>orchidectomie</td></tr>
<tr><td>cytoplasmic|ADJECTIVE</td><td>cytoplasme</td></tr>
<tr><td>g-protein|NOUN</td><td>protéine g</td></tr>
<tr><td>brachytherapy|NOUN</td><td>brachythérapie</td></tr>
<tr><td>fibroblast|NOUN</td><td>fibroblaste</td></tr>
<tr><td>radioactivity|NOUN</td><td>radioactiviter</td></tr>
<tr><td>cardiovascular|ADJECTIVE</td><td>cardiovasculaire (ADJECTIVE) > cardiovasculaire (NOUN) > cardiovasculairer</td></tr>
</table>

Table A2.39. *Ranked outputs by the English → French system*

Appendix 3

Comparable Corpora Lexicons Consultation Interface

The prototype can be freely accessed at http://80.82.238.151/Metricc/InterfaceValidation/.[1]

The interface gives access to the lexicons extracted from the BREAST CANCER English-French corpus and from the WATER SCIENCE corpus as well as the terminology records linked to the terms.

1 Username: "test". Leave the password field empty.

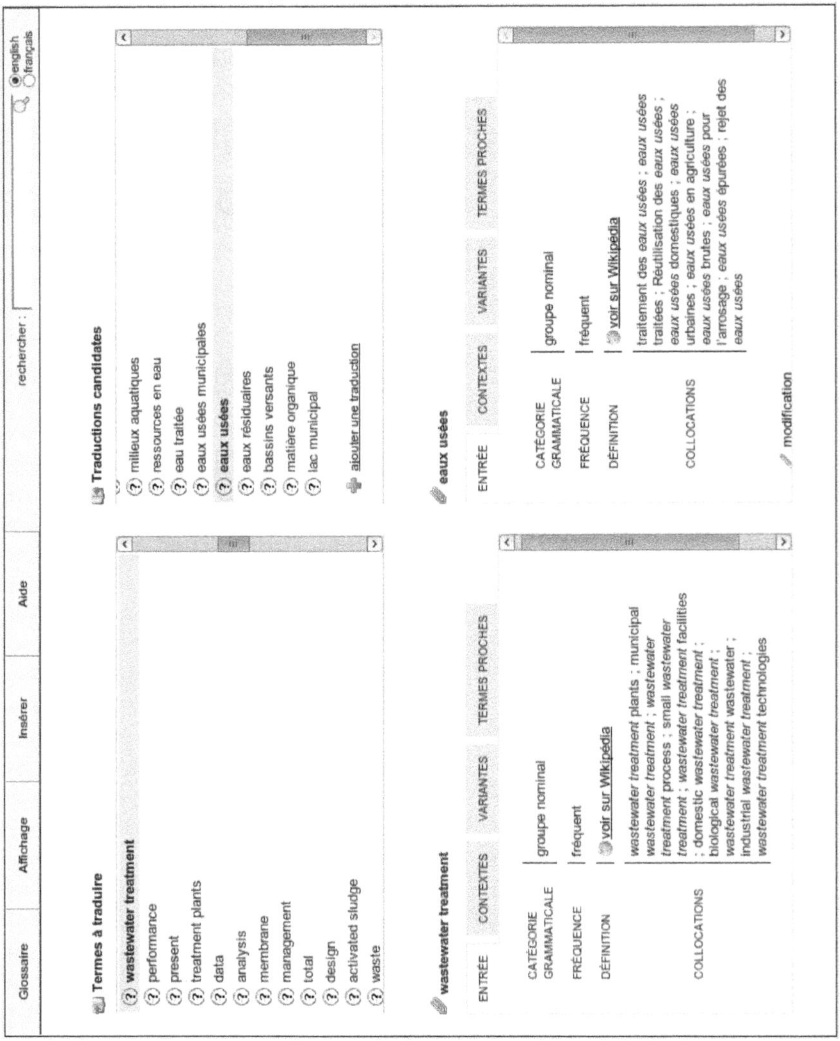

Figure A3.1. *Comparable corpora exploration prototype: translation equivalences and terminology records*

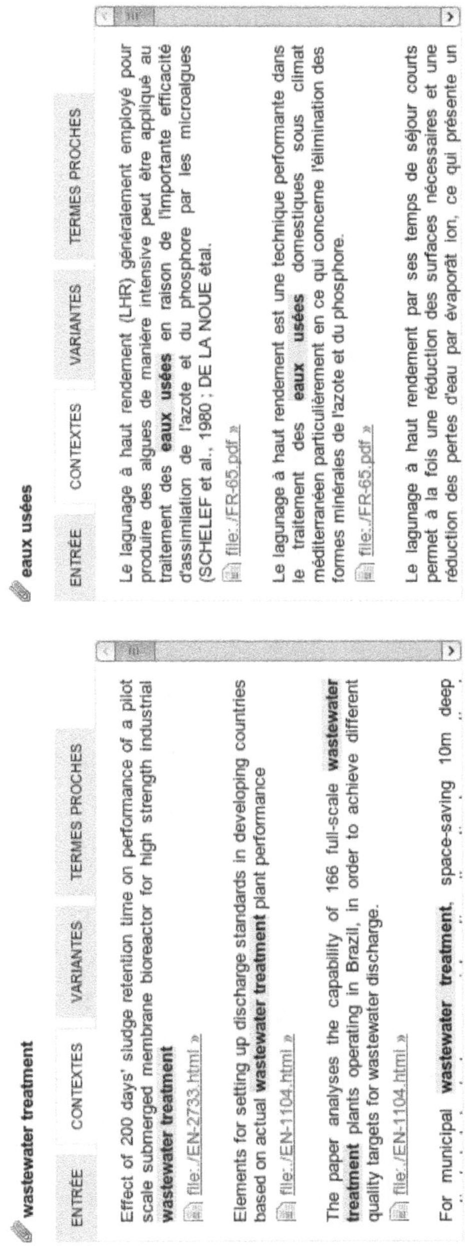

Figure A3.2. *Comparable corpora exploration prototype: bilingual contexts*

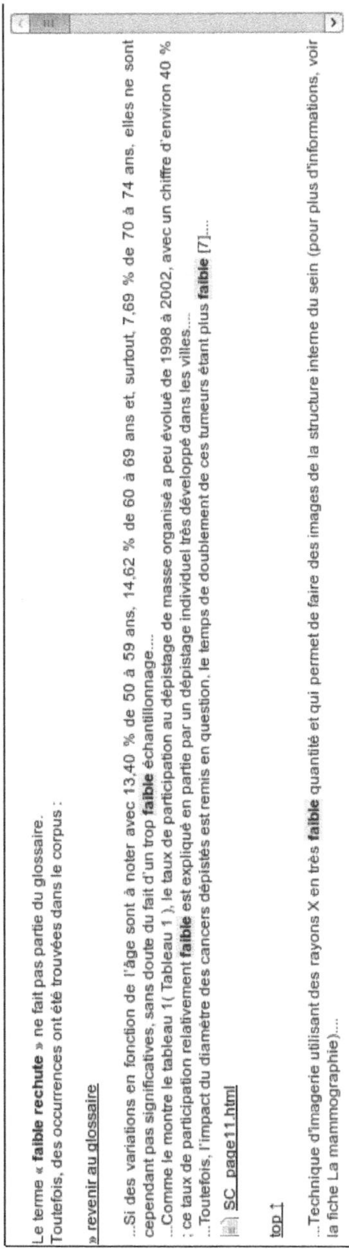

Figure A3.3. *Comparable corpora exploration prototype: monolingual contexts*

List of Tables

List of Figures

List of Algorithms

List of Extracts

Bibliography

[ALP 66] ALPAC, Languages and machines: computers in translation and linguistics, Publication no. 1416, Automatic Language Processing Advisory Committee – Division of Behavorial Sciences, National Academy of Sciences, National Research Council, Washington D.C., USA, 1966.

[BAK 96] BAKER M., "Corpus-based translation studies: the challenges that lie ahead", in SOMERS H., (ed.), *Terminology, LSP and Translation: Studies in Language Engineering in Honour of Juan C. Sager*, John Benjamins, Pays-Bas, Amsterdam/Philadelphia, PA, 1996.

[BAL 04] BALDWIN T., TANAKA T., "Translation by machine of complex nominals", *Proceedings of the ACL 2004 Workshop on Multiword Expressions: Integrating Processing*, Barcelona, Spain, pp. 24–31, 2004.

[BAN 05] BANERJEE S., LAVIE A., "METEOR: an automatic metric for MT evaluation with improved correlation with human judgments", *Proceedings of Workshop on Intrinsic and Extrinsic Evaluation Measures for MT and/or Summarization at the 43rd Annual Meeting of the Association of Computational Linguistics*, Ann Arbor, MI, pp. 65–72, 2005.

[BAU 83] BAUER L., *English word-formation*, Cambridge University Press, Cambridge, United Kingdom, 1983.

[BÉC 92] BÉCHADE H.D., *Phonétique et morphologie du français moderne et contemporain*, Presses Universitaires de France (PUF), 1992.

[BEN 00] BENNISON P., BOWKER L., "Designing a tool for exploiting bilingual comparable corpora", *Proceedings of LREC 2000*, Athens, Greece, 2000.

[BLA 07] BLANCHON H., BOITET C., "Pour l'évaluation externe des systèmes de TA par des méthodes fondées sur la tâche", *Traitement Automatique des Langues*, vol. 48, no. 1, pp. 33–65, 2007.

[BOU 94] BOURIGAULT D., LEXTER un Logiciel d'EXtraction de TERminologie. Application à l'extraction des connaissances à partir de textes, Thesis, Ecole des Hautes Etudes en Sciences Sociales, Paris, 1994.

[BOW 02] BOWKER L., PEARSON J., *Working with Specialized Language: A Practical Guide to Using Corpora*, Routledge, London/New York, 2002.

[BRO 90] BROWN P., PIETRA S.D., JELINEK F., *et al.*, "A statistical approach to machine translation", *Computational Linguistics*, vol. 16, no. 2, pp. 79–85, 1990.

[BRO 93] BROWN P., DELLA PIETRA S., DELLA PIETRA V., *et al.*, "The mathematics of statistical machine translation: parameter estimation", *Computational Linguistics*, vol. 19, no. 2, pp. 263–311, 1993.

[BRO 11] BROWN DE COLSTOUN F., DELPECH E., MONNERET E., "Libellex: une plateforme multiservices pour la gestion des contenus multilingues", in LAFOURCADE M., PRINCE V. (Eds.), *Actes de la 18ème conférence sur le traitement automatique des langues naturelles*, Montpellier, France, vol. 2, p. 319, 2011.

[CAL 07] CALLISON-BURCH C., FORDYCE C., KOEHN P., *et al.*, "(Meta-) evaluation of machine translation", *Proceedings of the 2nd workshop on Statistical Machine Translation*, Prague, Czech Republic, p. 136158, 2007.

[CAL 08] CALLISON-BURCH C., CAMEROB F., KOEHN P., *et al.*, "Further meta-evaluation of machine translation", *Proceedings of the Third Workshop on Statistical Machine Translation*, Columbus, Ohio, pp. 70–106, 2008.

[CAL 09] CALLISON-BURCH C., KOEHN P., MONZ C., *et al.*, "Findings of the 2009 workshop on statistical machine translation", *Proceedings of the Fourth Workshop on Statistical Machine Translation*, Athens, Greece, Association for Computational Linguistics, pp. 1–28, March 2009.

[CAL 10] CALLISON-BURCH C., KOEHN P., MONZ C., *et al.*, "Findings of the 2010 joint workshop on statistical machine translation and metrics for machine translation", *Proceedings of the Sixth Workshop on Statistical Machine Translation*, Uppsala, Sweden, 2010.

[CAO 07] CAO Z., QIN T., LIU T., *et al.*, Learning to rank: from pairwise approach to listwise approach, Microsoft Research, Report no. MSR-TR-2007-40, 2007.

[CAR 96] CARLETTA J., "Assessing agreement on classification tasks: the Kappa statistic", *Computational Linguistics*, vol. 22, no. 2, pp. 249–254, 1996.

[CAR 05] CARTONI B., "Traduction de règles de construction des mots pour résoudre les problèmes d'incomplétude lexicale en traduction automatique étude de cas", *Proceedings of RECITAL 2005*, Dourdan, France, pp. 565–574, 2005.

[CAR 09a] CARTONI B., "Les adjectifs relationnels dans les lexiques informatisés: formalisation et exploitation dans un contexte multilingue", *Actes de la 16e Conférence Traitement Automatique des Langues Naturelles*, Senlis, France, 2009.

[CAR 09b] CARTONI B., "Lexical morphology in machine translation: a feasibility study", *Proceedings of the 12th Conference of the European Chapter of the ACL*, Athens, Greece, pp. 130–138, 2009.

[CAR 11] CARL M., DRAGSTED B., JAKOBSEN A.L., "On the systematicity of human translation process", *Tralogy*, Kluwer Academic Publisher, Paris, France, 2011.

[CAR 12] CARPUAT M., III H.D., FRASER A., *et al.*, "Domain adaptation in machine translation: final report", 2012 Johns Hopkins Summer Workshop Final Report, 2012.

[CHA 11] CHANG C., LIN C., "LIBSVM: a library for support vector machines", *ACM Transactions on Intelligent Systems and Technology*, vol. 2, pp. 27:1–27:27, 2011. Software available at http://www.csie.ntu.edu.tw/cjlin/libsvm.

[CHI 02] CHIAO Y., ZWEIGENBAUM P., "Looking for French-English translations in comparable medical corpora", *Journal of the American Society for Information Science*, vol. 8, pp. 150–154, 2002.

[CHI 04] CHIAO Y., Extraction lexicale bilingue à partir de textes médicaux comparables: application à la recherche d'information translangue, PhD Thesis in Medical Informatics, University of Paris 6, France, 2004.

[CLA 09] CLAVEAU V., "Translation of biomedical terms by inferring rewriting rules", in PRINCE V., ROCHE M. (eds.), *Information Retrieval in Biomedicine: Natural Language Processing for Knowledge Integration*, Medical Information Science Reference, pp. 106–123, 2009.

[CLA 11] CLAVEAU V., KIJAK E., "Morphological analysis of biomedical terminology with analogy-based alignment", *Proceedings of the International Conference Recent Advances in Natural Language Processing 2011*, Hissar, Bulgaria, pp. 347–354, 2011.

[COR 87] CORBIN D., *Morphologie dérivationnelle et structuration du lexique*, Presses Universitaires de Lille, 1987.

[COS 07] COSTAOUEC D., GUÉRIN F., *Syntaxe fonctionnelle. Théorie et exercices*, Presses Universitaires de Rennes, 2007.

[DAI 94a] DAILLE B., Approche mixte pour l'extraction automatique de terminologie: statistiques lexicales et filtres linguistiques, PhD Thesis in Theoretical Computer Science, University of Paris 7, France, 1994.

[DAI 94b] DAILLE B., GAUSSIER E., LANGÉ J., "Towards automatic extraction of monolingual and bilingual terminology", *Proceedings of the 15th International Conference on Computational Linguistics*, Kyoto, Japan, pp. 515–521, 1994.

[DAI 05] DAILLE B., MORIN E., "French-English terminology extraction from comparable corpora", *Proceedings, 2nd International Joint Conference on Natural Language Processing*, Lecture Notes in Computer Sciences, Jeju Island, Korea, vol. 3651, pp. 707–718, 2005.

[DAR 79] DARBELNET J., "Réflexions sur le discours juridique", *Meta: journal des traducteurs/Meta: Translator's Journal*, vol. 24, no. 1, pp. 26–34, 1979.

[DE 11] DE GROC C., "Babouk: focused web crawling for corpus compilation and automatic terminology extraction", *Proceedings of the IEEE/WIC/ACM International Conferences on Web Intelligence*, Lyons, France, pp. 497–498, 2011.

[DÉJ 02] DÉJEAN E., GAUSSIER E., "Une nouvelle approche à l'extraction de lexiques bilingues à partir de corpus comparables", *Lexicometrica, Alignement lexical dans les corpus multilingues*, pp. 1–22, 2002.

[DÉL 09] DÉLÉGER L., Exploitation de corpus parallèles et comparables pour la détection de correspondances lexicales: application au domaine médical, PhD Thesis in Medical Informatics, University of Pierre and Marie Curie, Paris, 2009.

[DEL 10] DELPECH E., DAILLE B., "Dealing with lexicon acquired from comparable corpora: validation and exchange", *Proceedings of the 2010 Terminology and Knowledge Engineering Conference (TKE 2010)*, Dublin, Ireland, pp. 211–223, 2010.

[DEM 77] DEMPSTER A.P., "Maximum likelihood from incomplete data via the EM algorithm", *Journal of the Royal Statistical Society*, vol. 39, no. 1, pp. 1–38, 1977.

[DOD 02] DODDINGTON G., "Automatic evaluation of machine translation quality using N-gram co-occurrence statistics", *Proceedings of the second international conference on Human Language Technology Research*, San Diego, California, pp. 128–145, 2002.

[DRO 06] DROSDOWSKI G., *Das grosse Wörterbuch der deutschen Sprachen in 8 Bänden*, Duden, 2006.

[DUN 93] DUNNING T., "Accurate methods for the statistics of surprise and coincidence", *Computational Linguistics*, vol. 19, no. 1, pp. 61–74, 1993.

[DUR 10] DURIEUX C., *Fondement didactique de la traduction technique*, La Maison du dictionnaire, Paris, France, 2010.

[ENG 95] ENGUERARD C., PANTERA L., "Automatic natural acquisition of a terminology", *Journal of Quantitative Linguistics*, vol. 2, no. 1, pp. 27–32, 1995.

[FID 11] FIDRMUC J., The Economics of multilingualism in the EU, CEDI Discussion Paper Series no. n11-04, Centre for Economic Development and Institutions (CEDI), Brunel University, London, UK, 2011.

[FRE 99] FREUND Y., SCHAPIRE R.E., "Large margin classification using the perceptron algorithm", *Machine Learning*, vol. 37, no. 3, pp. 277–296, 1999.

[FRI 97] FRIEDBICHLER I., FRIEDBICHLER M., "The potential of domain-specific target-language corpora for the translator's workbench", *First international conference on Corpus Use and Learning to Translate*, Bertinoro, Italy, 1997.

[FUN 95] FUNG P., "Compiling bilingual lexicon entries from a non-parallel English-Chinese corpus", in YAROVSKY D., CHURCH K., (eds.), *Proceedings of the 3rd Workshop on Very Large Corpora*, pp. 173–183, 1995.

[FUN 97] FUNG P., "Finding terminology translations from non-parallel corpora", *Proceedings of the 5th Annual Workshop on Very Large Corpora*, Hong Kong, pp. 192–202, 1997.

[FUN 98] FUNG P., "A statistical view on bilingual lexicon extraction: from parallel to non-parallel corpora", *Proceedings of the 3rd Conference of the Association for Machine Translation in the Americas*, Langhorne, PA, pp. 1–17, 1998.

[FUN 04] FUNG P., CHEUNG P., "Mining very-non-parallel corpora: parallel sentence and lexicon extraction via bootstrapping and EM", *Proceedings of EMNLP 2004*, Barcelona, Spain, pp. 57–63, 2004.

[GAR 08] GARERA N., YAROWSKY D., "Translating compounds by learning component gloss translation via multiple languages", *Proceedings of the 3rd International Joint Conference on Natural Language Processing*, Hyderabad, India, vol. 1, pp. 403–410, 2008.

[GAU 00] GAUSSIER E., HULL D.A., AIT-MOKHTAR S., "Term alignment in use: machine aided human translation", in VÉRONIS J. (ed.), *Parallel Text Processing*, Kluwer Academic Publisher, London, pp. 253–274, 2000.

[GAV 97] GAVIOLI L., ZANETTIN F., "Comparable corpora and translation: a pedagogic perspective", in BEEBY A., RODRIGUEZ P., SANCHEZ-GIJON P., (eds.), *Corpus use and learning to translate*, John Benjamins Publishing, Bertinoro, Italy, p. 151, 1997.

[GEN 77] GENDRE F., *L'analyse statistique univariée: Introduction à son utilisation pratique*, Librairie Droz, France, 1977.

[GOE 09] GOEURIOT L., Découverte et caractérisation des corpus comparables spécialisés, PhD Thesis in Computer Science, University of Nantes, 2009.

[GRA 04] GRABAR N., Terminologie médicale et morphologie. Acquisition de ressources morphologiques et leur utilisation pour le traitement de la variation terminologique, PhD Thesis in Medical Informatics, University of Paris 6, France, 2004.

[GRE 99] GREFENSTETTE G., "The world wide web as a resource for example-based machine translation tasks.", *ASLIB'99 Translating and the computer*, vol. 21, 1999.

[HAG 06] HAGEN S., FOREMAN-PECK J., DAVILA-PHILIPON S., *et al.*, ELAN: effects on the European economy of shortages of foreign languages skills in enterprise, Report , CILT, the National Centre for Languages, England, 2006.

[HAL 09] HALL M., FRANK E., HOLMES G., *et al.*, "The WEKA Data Mining Software: An Update", SIGKDD, vol. 11, no. 1, 2009.

[HAR 12] HARASTANI R., DAILLE B., MORIN E., "Neoclassical compound alignments from comparable corpora", *Proceedings of the 13th International Conference on Intelligent Text Processing and Computational Linguistics*, pp. 72–82, 2012.

[HAU 11] HAUER B., KONDRAK G., "Clustering semantically equivalent words into cognate sets in multilingual lists", *Proceedings of the 5th International Joint Conference on Natural Language Processing*, Chiang Mai, Thailand, pp. 865–873, 2011.

[HAZ 12] HAZEM A., MORIN E., "ICA for bilingual lexicon extraction from comparable corpora", *Proceedings of the 5th Workshop on Building and Using Comparable Corpora*, Istanbul, Turkey, 2012.

[HUT 96] HUTCHINS J., "ALPAC: the (in)famous report", *MT News International*, no. 14, pp. 9–12, 1996.

[HUT 05] HUTCHINS J., "Machine translation: general overview", in R. MITKOV (ed.), *The Oxford Handbook of Computational Linguistics*, Oxford University Press, New York, pp. 501–511, 2005.

[IAC 03] IACOBINI C., "Composizione con elementi neoclassici", in GROSSMAN M., RAINER F. (eds.), *La formazione delle parole in italiano*, Tübingen: Niemeyer, pp. 69–96, 2003.

[ISO 09] ISO, Terminology work – Principles and methods, Report no. 704, International Organization for Standardization, 2009.

[JAC 96] JACQUEMIN C., "A symbolic and surgical acquisition of terms through variation", in WERMTER S., RILOFF E.S.G. (ed.), *Connectionist, Statistical and Symbolic Approaches to Learning for Natural Language Processing*, Springer, Heidelberg, Germany, pp. 425–438, 1996.

[JI 09] JI H., "Mining name translations from comparable corpora by creating bilingual information networks", *Proceedings of the 2nd Workshop on Building and Using Comparable Corpora: from Parallel to Non-parallel Corpora*, Suntec, Singapore, pp. 34–37, 2009.

[KEE 85] KEENAN E.L., FALTZ L.M., *Boolean semantics for natural language*, Dordrecht, Holland, 1985.

[KEN 83] KENDALL M., "A new measure of rank correlation", *Biometrika*, vol. 30, no. 1–2, pp. 81–89, 1983.

[KIL 11] KILGARRIFF A., AVINESH P., POMIKÀLEK J., "BootCatting Comparable Corpora", *Proceedings of the International Conference on Terminology and Artificial Intelligence*, Paris, France, pp. 123–126, 2011.

[KOE 02] KOEHN P., KNIGHT K., "Learning a translation lexicon from monolingual corpora", *Proceedings of the Workshop of the ACL Special Interest Group on the Lexicon (SIGLEX)*, Philadelphia, Pennsylvania, PA, Association for Computational Linguistics, pp. 9–16, 2002.

[KOE 06] KOEHN P., MONZ C., "Manual and automatic evaluation of machine translation between European Languages", *Proceedings of the Workshop on Statistical Machine Translation*, Association for Computational Linguistics, New York City, New York, NY, pp. 102–121, 2006.

[LAN 77] LANDIS J., KOCH G., "The measurement of observer agreement for categorical data", *Biometrics*, vol. 33, no. 1, pp. 159–74, 1977.

[LAN 08] LANGLAIS P., YVON F., ZWEIGENBAUM P., "Analogical translation of medical words in different languages", *Proceedings of the 6th international conference on Advances in Natural Language Processing*, pp. 284–295, 2008.

[LAN 09] LANGLAIS P., YVON F., ZWEIGENBAUM P., "Improvements in analogical learning: application to translating multi-terms of the medical domain", *12th Conference of the European Chapter of the Association for Computational Linguistics*, Athens, Greece, pp. 487–495, 2009.

[LAR 98] LAROSE R., "Méthodologie de l'évaluation des traductions", *Méta: journal des traducteurs/Meta: Translators' Journal*, vol. 43, no. 2, pp. 163–186, 1998.

[LAR 10a] LARDILLEUX A., Contribution des basses fréquences à l'alignement sous-phrastique multilingue: une approche différentielle, PhD Thesis, University of Caen Basse Normandie, 2010.

[LAR 10b] LAROCHE A., LANGLAIS P., "Revisiting context-based projection methods for term-translation spotting in comparable corpora", *Proceedings of the 23rd International Conference on Computational Linguistics*, Beijing, China, pp. 617–625, 2010.

[LEO 08] LÉON S., Acquisition automatique de traductions d'unités lexicales complexes à partir du Web, PhD in Linguistics – Natural Language Processing, University of Provence Aix-Marseille I, Marseille, France, 2008.

[LEP 03] LEPAGE Y., De l'analogie rendant compte de la commutation en linguistique, Mémoire d'habilitation à diriger des recherches, Joseph Fourier University, Grenoble I, France, 2003.

[LEV 66] LEVENSHTEIN V.I., "Binary codes capable of correcting deletions, insertions, and reversals", *Soviet Physics*, vol. 10, pp. 707–710, 1966.

[LI 07] LI H., XU J., "AdaRank: a boosting algorithm for information retrieval", *Proceedings of the 30th Annual International ACM SIGIR Conference on Research and Development in Information Retrieval*, Amsterdam, The Netherlands, pp. 391–398, 2007.

[LI 10] LI B., GAUSSIER E., "Improving corpus comparability for bilingual lexicon extraction from comparable corpora", *23rd International Conference on Computational Linguistics*, Beijing, China, pp. 23–27, 2010.

[LI 11] LI B., GAUSSIER E., MORIN E., *et al.*, "Degré de comparabilité, extraction lexicale bilingue et recherche d'information interlingue", *Actes de la 18ème conférence sur le traitement automatique des langues naturelles*, Montpellier, France, vol. 1, pp. 211–222, 2011.

[LIN 93] LINDBERG D., HUMPHREYS B., MCCRAY A., "The unified medical language system", *Methods Inf Med*, vol. 32, pp. 81–91, 1993.

[LIU 07] LIU T., "Learning to rank: from pairwise approach to listwise approach", *Pao-Lu Hsu Statistics Conference: Machine Learning*, 2007.

[LIU 09] LIU T., "WWW 2009 tutorial on learning to rank for information retrieval", 18th International World Wide Web Conference, Madrid, Spain, 2009.

[LIU 11] LIU T., *Learning to Rank for Information Retrieval*, Springer Verlag, New York, 2011.

[LOV 98] LOVIS C., BAUD R., RASSINOUX A., *et al.*, "Medical dictionaries for patient encoding systems: a methodology", *Artificial Intelligence in Medecine*, pp. 201–214, 1998.

[MAC 08] MACKEN L., LEFEVER E., HOSTE V., "Language-independent bilingual terminology extraction from a multilingual parallel corpus", *Proceedings of the 22nd International Conference on Computational Linguistics*, vol. 1, Manchester, UK, pp. 529–536, 2008.

[MAN 08] MANNING C.D., RAGHAVAN P., SCHÜTZE H., *Introduction to Information Retrieval*, HTML edition, Cambridge University Press, 2008.

[MAR 79] MARTINET A., *La grammaire fonctionnelle du français*, Didier, Paris, 1979.

[MAR 85] MARTINET A., *Syntaxe générale*, Armand Colin, Paris, 1985.

[MCE 07] MC ENERY A.M., XIAO R.Z., "Parallel and comparable corpora: what is happening?", in ANDERMAN G., MARGARET R. (eds), *Incorporating Corpora: The Linguist and the Translator*, Translating Europe, Multilingual Matters, Clevedon, UK, pp. 18–31, 2007.

[MEL 99] MELAMED I.D., "Bitext maps and alignment via pattern recognition", *Computational Linguistics*, vol. 25, no. 1, pp. 107–130, 1999.

[MEL 06] MEL'UK I., *Aspects of the Theory of Morphology*, Mouton de Gruyter, Berlin, New York, 2006.

[MET 00] METZLER D., CROFT W.B., "Linear feature-based models for information retrieval", *Information Retrieval*, vol. 10, pp. 257–274, 2000.

[MEY 01] MEYER I., "Extracting knowledge-rich contexts for terminography: a conceptual and methodological framework", in BOURIGAULT D., JACQUEMIN C., L'HOMME M. (eds), *Recent Advances in Computational Terminology*, John Benjamins, pp. 279–302, 2001.

[MOR 04] MORIN E., DUFOUR-KOWALSKI S., DAILLE B., "Extraction de terminologies bilingues à partir de corpus comparables", *Actes de la 11ème Conférence annuelle sur le Traitement Automatique des Langues Naturelles (TALN)*, Fez, Morocco, pp. 309–318, 2004.

[MOR 07] MORIN E., DAILLE B., TAKEUCHI K., *et al.*, "Bilingual terminology mining - using brain, not brawn comparable corpora", *Proceedings of the 45th Annual Meeting of the Association of Computational Linguistics*, Prague, Czech Republic, pp. 664–671, 2007.

[MOR 10] MORIN E., DAILLE B., "Compositionality and lexical alignment of multi-word terms", in RAYSON P., PIAO S., SHAROFF S., *et al.* (eds), *Language Resources and Evaluation (LRE)*, Multiword Expression: Hard Going or Plain Sailing, Springer, Netherlands, vol. 44, pp. 79–95, 2010.

[MOR 12] MORIN E., DAILLE B., "Revising the compositional method for terminology acquisition from comparable corpora", *International Conference on Computational Linguistics (COLING)*, Mumbai, India, pp. 1797–1810, 2012.

[NAG 84] NAGAO M., "A framework of a mechanical translation between Japanese and English by analogy principle", in ELITHORN A.B.R. (ed.), *Artificial and Human Intelligence*, North-Holland, Amsterdam, pp. 173–180, 1984.

[NAM 03] NAMER F., "Les mots composés morphologiquement", Note technique faite dans le cadre du projet umlf landisco, Nancy 2 University, 2003.

[NAM 05] NAMER F., "Morphosémantique pour l'appariement de termes dans le vocabulaire médical : approche multilingue", *Actes de la 12ème conférence sur le Traitement Automatique des Langues*, Dourdan, France, pp. 63–72, 2005.

[NAM 07] NAMER F., BAUD R., "Defining and relating biomedical terms: towards a cross-language morphosemantics-based system", *International Journal of Medical Informatics*, vol. 76, no. 2–3, pp. 226–33, 2007.

[OCH 00] OCH F., NEY H., "A comparison of alignment models for statistical machine translation", *Proceedings of the 18th Conference on Computational Linguistics*, vol. 2, pp. 1086–1090, 2000.

[OTE 05] OTERO P.G., CAMPOS J.R., "An approach to acquire word translations from non-parallel texts", *Progress in Artificial Intelligence*, Lecture Notes in Computer Science, Springer-Verlag, vol. 3808, pp. 600–610, 2005.

[OZD 06] OZDOWSKA S., ALIBI, un système d'ALIgnement BIlingue à base de règles de propapagation syntaxique, PhD in Linguistics, University of Toulouse II, France, 2006.

[PAP 02] PAPINENI K., ROUKOS S., WARD T., *et al.*, "BLEU: a method for automatic evaluation of machine translation", *Proceedings of the 40th Annual Meeting of the Association for Computational Linguistics*, Philadelphia, PA, pp. 311–318, 2002.

[PER 10] PEREZ M., Interview d'Héloise Portal, responsable francophone de Linguee, 2010.

[PLA 98] PLANAS E., TELA, Structures et Algorithmes pour la Traduction fondée sur la Mémoire, Computational science doctoral dissertation, Joseph Fourier University, Grenoble I, France, 1998.

[PLA 00] PLANAS E., FURUSE O., "Multi-level similar segment matching algorithm for translation memories and example-based machine translation", *Proceedings of the 18th International Conference on Computational Linguistics*, Saarbrucken, Germany, pp. 621–627, 2000.

[PLA 05] PLANAS E., "Similis : un logiciel d'aide à la traduction au service des professionnels", *Traduire*, no. 206, pp. 41–48, 2005.

[PLA 11] PLANAS E., MeTRICC : Rapport final sur l'évaluation de l'apport des lexiques bilingues pour la traduction, Délivrable ANR no. n28 lot 4.3, University of Nantes, 2011.

[POR 80] PORTER M.F., "An algorithm for suffix stripping", *Program*, vol. 14, no. 3, pp. 130–137, 1980.

[PRO 09] PROCHASSON E., MORIN E., "Points d'ancrage pour l'extraction lexicale bilingue à partir de petits corpus comparables spécialisés", *Traitement Automatique des Langues*, vol. 50, no. 1, pp. 238–304, 2009.

[PRO 10] PROCHASSON E., Alignement multilingue en corpus comparables spécialisés : Caractérisation terminologique multilingue, Thesis in Computer Science, University of Nantes, 2010.

[RAP 95] RAPP R., "Identifying word translations in non-parallel texts", *Proceedings of the 33rd Annual Meeting on Association for Computational Linguistics*, Boston, MA, pp. 320–322, 1995.

[RAP 99] RAPP R., "Automatic identification of word translations from unrelated English and German corpora", *Proceedings of the 37th Annual Meeting of the Association for Computational Linguistics (ACL '99)*, College Park, MD, pp. 519–526, 1999.

[RAU 09] RAUF S., SCHWENK H., "On the use of comparable corpora to improve SMT performance", *Proceedings of the 12th Conference of the European Chapter of the ACL (EACL 2009)*, Athens, Greece, pp. 16–23, 2009.

[REI 71] REISS K., *Translation Criticism, the Potentials and Limitations: Categories and Criteria for Translation Quality Assessment*, St. Jerome Publishing, Manchester, GB, 1971.

[REN 03] RENDERS M., DÉJEAN H., GAUSSIER E., "Assessing automatically extracted bilingual lexicons for CLIR in vertical domains: XRCE participation in the GIRT track of CLEF 2002", *Advances in Cross-Language Information Retrieval*, Springer Berlin Heidelberg, vol. 2785, pp. 363–371, 2003.

[RIE 05] RIEGEL M., PELLAT J., RIOUL R., *Grammaire méthodique du français*, Presses Universitaires de France (PUF), Paris, France, 2005.

[RIE 12] RIEHMANN P., GRUENDL H., POTTHAST M., *et al.*, "WORDGRAPH: keyword-in-context visualization for NETSPEAK's wildcard search", vol. 18, pp. 1411–1423, 2012.

[ROB 06] ROBITAILLE X., SASAKI X., TONOIKE M., *et al.*, "Compiling French-Japanese terminologies from the Web", *Proceedings of the 11th Conference of the European Chapter of the Association for Computational Linguistics*, Trento, Italy, pp. 225–232, 2006.

[SAD 03] SADAT F., YOSHIKAWA M., UEMURA S., "Learning bilingual translations from comparable corpora to cross-language information retrieval: hybrid statistics-based and linguistics-based approach", *Proceedings of the sixth international workshop on Information retrieval with Asian languages (AsianIR '03)*, vol. 11, Sappro, Japan, pp. 57–64, 2003.

[SCH 06] SCHULZ S., MARKÓ K., DAUMKE P., *et al.*, "Semantic atomicity and multilinguality in the medical domain: design considerations for the MorphoSaurus subword lexicon", *Proceedings of the 5th International Conference on Language Resources and Evaluation*, Genoa, Italy, pp. 1684–1687, 2006.

[SCU 08] SCURTU G., "Traduire le vocabulaire juridique français en roumain", *Meta: journal des traducteurs / Meta: Translator's Journal*, vol. 53, no. 4, pp. 884–898, 2008.

[SEC 05] SECAR A., "Translation evaluation - a state of the art survey", *eCoLoRe / MeLLANGE Workshop*, Leeds, UK, pp. 39–44, 2005.

[SFT 09] SFT, Commission statistiques et étude du marché, SFT enquête tarifs 2009, Syndicat national des traducteur professionnels, 2009.

[SHA 06] SHAROFF S., BABYCH B., RAYSON P., *et al.*, "ASSIST: automated semantic assistance for translators", *Proceedings to the 11th Conference of the European Chapter of the Association for Computational Linguistics*, Trento, Italy, pp. 139–142, 2006.

[SNO 06] SNOVER M., DORR B., SCHWARTZ R., *et al.*, "A study of translation edit rate with targeted human annotation", *Proceedings of Association for Machine Translation in the Americas (AMTA 2006)*, pp. 224–231, 2006.

[SOK 12] SOKOLOV A., WISNIEWSKI G., YVON F., "Non-linear n-best list reranking with few features", *AMTA*, San Diego, CA, p. 10, 2012.

[SOM 05] SOMERS H., "Machine translation : latest developments", in MITKOV R. (ed.), *The Oxford Handbook of Computational Linguistics*, Oxford University Press, New York, pp. 512–528, 2005.

[TAL 08] TALVENSAARI T., PIRKOLA A., JÄRVELIN K., *et al.*, "Focused web crawling in the acquisition of comparable corpora", *Information Retrieval*, vol. 11, no. 5, pp. 427–445, 2008.

[TIE 09] TIEDEMANN J., "News from OPUS – a collection of multilingual parallel corpora with tools and interfaces", in NICOLOV N., BONTCHEVA K., ANGELOVA G., *et al.*, (eds), *Recent Advances in Natural Language Processing (RANLP 2009)*, John Benjamins, Amsterdam/Philadelphia, vol. V, pp. 237–248, 2009.

[TUR 03] TURIAN J., SHEN L., MELAMED I.D., "Evaluation of machine translation and its evaluation", *Proceedings of MT Summit IX*, New Orleans, LA, pp. 386–393, 2003.

[VER 00] VÉRONIS J., "From the Rosetta stone to the information society. A survey of parallel text processing", in VÉRONIS J., (ed.), *Parallel Text Processing*, Kluwer Academic Publisher, London, UK, pp. 1–24, 2000.

[VIN 10] VINTAR Š., "Bilingual term recognition revisited: the bag-of-equivalents term alignment approach and its evaluation", *Terminology*, vol. 16, no. 2, pp. 141–158, 2010.

[VIT 67] VITERBI A., "Error bounds for convolutional codes and an asymptotically optimum decoding algorithm", *IEEE Transactions on Information Theory*, vol. 13, no. 2, pp. 260–269, 1967.

[WEL 11] WELLER M., GOJUN A., HEID U., *et al.*, "Simple methods for dealing with term variation and term alignment", *Proceedings of the 9th International Conference on Terminology and Artificial Intelligence*, Paris, France, pp. 87–93, 2011.

[WIL 01] WILLIAMS M., "The application of argumentation theory to translation quality assessment", *Meta: Journal des Traducteurs/Meta: Translator's Journal*, vol. 46, no. 2, pp. 326–344, 2001.

[WIL 04] WILLIAMS M., *Translation Quality Assessment: An Argumentation-Centred Approach*, University of Ottawa Press, 2004.

[WU 10] WU Q., BURGES J.C., SVORE K., *et al.*, "Adapting boosting for information retrieval measures", *Journal of Information Retrieval*, vol. 13, pp. 254–270, 2010.

[YU 09] YU K., TSUJII J., "Extracting bilingual dictionary from comparable corpora with dependency heterogeneity", *NAACL-Short '09 Proceedings of Human Language Technologies*, vol. Short Papers, Boulder, Colorado, pp. 121–124, 2009.

[ZAN 98] ZANETTIN F., "Bilingual Comparable Corpora and the Training of Translators", *Meta: journal des traducteurs/Meta: Translator's Journal*, vol. 43, no. 4, pp. 616–630, 1998.

Index